D1194592

PROBLEMS OF DESIGN

by **GEORGE NELSON**

Copyright © 1957, 1965 Whitney Library of Design Division
Whitney Publications, Inc.
18 East 50th Street, New York, N. Y. 10022
Publishers of Interiors and Industrial Design
Charles E. Whitney, President
First edition 1957
Second edition 1965
All rights reserved. No part of this book
may be reproduced without permission from the
publisher.
Printed in the United States of America
Library of Congress Catalog Card No. 57-14401

NK
1505
.N4

TABLE OF CONTENTS

DISCARDED
UNIVERSITY OF WISCONSIN - EAU CLAIRE

258868

v

DISCARDED

UNIVERSITY OF VIRGINIA - TAG D SAINT

FOREWORD

George Nelson is unique. He is an industrial designer with a sense of humor. This allows him —indeed compels him—to be candid about the intricate workings of Big Design. And yet he continues to direct an organization whose designs are profitable, popular, and good. How does he satisfy both the demands of his clients' advertising agencies and his own common sense? How does he remain an honest intellectual while actually making money?

Before revealing the answers to these questions, it would be well to explain that in my own dark view of the world all industrial designers except George Nelson are divided into two convenient categories. The first comprises an army of researchers, renderers and receptionists led by an immaculately groomed Salesman General. They are inundating the whole western world and parts of Asia with unnecessary objects, technicolored, globular, and largely plastic, and they and their designs must be resisted. The second category comprises both designers and manufacturers who years ago would have been craftsmen. They like to make useful objects neatly and quietly, but they exist now only in the narrow cracks left between really large-scale industries. In the United States they can make furniture and glassware and lamps, but not automobiles. Existence for them is perhaps not so precarious as it may seem; in a luxury market integrity can also be made saleable.

Some of the objects our first group of designers regularly fashions for industry have a vulgarity independent of any purpose. This is not because ugliness is valued in itself, or even because it is thought to be beautiful. Nor are such objects— the automobile is a good example—necessarily shaped according to some rigorously defined program of functions. Not only is its appearance and its usefulness unimportant: the object itself is of no importance. What is important is to sustain production and consumption. The individual object, even in an edition of five million, is only a means to an end, and the designers of our second group so often fail in their efforts to influence big industry just because they are interested in the object, any object, for its own sake.

Now, if an industrialized economy values process by which things are made more than it values the things, the industrial designer ought to have the training and inclinations of a psychoanalyst. Failing this, he ought at least to have the instincts of a reporter, or, more useful, of an editor. These George Nelson possesses in high degree, but as it happens he was trained to be an architect. His education at Yale was followed by postgraduate work at Catholic University, where in 1932 he won the Rome Prize in architecture. In Europe during the next two years he convinced himself that the great architectural styles of the past required no further emendations. His personal interest in modern architecture thus heightened, he interviewed a number of outstanding talents, among them Le Corbusier and Mies van der Rohe, already famous in Europe but only beginning to be known here. On his return to the United States these interviews were published by the magazine Pencil Points (now Progressive Architecture). Some of them were, and still are, remarkable combinations of enthusiasm and perception: enthusiasm for widely disparate theories, and perception in recognizing which aspects of a man's personality had colored his work. None of these articles could be described as abstract criticism, and yet each of them exhibited a perfectly clear picture of ideas. After their publication Nelson joined the staff of Architectural Forum, and from there his editorial activities eventually extended to special projects for Time and Fortune.

In 1936 he opened an architectural office in association with William Hamby. (Their most notable building was a New York townhouse for Sherman Fairchild, with two separate units facing an interior garden and connected by a spectacular ramp.) When World War II terminated architectural work Nelson's attention was again turned to writing. He produced two books: "The Industrial Architecture of Albert Kahn" and, with Henry Wright, "Tomorrow's House". For Life magazine he developed the storage wall, expanding the usefulness of an ordinary partition by compartmenting it to hold what seemed to be every household item ever made. Publication of this architectural piece of furniture led to a continuing association with the Herman Miller Furniture Company.

In 1947 Nelson opened an office in New York City for architecture and industrial design. I remember this office quite well. It was on the second floor of a narrow building on Lexington Avenue. The ground floor was occupied by a restaurant specializing in health foods. These were made of something which could offend neither God nor dumb beasts, but which smelled funny. The patrons of this restaurant had necessarily a certain dedicated manner, and I remember the unnerving contrast between the solemnity on the ground floor and the haphazard urbanity on the floor above.

Not that the Nelson office was without its own peculiar intensity. At that time it was engaged, as it is now, in the design of furniture. But because George Nelson was interested in doing many things at once, it seemed both professionally wise and morally imperative to explore aspects of what may be called New Techniques. During the day the office devoted itself to designing chairs, among other things, made of wood. But at night the staff gathered around Buckminster Fuller and labored with him over the birth of a Seating Tool. This was made of two aluminum reflector shields of the sort used by photographers, a sheet of celluloid, and, most important, a piece of piano wire. After the celluloid was properly cut and rolled to make a truncated cone, it was set down on the rim of the larger of the two reflectors. The small reflector was set on top of the cone; the wire was passed through it and was fastened to the underside of the base. Pulled toward each other by the wire, the two reflectors held the celluloid rigid and demonstrated what remarkable strength some materials have when used in certain ways. But unfortunately anyone sitting on this nearly invisible object completely overhung the seat, and appeared to be balancing painfully on a knitting needle.

Nobody expected this design to do very much, really, toward revolutionizing the production of chairs. And it would be a mistake to believe that a short time later the information thus gathered was found to have a marvelously logical use. That sometimes happens, but even so it is only a secondary benefit. What did happen, and what was of real importance was that a sense of the process by which ideas evolve was somehow sharpened; the process, not the thing itself, was its own reward.

For George Nelson, I believe, the process has always been most important. What makes Nelson different from other people thus engaged is the range of his curiosity, the variety of facts and beliefs and enthusiasms he seeks to integrate in one continuously evolving structure. Where other designers might proceed by excluding possibilities and limiting the frame of reference, Nelson seeks to expand it, and even to bring into the picture what may seem irrelevant, if not actually inimical, to the ultimate job of creating useful and beautiful things. His speculations include ideas conventionally regarded with distaste. The possibilities for design of artificial obsolescence, for example, and the changing ideas of utility this aspect of American industrialization is bringing about; as well as the exact observation of how the managers of large corporations arrive at decisions, are for Nelson appropriate considerations for the designer. This book is a collection of his essays on these subjects. Some of their value is that they document, at least in part, the history of his work and ideas. But they also constitute a kind of sketchbook of work in progress. Or more exactly, they are a sketchbook in which the author has drawn successive self-portraits. Taken all together they suggest a man whose personality becomes the more intact the more variously his energies are dispersed. For Nelson variety is not the spice of life; it *is* life. What for other people may be irreconcilable contradictions become, within this mode of human organization, intensely interesting bits of information to be fitted into the structure of awareness. Ensuring the maximum and continuous expansion of awareness is thus the only real problem. The work in progress, the first and most significant product to emerge from this study, is George Nelson. He is his own best design.

Arthur Drexler

PROBLEMS OF DESIGN

Because we live in a society which has come to rely heavily on language as a means of transmitting increasingly complex ideas and instructions, we tend—quite naturally—to think of communication as a process rooted in the use of words. Yet even now, before the semanticists have quite solved the problem of how to make the same word mean the same thing to different people, we know that communication has to do with more than the spoken or written word. The after-dinner doodle on the back of a napkin is a communication. So are the night noises of traffic in a big city. The scrawled equations of mathematicians or physicists represent extreme compressions of fact and idea, communications which could only be matched by the use of huge numbers of words. The painting of the painter, the sculpture of the sculptor, the design of the designer—these are all communications of a sort, despite the lack of words, regardless of the intentions of their creators.

The one question to be asked of any communication is, of course, what is it saying? Sometimes the answer is simple enough, as in the case of the ubiquitous scrawls in public lavatories. Sometimes it is not: James Joyce's "Ulysses" had to be taken to court for even a limited interpretation of its message. When one comes to the activities of a profession, the communication becomes even more diffuse and the message less distinct, and we therefore tend to draw conclusions and form estimates based on the work or words of leading people. We may have a high opinion of contemporary architects because of the example of Le Corbusier, or admire the social conscience of physicists on the basis of a paper by Dr. Oppenheimer. Similarly, the status of design—as practiced by industrial designers — is established through a composite communication of both action and words.

I have conveniently at hand an example of the latter. In a recent statement to the press, one of the leading members of our profession stated that the major social contribution of the industrial designer lies in the new comfort and ease he has created for the public. About this verbal communication I shall have two things to say—first, that it is not true, and second, that if it were, it would be of no particular consequence.

Before descending on this harmless remark and

DESIGN AS COMMUNICATION

tearing it to bits, let us play with the assumption that it *is* true. Let us pretend to accept as a fact the proposition that the designer has brought a new degree of physical ease to society, and that this is his highest achievement. Having done this we can now attribute to him a status of a sort: we know who he is and why he is here. Just as an architect is around to keep the rain off your furniture, and your lawyer exists to keep you clear of lawsuits and the clergyman is there to ease the steep climb to heaven. In any organized society people have to do things for each other, and the esteem they enjoy depends on the society's evaluation of the services performed. In our society, of course, the degree of esteem can change with extreme abruptness. Ten years ago, as far as popular attitudes were concerned, the nuclear physicist and his activities were strictly for the birds. Today they enjoy an almost superstitious respect—and why not? Anyone who offers the prospect of unlimited wealth and/or unlimited disaster is quite a guy—or if you prefer, quite a profession. Obviously such a professional will find himself higher on the ladder of status than one who merely offers an increase in creature comforts. Nobody really cares anyway if the missile with the atomic warhead has been subtly color-styled by Zilch Associates to look its very best just below the ionosphere. The color of the bomb going off is prettier and has greater impact on more people.

However, if we do think of the provision of greater comfort and convenience as a topflight social activity, we have to find significant examples and see what the contribution of the designer really has been. When I say "designer" please understand that I am referring to people like ourselves who have an identifiable trade known as industrial design. And when I talk about comfort I am not limiting it to the feeling of a hot water bottle at the foot of the bed, but am including anything which makes the mechanics of existence simpler and thus releases time and energy (theoretically) for other pursuits. Thus the electric toaster might be an example. It takes less fussing than sticking a slice of bread on a fork and holding it over a fire. The refrigerator is a genuine improvement over the technique of putting a box out the pantry window in winter. Or radiant electric heating. Or express highways. Examples such as these have indeed changed our ways of living, but the trouble is that they are not the creations of industrial designers. One can find examples which are, but they are far less

significant: secretary's chairs which won't snag nylon hosiery; more readable dials on dashboards and telephones; eye-saving colors on typewriters; luggage handles which are easier to grip; and so on. I am not trying to run down our perfectly useful activities—I am saying that I find no evidence to support the claim of a major contribution in the activity known as making life easier.

JET-PROPELLED SUPER-COMFORT

As one considers this lack of evidence a question naturally comes to mind: why should the claim have been made at all? The obstetrician does not pretend to be able to straighten teeth, nor does the lawyer claim he can shingle roofs. Why this attempt on the part of the industrial designer to establish a position in an area where others are quite clearly the real contributors?

There is a reason for this particular choice, and I believe it may go like this: we are members of a society which appears to have given itself over to the pursuit of what might best be described as "super-comfort." Anything making life easier in this society is viewed with instant, total and unanimous approval. In fact, the very phrase itself has acquired the aura of something approaching sanctity. This trend, which since the end of World War II has become virtually jet-propelled, has alarmed quite a few people. The basis for alarm is that nobody can find an end to the trend. First we traded the horse and buggy for the car. Then the car was enclosed and the rutted roads were paved. A self-starter replaced the crank and electric lamps the acetylene headlights. Then came heaters and radios. The two-man top evolved into the one-man top and finally power took over, as it is now taking over with the brakes and steering. The clutch withered away. Pushbuttons make the windows go up and down and there is an extra loudspeaker behind the rear seats. And now—optional at $600 extra—there is air conditioning. Parenthetically, none of these developments as far as I know can be credited to the industrial designer. Anyway, we have the accelerating trend towards super-comfort, the alarm about a society getting soft and decaying, and the unspoken but completely solid public approval for the whole thing.

PRETENSE OF SOCIAL MEANING
To the extent that he identifies himself with so formidable a social phenomenon, the designer is inserting a pretense of social meaning into his

work. It is also a relatively low order of meaning, by which I do not mean that it is "bad" but merely that it is not especially significant as expressed.

A trend as conspicuous as the one under discussion might be viewed with the contempt which stems from imagined superiority. Actually, it is hard to view what is going on with anything other than amazement. Here is a society which is dedicated—on the surface at least—to the creation of a civilization of super-comfort. This is a society which through a volume of production no one could have even conceived a generation ago has taken the good old economic pyramid of the textbooks, with its handful of idle rich at the top and a broad layer of crushed proletarians at the bottom, and converted it into a diamond where the big purchasing power is spread over an enormous number of middle-class people. With money in the hands of so many who never had it before, why not a vast demand for television sets, refrigerators in which the ice cubes are made without trays, air conditioning and outboard motors? It is plausible that ownership of such conveniences does not represent the highest objective society has ever set for itself, but this does not make it vicious. There is nothing on record to indicate that Plato or Lorenzo the Magnificent lacked the best that could be provided, but both managed to give a good account of themselves in spite of their soft surroundings. Comfort as such—"making life easier"—has nothing intrinsically good or bad in it. The race from its earliest days has been engaged in a battle to extract an easier, safer and more entertaining life from the world around it, and we have carried this struggle to a rather spectacular point.

In pursuing his day-to-day activities the designer must deal often with problems of making life easier. This is absolutely inevitable in the society to which we belong. The manager of a supermarket has to deal with these problems too. His is a service occupation and so is that of the designer, and there is nothing reprehensible or degrading in the idea of service. Jesus viewed his activities in this light and so did the great painters of the Renaissance. What is significant about service is not the fact itself, but the infinity of levels at which it can be rendered. The average architect who draws plans for building developments operates at roughly the same intellectual and social level as the attendant in a filling station. Frank Lloyd Wright is also an architect, but there is a qualitative difference in the nature of the service he provides. As the centuries drift by, society forgets the bad plans, the ugly buildings, the jerry-built houses. But the rest it remembers—the good work of the good men—and architecture gradually achieves the status of a noble profession. In casting about for its own historic role, industrial design will always remain where it began: within the framework of a service profession. Its crucial decisions will be those dealing with the *level* of the service.

LIKE BUDDHA AND BOTTICELLI

Within the limits of his trade, the designer can be viewed in a variety of ways. We have already considered him at some length as a purveyor of comfort. In many quarters he is accepted as an adjunct to the advertising agency, or as an aid to merchandising. On occasion he is used to develop a new product from scratch: some designers have clients who depend on them to tell them what to make and how to make it. Or perhaps the designer is a kind of business consultant who has specialized in matters of taste. While all of these descriptions seem to me to be valid in varying degrees, my own view is that the designer is in essence an artist, one whose tools differ somewhat from those of his predecessors, but an artist nonetheless. I prefer this view because I believe it has to be true if the designer is to perform his service at the top possible level.

"Artist" is not a word to be used without risking suspicion in some quarters, and it is even possible that some industrialists might shy away from designers if they heard the word applied to them. This would not be the case if people really understood what a remarkable fellow this artist is, how extraordinary the survival value he has shown, and what remarkable influence he has had. It is a curious fact, and one generally ignored, that the least imposing occupations have frequently proven the most durable. If someone were to go to the trouble of charting those aspects of human activity which have endured the longest, and made the greatest impression on posterity, the results would be a shock to many people.

Take, for instance, the case of Buddha. Buddha was an aristocrat who at some point in his life quitted the ancestral palace and went to live in a cave where he promulgated certain impractical doctrines regarding man's relation to the world. Who remembers how much money Buddha's father had? Or the name of India's military leader of the time?

What we do remember is that Buddha has affected the lives of hundreds and hundreds of millions of people, that he did this by sitting in a cave and saying something once in a while, and that the name of his most powerful contemporary is not even a whisper. Buddha was not an artist —he was a religious teacher. What the chart would show is that religious teaching (philosophy if you prefer) is the most durable thing yet produced by mankind.

Or take the case of Botticelli. Botticelli was an Italian painter who painted women's faces as they were never painted before or since. Many people remember Botticelli and his pictures, but who can tell you the name of the political boss of Florence at that time? Or who had the biggest importing business in Venice? Or which city was at war with which, and who won? What the chart would show is that art is the next most durable thing yet produced by man.

THE OUTSTRETCHED HAND

Just what is an artist? We know he isn't a chap who starves in garrets. Matisse has pots of money, and plenty of non-artists have starved in garrets. We know he isn't necessarily a painter or a sculptor—D. W. Griffith neither painted nor carved, but he was an artist. My own definition may not suit you, but it is yours for whatever it may be worth: *an artist is someone who gives form to the essence of something.* He is a purveyor, not of comforts, if you please, but of truths. You can always tell when his communication comes through because in the shock of understanding the message there is also the feeling that you had known it all your life.

Consider an example of how this communication takes place within the framework of a society. In the early 16th Century the Pope—was it Julius II?—decided to undertake the decoration of the Sistine Chapel. This decision was not an arbitrary whim: it was taken for granted at the time that the only proper way to treat an important interior was to decorate every available

inch of it with murals and sculpture, and because of this there existed a whole series of service occupations, of which painting was one. Michelangelo was retained to do the job. Among the items in this vast mural was the figure of God reaching out to touch the hand of Adam, and so completely has this painting been taken over by the eastern world that today, almost 500 years later, even a detail of the hands is enough to identify the mural and its author. The communication established by Michelangelo in this painting is an exceedingly complex one and I do not propose to analyze it, but this much is evident—a job initiated to glorify a pope became, in the hands of a genius, an imperishable statement that man is not alone.

To assume the role of the artist means that the designer must concern himself with the essence of the problem he is dealing with, and this is extremely difficult. It does us no good to complain that designing a bathroom scale is a very different thing from painting the Sistine Chapel. Of course it is different. A ladybug is not an elephant, but the biologist does not despise it because it is smaller. Nor does it prove anything to hide behind the problems created by clients or production costs. The architects of French cathedrals had problems with clients and costs too.

Every design is in some sense a social communication, and what matters is not so much the importance of the object—this is generally out of the designer's control—as the emotional intensity with which the essentials have been explored and expressed. Truth is a most important quality in design of any dimension and people tend to recognize it when they see it. I have at home in my kitchen an automatic laundry, an anonymous white cube which gives no inkling of its purpose, and I find after looking at it for a couple of years that I have very mixed feelings about it. What I dislike very much is the visual evidence of the machine—I would greatly prefer having it out of sight, like a furnace. What I like and admire is that the designer did everything he could to reduce its visibility—its shape is the simplest possible and ornamental tricks are at a minimum. I get from this design a distinct sense of communication: the designer obviously believed that the washing machine should not be a prominent object and he did everything he could to say so. That he did not take the final step and integrate it into the structure of the house was beyond his control, and one therefore accepts the statement and respects the effort. In the automotive field one can find similar examples. All car design, today, is beginning to "go Italian." You can see the evidence in many recent British and American cars. What this means is that an Italian designer made a statement regarding the nature of the automobile which more and more people are coming to accept as a closer approximation to the truth than the work of other designers. Inevitably, this statement had an effect on the thinking of designers everywhere.

I chose to discuss design as communication, in spite of the fact that there are many ways to consider it, because this approach puts a maximum of responsibility on the designer. An important aspect of great art is that the artist has assumed total responsibility for communicating the truth as he perceives it.

This responsibility of the designer is to develop an artist's awareness of the modern world, and by this I mean a total awareness which integrates the outlook of the scientist, the mathematician and everyone else who is acting creatively. This world of ours has become a strange and explosive place where accelerating change seems to be the only remaining constant, where intangible relationships are more concrete than tangible things and where cooperation has replaced competition as the only possible technique for survival. Technically it is a world in which more is always being done with less, with the ultimate object of doing everything with nothing. It is our responsibility as artists in industry to make these things manifest, and thus to extend through our work a growing comprehension of the modern world. Until we learn to comprehend it, we haven't a chance of learning how to control it.

GOOD DESIGN: WHAT IS IT FOR?

"Good Design" is neither a book of etiquette nor a social register. What follows is one of many attempts to remove the heavy hand of authority from what should be an area of personal enjoyment.

Within the past few years the phrase "good design" has taken on a new meaning over and above its original one: a program jointly sponsored by the Museum of Modern Art and the Merchandise Mart of Chicago. Such is the power of an idea when backed by effective publicity. I make mention of this at the outset because my subject has the same title as this program, but otherwise no connection. "Good design," as popularized by the Museum and the Merchandise Mart, has come to mean a certain number of objects selected by Mr. Kaufmann and his juries, objects which may then carry a kind of label of approval when displayed for sale in stores. What I plan to discuss is much less specific, and it would be well, therefore, to avoid any possibility of confusion.

Among these "less specific" matters is the question of how a design comes into existence and how it is refined to a certain degree of excellence. The process is not a simple one, and I doubt seriously if anyone understands it with any degree of completeness. In spite of this, a tentative exploration of the question has some value.

TRADITION VS TECHNOLOGY

For a design to emerge at all, a definite situation has to exist. There has to be a need—or at least a possible use for it—and there has to be a designer. The designer may think of himself as a farmer or a machinist, or he may call himself a designer. It doesn't matter particularly as long as there is someone around with the urge and the competence to give form to an idea. The channel through which the designer's idea flows to become a finished object is shaped by tradition and by technology. These two do not always function smoothly together. In primitive cultures the need for designed products is expressed in a series of relatively simple implements, utensils and religious objects. The designer is frequently the maker and the user as well. With technology moving slowly, tradition becomes the main guide towards suitable form, and design development tends to go on over generations. Once developed, forms settle into fairly rigid molds and "design" would be described more precisely as imitation of standard patterns, with individual variations. There are any number of examples of forms which have persisted virtually unchanged over centuries and even millennia. In societies which saw themselves as permanent—Egypt is an outstanding example—the persistence of established forms also served to support prevailing belief in an eternally static situation.

FUNCTION HIGHLY OVERRATED

When we talk about the "need" for a certain kind of object, it is a good thing to realize that there is no necessary connection between the level or type of need and the quality of the design. This is an important point in any discussion of design and it is worth expanding. Let us say that the "need" in question concerns a vessel to hold liquids. The response to the need—a designed and manufactured object—may be a perfectly adequate container with no esthetic interest, or it may be a thing preserved through the ages as an incomparable work of art. In other words, functional sufficiency is no guarantee whatever of good design—it is merely the floor below which a design cannot go without failing to serve its purpose. I think it important to realize this because there is a widespread misconception today regarding the role of function, and a very general tendency to overemphasize its significance. And just as the role of function is not necessarily a major one, so with the type or level of the need. It makes no difference, from the viewpoint of good design, whether a container for liquids was made for a prince or a pauper. To be sure, until relatively recently the princes had a better time of it because they were better able to take over the production of the best designers. But the level at which the artist or designer worked has always been far more significant a factor than the social or financial level of his client.

The emotional and intellectual level at which the designer works is also more important a factor than the type of object on which he is required—or inspired—to work. I have just mentioned princes, and among the needs of princes are palaces. Yet here, as in the case of the simple container, there is no guarantee of good design in the exalted nature of the assignment. If you compare the residence of Haile Selassie in Addis Ababa, and Holyrood Palace in Edinburgh, it takes no excess of critical sophistication to realize that the latter is an exquisite, though minor work, and that the former is the quintessence of vulgarity. The fact that the Ethiopian structure is more "functional" is really of no consequence.

PALACES ARE AMORAL

The example of a royal palace can be used to illuminate another aspect of current attitudes towards design: the tendency to confuse esthetic and moral judgments. We come at the end of a long and successful struggle to destroy monarchy as an institution, and the demand for palaces is currently at an all-time low. But the revulsion against royalty has spread in some quarters to include the rich, and I have heard a few intelligent and serious architects state that in our time the only chance for great architecture is in public housing. This is a very clear case of the injection of moral or political judgments into situations where they have no application. The fact in this instance happens to be that at least three of the peaks of architectural achievement in the first half of the 20th Century are homes for the rich: Wright's Kaufmann house near Pittsburgh, the Villa Savoye of Le Corbusier and the Tugendhat house in Czechoslovakia by Mies van der Rohe. Design is amoral and non-ideological, and any attempt to give it meanings it cannot possess merely obscures the communication it can make. I remember wandering around Versailles as a student and hearing other tourists deplore it as an expression of the greed and ostentation of Louis XIV. It is possible that Louis should have given the money to his starving subjects, and it is also possible that fewer starved than otherwise would have because of the employment created by this vast project. But it is certain that what Versailles has to say *as a design* has a great deal to do with the boldness of the human spirit and very little with the greed or generosity of Louis XIV.

DAMS HAVE NO POLITICS

Some months ago one of the business weeklies published a photograph of the dam at Kuibyshev, a huge structure spanning the Volga, and part of a river reconstruction system similar to TVA. From the distance at which the photograph was taken it was absolutely impossible—for a layman at least—to determine whether the dam was in the U.S.S.R., the U.S.A., or anywhere else. Dams have no politics; seen as designs they can be judged only by criteria which are timeless, universal and non-ideological. I am stressing this point for reasons which will become more evident as we continue. I consider it important because it is not possible to see a design with any clarity if vision is distorted by irrelevancies. The "good" in good design has no connection whatever with the same word as applied to human behavior. I have never seen a liturgical object from a Jewish place of worship which could be described as beautiful. The Aztecs, on the other hand, left many which show extraordinary sensibility. Yet the Jewish religion marks one of the high points in human development, while that of the Aztecs was indescribably savage and bloody.

Some of you who may be reading this to learn my views on the current state of design in vacuum cleaners or eggbeaters, or to pick up some handy formula for making infallible judgments in these matters, may be getting a little restive at this point, and wondering what Egyptian palaces and Soviet dams have to do with the subject at hand. If this should be the case, I can only observe unsympathetically that it serves you right. There are too many quick and easy answers. Oceans of hogwash have been poured over unresisting readers regarding this matter of good design, and I am trying not to swell the flood any further.

CONSERVATIVE EVOLUTIONARY DEVELOPMENT

In pursuing this modest objective I am going to continue to digress—this time to entertain you with a short lecture on the theory of evolution. Since this is a field in which I am deeply uninformed, what I shall have to say will combine the illusion of clarity which goes with ignorance, and the brevity which stems from the lack of possession of facts.

For the purposes of this discussion there are three aspects to evolutionary theory which appear to me to be relevant. Number one has to do with the manner in which organisms reproduce. The apparatus consists of complex chemical units —genes—which are clustered into groups of chromosomes. The whole design is set up for perfect self-reproduction, rather like a cosmic typewriter whose output can make endless carbon copies of itself. The point which is intriguing

about the process is its utter conservatism; there is no room in the system for change. Long-lived ancient cultures like Egypt and China show a roughly parallel type of behavior.

REVOLUTIONARY MUTATIONS

Item number two is that the apparatus does not work perfectly. A few times in a million something slips up and a slight mutation appears. Now a mutation is not conservative. It is revolutionary. What permits biological evolution to take place is the combination of conservatism (which perpetuates the species) and a long, slow series of successful revolutions (which permit it to adapt and develop). Again, it is not hard to think of parallels in the history of human societies.

NEITHER CONSERVATIVES NOR RADICALS ARE "BAD"

The third and final point has to do with the conditions under which these mutations are successful. The conditions for success exist in the world outside the organism, and if they should happen to favor the mutation (they usually do not) the now-modified gene-chromosome pattern gets the chance to survive and reproduce itself. The results of this interaction of conservatism and change, spread over periods of fifty to two hundred million years, have been quite extraordinary

If one doesn't mind stretching analogies a bit, the process of evolution can be described as a never-ending battle between conservatives and radicals. What they are fighting about is, so to speak, design. The quality of the design is rated very simply, in terms of survival or extinction. Please note that this quality of design is never an absolute, but always related to an external situation. For example the marsupials survived and even flourished in Australia not because they were better equipped to compete with the placental type of mammal, but because they were isolated from the competition. What determines the temporary victory in all of these struggles is not only the relative strength of the contestants, but the conditions under which the contests take place. Incidentally, from the evolutionary point of view, neither conservatives nor radicals are "bad." Both are necessary for the process to go on. Their roles are also interchangeable; the successful mutation instantly becomes "conservative." For any possible human purpose, biological evolution seems to be finished, but an almost identical process continues to determine the emergence and disappearance of social patterns. The main difference, of course, is that human evolution proceeds at a vastly increased rate of speed.

What I have been trying to suggest is that there is a larger pattern in the design process than the undisciplined whimsy of talented individuals, and that in this area of activity there are the same conservative tendencies, the same periodic emergence of mutations, and the same relationships to environment which are now more social than physical.

CONSERVATIVE EVOLUTION OF THE CHAIR

We can observe this process at work in any object which has a history. The chair, for instance, is traditionally a four-legged structure of wood sticks held together with nails, glue, pegs, dowels, screws, or joints in the sticks themselves. The differences between chairs over a long period of time are very slight, just as the differences between a native European and a native African are slight in comparison with the basic similarities of design. A Louis XV chair and one made by a farmer colonist in New England look different only if viewed out of context. There have, to be sure, been chairs which differed basically in their structure, such as the beautifully carved stone blocks one finds in the ruins of a Greek amphitheatre. A more successful mutation—successful because it was portable, among other things—was the rocker. There were many attempts at three-legged chairs over the centuries, but they were not successful except in very limited uses, such as milking stools. In Japan, no chair design was successful for milennia because of the unfavorable environment; a nation which squats has no need for a chair.

TECHNOLOGY AS A REVOLUTIONARY FORCE

One could go on for a long time, developing the picture of the chair as an object in process of evolution. Within the past century the pace of the process has accelerated. With the Thonet chair of bent wood a new structural principle replaced the old one. Laminated wood showed the way to further refinements with greater strength and less weight. Metal chairs appeared in the late 19th Century. In many chairs of today, with plastic shells and other devices, the traditional structure has almost disappeared. Behind these accelerating changes you will not find shifting tastes as a determining factor, but a developing technology. The technology provided the changing environment within which certain design mutations could survive. It provided the new processes and materials for chairs, was the basis for houses with glass walls and open plans, created the need to economize on household labor, and thus fostered a widespread willingness to change tastes and accept new things.

THE "DESIGNER" NEED NOT BE AN INDIVIDUAL

No design can exist in isolation. It is always related, sometimes in very complex ways, to an entire constellation of influencing situations and attitudes. What we call a good design is one which achieves integrity—that is, unity or wholeness—in balanced relation to its environment. The reason good design is hard to come by is that its creation demands a high degree of emotional and intellectual maturity in the designer, and such people are not found too often. Earlier generations solved this problem by using many hands and minds over periods of centuries, as in the case of the axe, or the teacup. The "designer" then was not an individual, but an entire social process of trial, selection, and rejection. Today he is still that, though in a somewhat different sense, and we tend to overestimate his significance as an individual.

AN IMPOSSIBLE COMPARISON

If someone posed a question like "which is better design, a Roman chariot or an Italian automobile?" an interesting characteristic of all design would reveal itself. It is that the usual yardsticks for measuring relative excellence do not work. If the question were "which is better for stopping a headache, aspirin or baking soda?" we are well equipped to find an answer. In the case of the first question, you can say that a modern motor car is faster, more powerful or more comfortable than a chariot, but you cannot say that it is better designed merely on the basis of these technological improvements. Each is a unity, created in response to the opportunities and limitations of a given environment. The quality of each, as a design, relates to the emotional intensity and clarity of thinking brought to bear on each problem. This is why many old things, functionally unsuited for present-day use, still look good to us. This is why we can enjoy museums; differences in time and techniques do not act as barriers in this area. To paraphrase a very profound observation of Picasso, there is no past in art.

A KLEENEX CULTURE

We live in a period which tends to reject old things and to get bored with new ones. This is not entirely bad. In part, at least, it is a logical consequence of the fantastic increase in knowledge and expansion of productivity, both of which generate new and exciting opportunities. And in part it reflects an apparently irresistible move toward what might be described as a "Kleenex culture," in which more and more consumer products shift from a semi-permanent to a disposable basis. To the extent that this shift reduces interest in possessions I suspect that it is all to the good. But the concomitant emphasis on novelty as *the* desirable quality tends to obscure the facts of design development and the understanding of superior performance in this area. New designs, like biological mutations, may represent a better adaptation to changing conditions, and they may not.

RAPIDITY OF RECENT CHANGES

The past twenty years have seen a rapidly accelerating development of what we call modern or contemporary design. By this I mean an approach which begins with rejection of the forms and symbols of earlier periods in an effort to find something more accurately expressive of the contemporary environment. This movement, as you know, has been worldwide in scope and it has embraced all the arts. Painting especially, which made some of its most important statements around the turn of the century, not only became a major center of controversy, but also contributed substantially to developments in other arts,

notably architecture. The seeds of change were first visible shortly after the mid-19th Century. Since the last war so much progress has been made that for all practical purposes one can consider the battle won. To use the biological analogy for the last time, this century-long history provides an almost perfect example of a series of design mutations appearing, taking hold and flourishing in a steadily more favorable climate, to the point where the new forms become dominant. As a result when we talk about good design today, it is contemporary design of one variety or another we are talking about.

By pretty general consensus, the only good design today is contemporary design. But it is pretty hard to explain to the enthusiasts that not all contemporary design is good design. And it is even harder to explain that just because modern has taken over in the design of houses, interiors, accessories, and consumer products, this is not because it makes for easier living, less maintenance and so on. The fact happens to be that *all* design in this general area today, whether modern or period, makes for these things, and for the simple reason that nobody—rich or poor, old or young—can any longer put up with design that doesn't. All this takes us back to the earlier discussion of the relation of functionalism and good design, and what I am again saying is that the requirements of function have to be met regardless of quality or type or design.

It may shock you to learn that when some of these requirements happen to conflict with the overall scheme in the designer's mind, they are quite as likely to be honored in the breach as in the observance. Some years back, when I was trying to do my first houses, there were repeated discussions with clients about the relative merits of one- and two-story houses. At that time it was taken for granted that all houses outside of Florida and California should be two-story houses, and we wanted to keep ours down to one. Why did we want to do this? We wanted to keep our houses down to one story because we found them more satisfying esthetically. What we said to our clients, however, was quite different: we said one-story houses were more functional. The same arguments were used in favor of the glass wall and the open plan, although both have serious disadvantages. What the architects and designers were driving at was a new kind of total expression which made more good sense in terms of a changed environment than the older kinds. Functionalism was emphasized partly because it had a grain of truth in it, but mainly because it offered the most convincing argument to laymen.

EXTRAVAGANT CLAIMS FOR GOOD DESIGN

A good bit of the support given the modern movement came from people imbued with a real crusading spirit, and it is inevitable that enthusiasts make extravagant claims. Yet these unfounded claims do not further the modern movement in any substantial way, and they have nothing whatever to do with good design. The dedicated folk who still buttonhole me from time to time give the impression that if one could live in a well-designed modern house, fitted out with discreetly furnished and accessorized contemporary interiors, life would somehow become very full and very beautiful. Since my trade has to do with the design of houses, interiors, and products, I suppose I should be very pleased to hear all this, but somehow it never works out that way. I find it impossible to believe that life is so simple that a new garment of whatever description can transform it. Albert Einstein lived in a drab, ill-furnished little house (to judge from published photographs) on a side street in Princeton. Can you see this man's life enriched or deepened in the slightest by an immersion in good, modern design? Or Picasso's? Picasso could

have the services of the best architect in the world any time he wanted; he happens to have three dwellings, none of which could be accused of being either good or contemporary design. Braque lives in a conventional Normandy farmhouse. Matisse has occupied a very commonplace hotel suite for years. Yet all of these people are extraordinarily sensitive and fully aware of what has been going on. One could hardly accuse them of not understanding the meaning of good design. And yet, as consumers, they ignore it.

WHAT GOOD DESIGN IS NOT . . .

All of this brings me to the main, and concluding point. Good design, like good painting, cooking, architecture, or whatever you like, is a manifestation of the capacity of the human spirit to transcend its limitations. It enriches its maker through the experience of creating, and it can enrich the viewer or user who is equipped to respond to what it has to say. But it is a statement and not a gadget. If it happens to make something easier or more comfortable, this is quite incidental—a bad design could do just as well in this respect, and very often does. Used to demonstrate one's superior taste to the neighbors it loses its essential quality and becomes one more item of conspicuous consumption, like a yacht or a Cadillac. It cannot transform a dark brown little life into a large, brightly colored one—only the person living the life can do that. It is not a vitamin pill or a sulfa tablet. It reaches its full potential when it is experienced by a person fully equipped to understand and enjoy what it has to communicate. But such a person has no need of it for enrichment, for he is already rich. This, I think, is why people like Einstein and Picasso seem to ignore its more general manifestations—they are busy making good designs of their own and need no further distraction.

The purpose of good design is to ornament existence, not to substitute for it.

ART X = THE GEORGIA EXPERIMENT

*The account of a tremendous personal
involvement in a very large problem. The proposal — "tooled
education" — was violently resisted by the
educators exposed to it. But it is happening anyway.*

Anyone who has ever meddled with activities outside his own specialty knows that the amateur approach contains two sets of possibilities: there is always the chance that its fresh view of a problem may open unsuspected avenues of thought; there is also the likelihood of its leading the enthusiast up blind alleys long since explored and abandoned by the professionals. The experience I am going to describe was initiated by amateurs in the field of education, and the ideas which developed from it may turn out to be valid —or they may not. I suspect that they are by no means unfamiliar to workers in the field. The reason for presenting the story to an audience concerned with problems of business and industry rather than education is in part the steadily growing evidence that the barriers between these two areas are not as solid as we have led ourselves to believe; also because I have come to believe that the industrial approach can play a vital role in helping education cope with the difficulties that currently beset it.

The experience that led to this conclusion began at the University of Georgia. Early in the summer of 1952 the phone rang and the caller identified himself as Lamar Dodd, head of the university's department of fine arts. His reason for calling was an invitation to fly down and give a lecture. I declined. It was June, there had been too much talking at schools the past winter, and it was sure to be uncomfortably hot in Athens.

As things turned out, it was. Two days later the persistent Mr. Dodd was again on the phone. It seemed that what they wanted wasn't really a lecture, but consultation with the faculty on some problems of educational policy. This was a ready-made opportunity to get out from under, and I quickly explained that nobody could possibly know less about educational policy. "I know," drawled the voice at the other end of the wire. "That's why we want you."

FOREGROUND

Georgia's department of fine arts is a large one, and like similar departments at other universities its functions are widely varied. The majority of the student group consists of undergraduates taking art as a major, not as a rule with any intention of making it a career, but simply because they like it. Many of them are girls who believe it will help them as future homemakers, presumably by improving their taste in decoration. Each year a sizable group comes in from the department of home economics, no doubt for the same reason. A small percentage of the students, particularly those in textiles and ceramics, go on to establish careers in these fields. But essentially the department is one which turns out laymen interested in the arts rather than professionals.

As a necessary part of the discussions I was to have with the faculty, a tour through the various classes was arranged. Everything I saw was familiar: courses in theory, classes in drawing and painting, classes in design, craft workshops for weaving, screen painting, ceramics and so on. At this point several uneasy thouhgts came to mind. Here was a place functioning exactly like any art school, but it was supposed to turn out non-professionals. All art schools, obviously, turn out one or the other, but what seemed a little odd was the lack of visible differences between the two kinds of instruction. To the outside observer, it seemed that there was possibly a confusion in both methods and objectives. Does it make sense for a girl whose main ambition is to become a homemaker to pretend for four years that she is aiming for a career in sculpture or painting? Perhaps it does, but isn't the real problem to foster understanding and creative capacity so that these qualities could be employed in any situa-

tion? And if this were the real problem, how would a school go about meeting it? Is intensive instruction in drawing and modeling the best way? Or is this method used simply because it has always been the art school method?

In the discussions which followed, these questions were put to the faculty rather tentatively. The response was quick and intelligent. A feeling gradually developed that it might be worth re-examining objectives and perhaps trying some experiments in educational techniques—though at the time no one had any very clear idea of what the experiments might be. We decided to have another session in the fall and Lamar Dodd, who had guided the discussions with an extraordinary combination of firmness and sensitivity, suggested the formation of a small advisory committee. I asked him to invite Charles Eames.

BATTLEGROUND

At the beginning of the fall meeting we again went through the routine of visiting the various classes. Now that we had asked the basic questions, it was perfectly clear that much time was being wasted through methods originally developed for other purposes. For example, one class was finishing a two-week exercise demonstrating that a given color is not a fixed quantity to the eye but appears to change according to the colors around it. In a physics class such a point would have been made in about five minutes with a simple apparatus, and just as effectively.

We cited this example in an effort to establish a principle by which teaching effectiveness could be evaluated. We suggested that if a school knew fairly precisely what it wanted to communicate, a yardstick could be used for checking its methods. The yardstick was a clock. In other words, given the intention of communicating something

15

specific, the shortest time taken to do this—*without loss of comprehension or retention*—represented the best method.

At this point storm warnings began to go up. Were we proposing to apply time-motion studies in the painting studio? Maybe, we retorted, such schools as this had no business teaching painting. The discussion became an argument, then a free-for-all.

From the faculty's point of view, there were good reasons for opposing mass educational techniques at a college level. For many of them college is the last stronghold of individualized instruction, where the student-teacher relationship is the vital core of education. Others, we realized, were exasperated by proposals which would mean new burdens on the school budget and their own scarce time. There exists in the art professions a strong feeling that their problems are unique and that methods sanctioned by tradition need not be questioned too closely. All of this was perfectly understandable, for in education, standards of performance are not under the same pressure as in industry, and the price of inefficiency is not exacted as swiftly or as ruthlessly.

That night Eames and I discussed the turmoil created by what we had believed were innocuous proposals. It was our feeling that the most important thing to communicate to undergraduates was an awareness of relationships. Education, like the thinking of the man in the street, was sealed off into too many compartments. If a girl wanted to know something about decorating her future home and what she got was a class in painting, this might make perfectly good sense, but perhaps it was up to the school to build a bridge between the two so that she might see how they were related. Whether this was accomplished by personal or impersonal methods seemed of little consequence.

PREPARATION

It occurred to us that if the faculty was confused and uncertain about what we wanted, it might be because we were too. The following day, in an atmosphere of interested cooperation, we proposed that we present a specific example of our thinking in the form of a sample lesson for an imaginary course (the course was promptly labeled "Art X"). We asked, too, that Alexander Girard be invited as the third member of the committee during preparation of the lesson.

It was a relief to have our part in this exploration now placed on a "put up or shut up"

basis, but it was only after leaving Athens that we realized what we had let ourselves in for. The idea was to develop high-speed techniques for exposing the relationships between seemingly unrelated phenomena. This meant films, slides, sounds, music, narration—the familiar world of audio-visual aids—and it soon became clear that we were committed to a job which might easily demand the resources of a Hollywood production unit. There was also the problem of how the three "producers" were going to work together: Girard lived in Michigan, I worked in New York, and Eames, in California.

Problems are made to be solved. We solved ours by outlining the lesson and dividing it into "packages" which could be produced separately. Girard agreed to make a facsimile exhibit which was supposed to accompany each of the canned lectures. Eames and I divided the one-hour lesson between us. Slides were to be made as needed and movies were to be made or, if possible, borrowed. The subject of the lesson was "Communication," and if anyone should ask why we started with so impossibly difficult a theme I can only answer that at the time we did everything the hard way. We wanted a subject permitting the exploration of relationships and "Communication" offered plenty of opportunities. And there was the easily comprehended starting idea, that art was a kind of communication.

PRESENTATION

Five months later the "Art X" company met in Athens, burdened with as much equipment as a traveling medicine show. There was a 16-mm. projector handling both film and magnetic sound. There were several tape recorders. There were three slide projectors, three screens which filled the end of the auditorium, cans of film, boxes of slides, reels of magnetic tape. Girard's exhibit arrived in a series of mammoth packing cases and he also brought a collection of bottles of synthetic smells, to be introduced into the room via the air conditioning system at various points in the show. Seventy-two hours later when we had staggered through the first creaky performance, we found that it took eight people to run it.

What had happened during the months of work was that our ideas had outstripped technical resources. As an example, while running off some slide sequences, it occurred to us that two slides run at once could illustrate certain contrasts. We liked the simultaneous projection so much that we tried three slides and found ourselves with a kind of poor-man's Cinerama on our hands. But to carry out this simple notion required three projectors, three screens and a magnetic tape playback.

The reason for the complexity was lack of money. Technical means for wide-screen projection already existed, but they were out of reach. Our dream had been to produce a one-hour lecture which could be transported in a few small cans; ultimately we decided that it was more important on the first try to explore as many possibilities as we could and to worry later, if the need should arise, about making the results portable.

What was the show about? The illustrated chart gives an idea of the subjects touched upon, but any audio-visual presentation that is more than a series of stills strung together cannot be described except in its own terms. Take, for instance, the small section which relates to the idea of "abstraction":

A slide goes on the screen, showing a still life by Picasso. A narrator's voice identifies it, adds that it is a type of painting known as "abstract," which is correct in the dictionary sense of the word, since the painter abstracted from the data in front of him only what he wanted and arranged it as he saw fit. The next slide shows a section of London. The dry voice identifies this as an abstraction too, since of all possible data about this area, only the street pattern was selected. Then follow other maps of the same area, but each presents different data—routes of subways, location of garages, etc. The voice observes that each time the information is changed, the picture changes. The camera closes in on the maps until only a few bright color patches show; the communication is now useless to the geographer, but there is something new in the residue of colors and shapes. Then a shift to a distant view of Notre Dame, followed by a series which takes you closer and closer. The narrator cites the cathedral as an abstraction—the result of a filtering-out process which has gone on for centuries. The single slide squence becomes a triple-slide projection. Simultaneous exterior views change to interior views. Organ music crashes in as the narration stops. The interior becomes a close-up of a stained glass window. Incense drifts into the auditorium. The entire space dissolves into sound, space and color.

What I have tried to describe is a fragment which may have taken four minutes in its entirety. But even in this flash presentation a very complex communication was completed. The students were shown a modern painting to which they reacted with feelings ranging from hostility to exaggerated reverence. They were then forced to make a swift adjustment to the unexpected idea that maps and cathedrals were also kinds of abstractions, and finally introduced to a sample of medieval architecture in a way which tried to communicate atmosphere rather than fact.

To describe all this with anything approaching adequacy might take a competent lecturer an hour, and still the emotional impact would be lacking. The degree to which learning can be accelerated through audio-visual methods is perhaps its best known characteristic; what may be even more significant is the extraordinary force with which it can be used to relate idea and concepts. Its significance lies in the extreme delicacy and complexity of relationships which go to make up the modern world. The success of leadership, even in relatively small ventures, depends to an ever-increasing extent on comprehension of these relationships. Industry, in recent years, has shown an awareness of the problem by sending off more and more of its most talented young executives —not only to the business schools—but to the liberal arts departments of the universities. Superior performance as a specialist is no longer enough. And dependence on the traditional tools of communication is no longer enough either.

MONEY

The first thing one learns about audio-visual techniques is that they are expensive, and our own experience with the "Art X" show quickly taught us that a course prepared in this way could add up to a fantastic total. The cost of film-making in a commercial studio (16 mm. color with sound) rarely averages out at less than $1,500 per minute—and a lecture takes fifty minutes. Even assuming every possible economy, a full course on almost any subject, prepared for wide distribution, could easily cost $1,000,000.

At first blush it may seem idiotic even to consider this kind of thing for institutions so chronically short of funds as schools, but the industrial designer has a somewhat different viewpoint than the professional educator. The sum of $1,000,000,

17

for instance, is not large if it is the new tooling for a refrigerator which is being considered; $50,000,000 is a modest sum if the product is to be a new line of cars. To an educator such comparisons might seem meaningless, since the two kinds of investment are totally different. But for us it brought up a question: are they so different? With the question came a new picture of education as a "handicraft" process in a society geared to other methods. With the picture, a hypothesis: many of the difficulties facing education today are related to the persistence of outmoded methods.

If, by some miracle in reverse, two men could make one automobile by hand in a year, the industry would require a working force of 10 to 12 millions. There would be a labor shortage, as there is in teaching today, and cars would be very expensive.

Two or three centuries ago in the European universities there existed a numerical ratio between faculty and students which may have been on the order of one to fifteen, or perhaps one to five. This could be described as a production ratio: it took x faculty members to produce y graduates. Today's ratios are: University of Illinois, five to six students per faculty member; Iowa, nine; Harvard, three or four; Michigan, sixteen. Now it is possible that education is one activity immune to the effects of the Industrial Revolution, and that nothing will ever change its production ratios. But I wonder.

Let us consider something else. There are listed in the World Almanac some 1,000 colleges and universities. Let us assume that certain common denominator courses, such as physics, biology, art appreciation, etc., are taught in all of them. Let us also assume that in each institution an average of $1,500 is budgeted for the instructor's time and other costs. If this figure were accurate (it is probably low) you would have a recurring annual bill of $1,500,000 for instructing the nation's undergraduates in, say, elementary biology. This is hardly low-cost production, by industrial standards. Nor can it possibly be claimed that the present "handicraft" method results in production of a uniformly high level.

With what has already been said, the contrasting industrial approach to this problem needs no detailed explanation. The big investment would be made *once*, at the beginning. The most gifted teachers in the field would be retained, and they would be backed up with all needed technical facilities. The result: a series of "packages" available to students everywhere. The cost per student: a fraction of what it is today. I cannot say that this procedure would solve the financial problems of the schools, but it seems reasonable to hope that it might relieve them. And much more than money is involved.

TIME

One of the most irksome problems confronting the educator is the competition for the student's time. On the one hand are the pressures for a more highly specialized education-training which covers more ground more intensively than ever. (Consider what a physicist has to learn today.) On the other, is the insistence that everyone have a liberal dose of the liberal arts. Both pressures, moreover, will increase. The demands of business, science and industry will become more exacting, not less. Public awareness of the dangers of a society run by half-educated specialists is also greater.

It is hard to see how, with present teaching methods, the schools can hope to turn out the competent technician who is *also* a mature, educated individual. A clear distinction between the two objectives, however, might open the way to improved methods. When a school turns out a professional, his capacity to perform is of crucial importance. To date, the best way to learn to do something is to *do* it, preferably under expert guidance. This is time-consuming, and there are few short-cuts. The procedures involved in a general liberal education, however, are different. It is not necessary for the student to be able to write Latin poetry, remember the date of the battle of Thermopylae or the name of the barroom where Kit Marlowe got into his final brawl. The objective is to help him form a coherent picture of human activity, a capacity to understand its great achievements, an ability to form independent judgments, and above all, to learn to relate isolated bits of information in terms of a large context.

To meet the second of these objectives, the approach tried in the sample lesson offers rich possibilities. It can communicate with great force and tremendous speed; it can establish relationships in minutes which would take a classroom lecturer hours. If the "briefings" such a method makes possible were substituted for many current elective courses, whole sections of time would be freed, and the specialist could be powerfully exposed, during his undergraduate years, to many important areas of human activity.

We are aware of the widespread feeling that canned education destroys the value of the personal contacts that schools and colleges make possible. People used to be suspicious of food out of cans. One cannot deny the inspirational value of direct contact with a great teacher, but how many great teachers are there? And why shouldn't a great teacher, in addition to inspiring one small group of students, be passed on to students in other schools?

Interestingly enough, the audio-visual methods, so rich in educative potential, have been confined largely, to date, to the teaching of trade skills and to conveying isolated bits of information. And the best of the experiments in education—as distinguished from training—have appeared in television.

RESULTS

If the result of work on the Art X lesson was to give us a new insight into some aspects of education, it does not follow that the result at the University of Georgia was the prompt allocation of a million dollars for the production of a course in art appreciation. What happened was far more constructive.

The Art X sample lesson was run through six times before the demands of students and faculty were satisfied. It produced both confusion and enlightenment, generated enthusiasm and hostility, and a rather depressed conviction that this kind of project was simply out of the grasp of a single school. Then one faculty member happened to remark, "Well, if we had about $25,000 for equipment . . ." and Eames and I both erupted in unrehearsed but perfect unanimity. We pointed out that nobody had given us $25,000, or fancy equipment, or a staff of technicians, and that we had offices to run while making Art X. It apparently made the point. The weekend following the showings, a number of faculty members descended upon one of the larger classrooms and began ripping out its insides wtih their own hands. That summer they ripped down the barriers between courses which had previously been rigidly separated. In the fall, new students walked in on a new kind of learning experience, one which gave them drawing, modeling, painting, carving and automatically projected lectures as a single integrated activity. Miraculously, two faculty members have managed to turn out over thirty of these presentations in one school year, and though there are immense obstacles to overcome, I doubt very much that it will stop.

It is early to draw conclusions but two things are quite clear: (1) given the determination, a school can produce its own audio-visual material with limited resources. The results are far from technically impeccable, but it doesn't matter; (2) creative use of the industrial approach does not eliminate the teacher—it upgrades him. It also gives an entirely new direction to the curriculum.

PROSPECTS

The emergence of a valid new concept is like suddenly turning on a light in a dark room. One no longer feels one's way from one separate object to another; the room and its contents become visible as a unity. The Art X lesson was innocently undertaken as a device for the clarification of certain ideas about teaching: it ended up by illuminating some of the immense enrichment which could come about through application of the industrial method to education. Its costs, by advance calculation, were prohibitive—so it goes ahead anyway. It presents all the dangers which stem from centralized production and control—but in practice it takes form at the grass roots level as an activity in which any institution can participate. The speed of communication is so great that the conventional course can be compressed into a kind of briefing. This, in turn, suggests one kind of answer to the education needs of industry, and to the growing demand for general adult education. It relates automatically to the emergence of non-commercial television. It suggests the merging, in a future not too far off, of the many current experiments in communication into a new pattern of continuing education.

Art X said its piece in an industrial vernacular because industry has given us more and better ways to say things than we had before. The pictures which flickered across the multiple screens were made by machines, developed by machines and projected by machines. The voices, music and sounds were electronically recorded, amplified and played back. But it was people who said the words, wrote the music, and made the final statement. This is why there is no need to be afraid of our tools—even in education. The teacher may become less visible in the new classroom, but he will still be there.

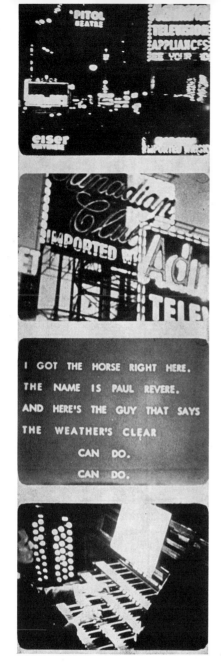

A sample lesson: *subject* **"COMMUNICATION"**

Excerpts from a visual lesson prepared by Charles Eames and George Nelson from original and borrowed films and slides; presented at the University of Georgia and U.C.L.A.

1 Introduction

Opening film (10 minutes) makes one point: the completion of a communication requires not only a message and a transmitter, but a receiver capable of tuning in.

Message: song from "Guys and Dolls,"

"Receivers" include student in American history (not used to thinking of Paul Revere as a horse).

constructed in the form of a fugue.

bookie, who knows all about race horses, nothing about fugues,

specialist in oriental literature. who does not speak English.

Each can receive only a portion of the apparently simple message.

2 Visual Communication

Film dissolves in triple color slide sequences, simultaneously projected. The sequences (about 50) cover an extreme variety of visual communications: painting, artifacts, sculpture, equipment, landscape design, structures, type faces, etc.

Here again the intention is to show that comprehension of a message varies with the capacity of receiver. Music background, no narration. Running time, about 10 minutes. Both sections by Nelson.

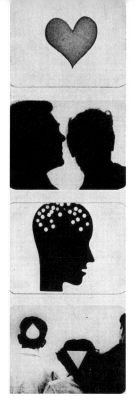

The process of communication is shown as it takes place between two people ("I Love you") between artist and audience, etc. Running time: 10 minutes. By Eames.

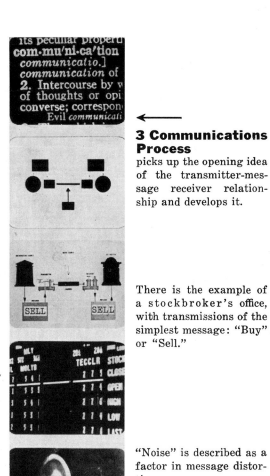

3 Communications Process

picks up the opening idea of the transmitter-message receiver relationship and develops it.

There is the example of a stockbroker's office, with transmissions of the simplest message: "Buy" or "Sell."

"Noise" is described as a factor in message distortion.

4 Abstraction

The point: The use of abstraction is necessary in communications, since it is rarely possible to send a *total* message. Examples: a Picasso still life, maps of a section of London ("change the information and you change the picture") and cathedrals in England and France.

Presentation of abstraction in communication changes from single slides (above) to simultaneous triple projections shown below. Smell effects (incense) accompanied slides of cathedral interiors. Detailed description is given in text. Slides, 35 mm color. Running time, 8 minutes. By Nelson.

La Lettre

Excerpts from a French film on the evolution of lettering and calligraphy. 16 mm black and white. 4 minutes.

6 UPA

← UPA

UPA

"The animated calligraphy of sound"—a 3-minute fragment taken from a 16 mm color film made by UPA for CBS. Edited by Eames.

→

7 Egypt

A 10-minute 16 mm film in color, taken from the magnificent footage shot by Ray Garner, generously made available for the lesson. Here a dead civilization is shown as a live transmitter. Its ruined architecture, sculpture, jewelry, hieroglyphics add up to a communication on a variety of levels. Again the success of the transmission depends on the ability of the receiver to decode the silent messages. Edited by Nelson.

8 Communications Method

→

Communications Method

An extension of the "Process" film, which penetrates still more deeply into the procedures used in communication. It shows, primarily, how the most complex of messages can be broken down into myriads of individual on-off, yes-no, stop-go decisions.

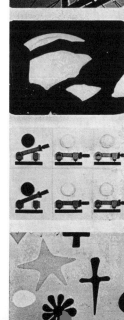

←

Communications method (continued)

Example of ways messages may be broken individual decisions: halftone photograph of a face is made up of several hundred thousand black-or-white decisions.

An electronic computer presents as many possible decisions as the halftone.

"The simplest human act" — picking a flower — takes infinitely more stop-go decisions than the most complex computer or printing plate.

Mosaic and pointilliste paintings are examples of complex productions visibly based on great numbers of separate, decisive acts.

Note: Both the "Process" and "Method" films, by Eames, have been merged into a single 16 mm color films which runs about 20 minutes, entitled "A Communications Primer." The film is available for distribution.

When it comes to cutting itself off at the knees by selfish and short-sighted action, the design profession is no better or smarter than others. This was an attempt to combat one segregation-type move before it got anywhere.

"CAPTIVE" DESIGNER vs(?) "INDEPENDENT" (!) DESIGNER

Are there real differences between the consultant designer and his company colleague? Can either claim to be superior?

In discussing an upheaval in the relationship among designers for industry, one consultant describes some visible differences—but debunks the classic debate.

In the golden days of pre-industrial design when a manufacturer needed some product design he generally went down to the shop and got one of the foremen to do it. Or did it himself.

In the golden days of industrial design he began turning to the gilded industrial designers, and got the full treatment.

Since the full treatment was quite often followed by an interesting rise in sales, the manufacturer was presently sold on design and designers.

Finally he realized that if he put the designers on a payroll instead of a retainer he got equivalent services for less money. Or thought he did, which had the same results.

Among these results was an economic threat to the independent designers. Or so it seemed.

It is a harmless foible of many professionals, designers included, to believe that they are somewhat differently motivated than workaday mortals. Workers may strike for seven cents an hour and corporate vice presidents may garner ulcers in reaching for that eventual $100,000-per-year-before-taxes paycheck, but the creative, dedicated professional has higher-level fish to fry, or so we sometimes like to think.

The facts, alas, fail to support the assumption. Workers and vice presidents often get non-monetary satisfactions out of their jobs, and there is evidence that the heart of the dedicated professional—when confronted with a stranger working his side of the street—beats with the same pure indignation as the heart of the oldest of all professionals.

For years, one of the most unusual and instructive sights on the professional scene was the battle of the American Institute of Architects to keep public agencies (hospitals, jails, etc.) from operating their own architectural offices. Needless to say, what officially pained the AIA so deeply was not the loss of fees to members, but rather the threat to the purity of the architectural profession. The battle was waged with great decorum, and public discussion concerned itself only with the moral issues at stake (*which* moral issues were at stake some of us never managed to figure out). However, the AIA leadership would have been deeply shocked by any suggestion that its motives were not much different from those of the CIO.

Now, in the profession of industrial design, we are doing it again. After barely a quarter-century of existence, we have divided ourselves into two opposed categories: "independent" designers and "captive" designers. The latter are full-time employees of businesses, mainly manufacturers.

The term "captive" is in itself revealing. It is derogatory, and it was brought into being by the "independents." It seems fairly obvious that no designer on a corporate payroll, particularly if he is getting a fair day's pay for a day's work, is going to think of himself as a prisoner. Meanwhile, independent designers work contentedly for clients who are almost without exception high-level corporate employees. Has anyone ever heard such a designer refer to his client as a "captive" executive?

The reason for pushing so hard at the point of economic competition as the basis of the existing professional split is that it seems to be *the* point, and that all other arguments are window dressing.

The reason for trying to deal with the subject at all, as far as I am concerned, is that it is an unhealthy situation. The division that has occurred in the design profession confuses its younger members, particularly students, reduces the effectiveness of the contribution required from it, and impairs its dignity. The industrial design profession has established a place for itself in a phenomenally short time. It is widely accepted as a useful service. But it is also still in the process of realizing its full potential as a service to a society going through a series of tremendous transformations.

Consider the matter from the viewpoint of an outsider. People who are not industrial designers —i.e., practically everybody—i.e., society in general—could not possibly care less how the needed service is provided or which category of professionals provides it. Why should they? Does anyone care if his paycheck is figured out by a bookkeeper or computed by a machine? The real problem is to furnish needed services, economically and at the highest reachable level. *How* this is worked out is of course a matter of concern to us as individuals, but numerically we are an all-but-invisible speck in the population, and the population just doesn't care. Does it make the slightest difference to the woman who just bought that pretty eggbeater whether it is a "captive" or "independent" eggbeater?

EITHER-OR VS.-TOTAL FLEXIBILITY

Consider, too, the behavior of business in areas where design is not involved. All manufacturers constantly face the problem of which components to make in the plant and which to buy on the outside. The problem is a complex one, and in an overall sense it never really gets "answered." More and more manufacturers do some of both, with each separate decision being made on the basis of many factors such as tooling investment, availability of skills, probable life of product, accessibility of sub-contractors, plans for future company development, and so on.

If industry meets its production problems using a wide variety of methods based on a totally flexible approach, why should the need for design service be resolved on an either-or basis?

Consider the matter of economy, which is of some importance to manufacturers. The costs of design service are not as a rule publicized, and it would seem reasonable to assume that the fees of independent designers vary within fairly wide limits. Nevertheless, it is probably not too far out of line to say that hourly drafting charges have to be somewhere in the neighborhood of three times the draftsman-designer's hourly pay.

Thus a man paid four dollars per hour would be billed out around twelve.

It does not matter greatly whether this basis for design charges is used generally or not: whatever the private designer's method of billing, the manufacturer with a flow of design problems can run his own design studio for less. This service, like the selection of the kind of production used, is determined by more factors than direct cost.

Like other design organizations, our own works for a variety of companies in a variety of ways. There are a few which depend on us, not only for all design, but for product development as well. Other clients have procedures for working with a number of outside designers. Still others have their own staffs, but choose to supplement this facility with design consultants. In reviewing these very different situations within our own office, we have yet to find anything fundamentally good or bad about any of them. There is always a valid reason for the method adopted, and we have consequently fallen into the habit of recommending to clients that they never use our facilities before checking on the adequacy of their own.

The reasons for differences in the methods of handling design service are very numerous. Automotive and major appliance manufacturers have demonstrated that it is almost imperative to maintain an in-plant staff: their problems are complex, fast-moving, and highly specialized. Another company might set up a design studio to implement a policy of complete integration. A company of similar size and product might retain an independent office simply because it didn't want to be bothered forming its own staff, or because it felt it had more freedom in buying the kinds of service it wanted.

Whatever the full list of reasons for the varied choices being made in industry today, those which come to mind might lead to the conclusion that there is a trend to concentrate on staff designers in certain types and sizes of industries, leaving the rest of the field open to independent offices. But this is not what seems to be happening. Apparently the overall situation is too fluid to permit the rigid classification of categories.

To illustrate what does seem to be happening, it is necessary to indicate some of the differences between staff designers and the independent group. For there *are* differences. It is as far from the truth to say that both are *alike,* as to say that one is "captive" and the other "free."

PRESUMED DIFFERENCES
In discussions of the two general categories making up the design profession today, much has been made of supposed differences between the kinds of people who elect one career as against another. Independent practice, according to this view, offers high possible rewards combined with large risks, whereas company employment is less spectacular but more secure. This contention, naturally, leads to the conclusion that the risk-taking independent is superior to the individual who scuttles under the protecting wings of a benevolent corporation. There may be some truth in this argument, but I have not yet been able to locate it. The idea that security and corporate employment are synonymous does not check with the facts. I know companies that have drastically cut design staffs to fit changes in policy, and there are top company designers who have lost their jobs. You can find men in independent offices who have had steady employment for twenty years.

Other pieces of the argument fail to fit. For instance, there are some pretty exciting jobs being done by company designers. Who can say that these men are motivated by fears of insecurity? Also, the notion that risk-taking is associated exclusively with independent practice is hard to substantiate.

Doesn't the top company designer stake his job, so to speak, on the success of each new product group? Doesn't he also stake a large chunk of his company's security? Isn't unsatisfactory performance ever penalized within the corporate setup?

What is probably true is that few people are willing to make decisions where risk is involved. It is likely that these few are "superior," at least in a competitive sense. To date there is nothing to show that such people are found only in independent offices.

There is another argument heard occasionally. Men in both branches of the profession, impatient with the lack of harmony and understanding they sense in prevailing attitudes have said, in effect, "What is all the noise about? A good designer is a good designer and it doesn't matter where you find him." With the spirit of the argument I could not be more in agreement, but the well-intended effort to heal a breach obscures the most interesting and productive possibility in the whole situation: there *are* differences, and they could be exploited with benefit.

REAL DIFFERENCES
The significant differences between the two groups *stem from their conditioning through work experiences.* The designer is not a finished product when he leaves school, but is continuously modified by what happens to him as he pursues his trade.

Consider, for instance, some of the things that happen to the typical independent professional. For one thing, nobody else cares whether he stays in business or not, so he has to develop whatever resources he has for this purpose. He becomes highly sensitized to passing opportunities he might otherwise overlook. He has to explain the value of his services to strangers, and in the process learns to become a better than average communicator. If he is at all successful, he will work for a number of companies, often in areas which have little in common with each other. This spread of design problems, usually quite unpredictable in its variations, inevitably creates certain attitudes, methods and techniques designed for the widest possible applicability. In the end you get an organization which is strongly permeated by a special attitude and equipped with special—but unspecialized—facilities.

The designer who works as easily with a lathe as with a pencil, who sees no insuperable barrier between the making of a piece of furniture and a film, tends to be extremely fluid in his attitudes and confident when faced with a new kind of problem. This particular kind of skill has its disadvantages, of course, but it develops tremendous strength as well.

The strength of the independent office lies in the range of its experience, the relatively large number of "testing" situations through which its personnel must go (in dealing with new clients, unfamiliar kinds of problems, etc.) in its highly developed ability to communicate, and in its general flexibility in relation to almost any situation. Translated into action, this means an ability to bring a high level of detached perception to any problem, and this has a very special kind of value to management.

NO PLACE FOR PRIMA DONNAS
Although in the largest of the manufacturing

establishments some of these experiences are duplicated, the work experience of the staff designer, as a general rule, is different from that of the independent professional. One very significant difference is that it is made clear to him from the outset that design is just one phase of a cooperative process, and not by any means the most important. The company is not dazzled by its designer's spectacular publicity because as a rule he gets no publicity at all. In other words, the staff designer quickly learns some very important things about the relationship of design to overall product development and to corporate success.

The prima donna attitude is not encouraged within the corporate organization, which has very few jobs which can be handled by a single individual, no matter how brilliant. A staff man would not be likely to commit the egregious error of the independent designer who said that he had "designed" the such-and-such plane. He would take it for granted that a plane's most important characteristic, its ability to stay in the air, is quite unaffected by the industrial designer's contribution. This is a small point, since few designers are overburdened by delusions of grandeur. But the conditioning of the staff designer, which stems directly from his role as a functioning member of management, is not a small point at all. It is the core of his entire working education.

The practice of management today is more and more a matter of education. The growing size and complexity of business tends to impose stiff penalties on unsound procedures. The daily financial pages are testimonials to the speed with which poorly managed companies, even large ones, can slip into a tight spin. Modern management, in consequence, keeps putting itself through school in a variety of ways. The company designer, as part of management, also goes through this process.

Design training and management training have some elements in common, but not many. The design school necessarily creates a situation in which individual performance is almost everything, and the emphasis on esthetics—also necessary—does not always make for sympathetic comprehension of the problems of business and industry. Management training stresses the need to learn how to get people, particularly groups of people, to do things. "Doing" therefore acquires two completely different meanings in the mind of the company designer, and as a result of his double education he becomes a most interesting kind of hybrid—and, incidentally, an adjunct to management with enormous potential value. The capable individual who can talk the language of business while retaining the designer's ability to see problems in an overall way is not in large supply at the present moment.

This, however, by no means exhausts the staff designer's value. Every company, no matter what the nature of its business, presents some kind of image to the world at large. This image is hard to describe in words, but it is a most valuable asset. It is a large part of what is in the customer's mind when he buys product A instead of product B. Any company's image is created by management (including design) through millions of daily acts which pile up to crystallize, not only into stated policy, but a kind of "feel" which the company acquires both for its own people and for outsiders. Because the staff designer lives and works within this framework—indeed, has helped build it—he can communicate its meaning with far more sureness and effectiveness than the outsider. But for this he pays a price: like other members of management he runs a constant risk of jelling when what is called for is fluidity.

Which is where the outside design consultant seems to be coming in.

Please note the use of "consultant." The independent designer has for many years played out the role of the expert—that is, he moved in, looked things over and wrote out a prescription. Management was eager—anxious—not to "inhibit" him. Sometimes the procedure worked and sometimes it didn't. With today's moves towards fuller integration of the skills available to a company, the indigestible "expert" has become something of a nuisance, and a menace to boot.

The new look in designers—whether staff or otherwise—includes an attitude of attentive listening.

The "captive" versus "independent" issue has just one thing wrong with it—it is not a real issue. If there is any question at all, it is whether the profession can mature to the point where each group understands and accepts the value of the other to its own work. This will probably not come easily. *It requires a change of attitude on the part of both groups.*

As industry is developing today, there are roles to be played which require the use of design professionals who have been differently oriented, but can work in harmony. Some of these *must* be staff people; others *must* be outside consultants. Actually, while the design problem is not looked at very often in this way, there is nothing especially new about the idea. A company with an advertising department also has an agency. Most companies with legal departments also retain outside firms.

POACHERS INVITED

As long as the staff designer was primarily a designer (in his own eyes) he naturally had to guard his own preserve and chase off poachers. But he is beginning to become an integral part of management. A typical management attitude is that it couldn't care less through what channels it gets results as long as it gets them. When the management-oriented designer finally realizes that results are what he too is paid for, he begins to lose interest in massaging his own ego. Then the outside designer looks less like competition and more like a possible assist.

In this process of transformation the independent practitioner has been learning too. Humility, mostly. A respect for creativity in non-visual areas such as corporate management. One cannot possibly go through one product development program after another without ultimately learning that to create and maintain a successful company takes quite a bit of doing, most of it outside the province of the industrial designer. The lesson, when learned, releases an urge to join the team, though not necessarily on a full-time basis. This urge can be processed by management for its own purposes, which include not only the maintenance of stability, but the early recognition and acceptance of change.

The special qualifications being developed in the two groups making up the design profession are not basically in conflict, but complementary. Both, actually, were called into existence by the widening requirements of industry, which must have highly skilled specialists, and highly skilled non-specialists.

The barriers between the groups are, in any practical sense, meaningless and anyway ours is a time for pulling barriers down, not putting them up. Design, like technology, politics and war, is becoming an open game, and open games demand far more in the way of personal resources than closed games. We could be a lot worse off, for there are more road blocks behind us than ahead.

ENDS AND MEANS

*I remember this mainly because when it was
given as a lecture at the Chicago Institute of Design
about ten years ago, it led to a question-and-answer period
which, in turn, precipitated a near-riot. In retrospect
it is a little hard to see why this restatement of the obvious produced such turmoil.*

LACK OF INTEGRITY

It is difficult to resist the conclusion that U. S. industry is being served by a group whose technical qualifications are admirable. I get the impression that the designing professions are filled with men and women whose knowledge of materials and processes leaves little to be desired. I also get the impression that these qualifications and skills are being used to convey the most mediocre of ideas. I marvel at the extent of the knowledge needed to design, say, the Buick or the new Hudson—but I am also struck by my inability to get the slightest pleasure out of the results. From where I sit, therefore, the whole matter of skills and techniques seems irrelevant compared to the lack of integrity with which these skills are employed.

Since I mentioned automobiles, let us pursue the subject for a moment. You recall that when the new Studebaker came out it aroused considerable interest because it was the only postwar car that showed any freshness of design. I had occasion to mention this to a General Motors vice president shortly afterwards, and was told that General Motors has no interest in pioneering in radical design changes. If we assume that the competence of the designers working for General Motors and for Studebaker is roughly the same, then we are pushed to the conclusion that the basic instrument in the redesign of the Studebaker was neither talent nor engineering knowhow, but company policy. If this is true, it means that the results of the designer's activity may be in large part determined before he is even hired. It also means that unless a voice in company policy is one of the tools at the designer's disposal, his entire work may be negated. Anything that can negate a designer's total effort is worth considering.

Another example: about ten years ago I was sent down the Tennessee Valley to put together a special issue for *The Architectural Forum*. Among the people interviewed was the engineer in charge of designing the dams, and I recall with particular vividness his answer to one question. The question was, "How many dams would have to be built to exploit fully the resources of the Valley?" His answer was, "Twelve"—the number of dams then completed or under construction. TVA at that time was viewed as a threat to private enterprise and was under severe fire in Congress. A few years later war changed the picture, and the number of dams at TVA increased to twenty-four. In other words, the answer had been 100% off.

Now this is interesting. Engineering is supposed to be a fairly exact discipline. With all needed facts at his disposal, how does an engineer make so great an error? I am tempted to conclude that even so precise an instrument as a slide rule can be affected by political pressures.

UNDER PRESSURE

It is not often that a designer finds himself in a position free from pressures. Whether the object in question is a house, a product or an advertising brochure, he is subject to budgets, technical limitations, marketing problems, conflicting demands from many people. Under these circumstances it is important for him to know where he stands in relation to the pressures. If he is at all concerned with the integrity of the product he is designing, he must establish some contact with reality, and this involves an understanding of the pressures brought to bear on him, and a decision to accept or reject them. One of the means at the disposal of the designer, therefore, should be a method of establishing his position in the process of bringing an idea to the point of production and sale. Illustrations may clarify this statement.

Let us imagine that a designer is engaged to design flat silver for a small manufacturer. And let us further assume that this designer is convinced that his function is to bring good design to vast numbers of people—a conviction held almost unanimously by the students preparing to enter the profession. In this instance he would discover that the technical limitations of a small silverware plant make mass production and low prices impossible. He must either accept this situation or reject the commission. Should he accept these limitations for what they are, he will learn something rather important: there is nothing wrong with designing for old materials and techniques, for they are as much a part of the current situation as new materials and new techniques. He might also learn that under such conditions, spectacularly "modern" design is as illogical as the use of machines to imitate hand-produced details. And finally, through acceptance of real limitations with his eyes wide open, the designer could get himself into a position to formulate a program designed to destroy these limitations—something he could never do if he rejected them in the first place.

THE AMERICAN MYTH OF MASS PRODUCTION

When a designer formulates a program he is merely stating a problem in its largest sense, and the capacity to state the problem is one of the indispensable qualifications of the designer. If a plant is backward in a technical sense, as in the hypothetical example just given, there are two problems with which the designer must cope. He must determine how to shape his design so that it relates most naturally to the process being used—not, if you please, to the process he wishes were used. His other problem is how to help bring the plant up to the highest technical level. Some designers consider this outside their scope; it is my feeling that to whatever extent the designer limits his responsibility, he also limits his potential.

Problems related to technique are no more important than those connected with merchandising. Because merchandising is apparently a complete field in itself, there is a natural temptation to accept as Gospel the findings of the specialists in this area. Convenient as this may be, it is not wise for the designer to do so, for his work is basically influenced by his attitude towards the market. If this seems far-fetched, take the table radio as a case in point. Over 12,000,000 of these units were produced in 1947, and the vast majority differ from each other only superficially. The standard solution is a decorated plastic case with certain limited variations in dials, knobs, and grilles, and the design level is several notches below mediocrity. The impression I get from this mass of indifferent merchandise is that at some level of policy there is general agreement on what the public will or will not accept, and that this policy is then accepted by the designer. Yet if the designer is genuinely concerned with arriving at an accurate statement of his problem, he may come to an entirely different conclusion. Let us assume that he reexamines the whole question of the merchandise and the public.

First of all, he begins to wonder what this "public" is. He does a little research and discovers that twelve and a half million table radios were made in 1947, and that his client produced 3 per cent of them, or 380,000. Furthermore, he learns that there are eleven models in his client's line, so he estimates that one design should sell somewhere between 30,000 and 40,000 radios. At this point he has discovered something: his "public" is not 140,000,000 people, it is less than 1/20 of 1 per cent of that number. The American myth of mass production and distribution is largely a myth without meaning. And consequently, most consumer research that develops neat little pictures of what the public will or will not buy is also without meaning. The designer may also come to the conclusion that in a market where manufacturers compete by imitating each other's designs, the safe design policy, in a business sense, is often a radical one. If he can persuade his client that his reasoning is correct (and it isn't nearly as difficult as you might think) he has a design assignment where his only limitations are real ones—the shape of the chassis, the nature of the materials he can use, and the characteristics of the process. Now he is free to state his problem *in terms of the problem* and there is a chance (though no guarantee) that he may come up with a good design.

CREATIVE DESTRUCTION

If stating the problem were as easy as it sounds, there would be more great artists and designers. It took a Cezanne to formulate the problem of the painter so sharply that everyone who came after him was affected. Wright, with his insistence on the nature of materials, helped change the course of architecture. Fuller, with one idea of greater performance per pound, created a tool of tremendous importance for the designer. To arrive at statements of this kind takes, paradoxically, a capacity for destructive action. And since the desire to hang on to what we have is bred deeply into the structure of the race, to destroy anything deliberately—even a concept—takes a particular kind of courage. I have come to feel that the outstanding creative artist could not exist without it. I have also come to feel that this particular capacity is not the monopoly of any group of geniuses, but is available to anyone who wants to realize his own creative potential as fully as possible.

I first came across this paradox in *War and Peace.* Tolstoy referred to the "creative destruction" that accompanied the War of 1812, and I found myself puzzled and irritated by his bland acceptance of what seemed to me a contradiction. As time went by, it finally resolved itself into a description of the process of life itself. The whole of nature is an example. And anyone can illustrate the process from his own experience.

I can remember, for instance, the moment that the Storagewall concept came into existence for me. Henry Wright and I had been working intensively on problems of storage, and we had done a lot of research and a lot of analysis. We had stuffed ourselves with facts, one set of which indicated that a phenomenal number of household items could be stored in a space only ten inches deep. But what to do with these facts had us baffled for months. One day, in looking at a wall in the office, I had the nagging feeling that something was wrong with that wall, and gradually the feeling sharpened to a conviction that what was wrong was the existence of a six-inch barrier containing nothing but air. The notion of adding a few inches on either side and using the interior for storage followed almost instantly. I want you to note that what set off the trigger mechanism was an unpremediated, destructive act: annihilating the concept of a partition as a single-purpose divider. Once the act was performed, the vacuum thus created was filled by a new idea in less time than it takes to tell about it.

The relative value of a creative act should be of no importance to the individual. In fact, he should consider it of absolute value. When Galileo, in affirming that the earth did move, simultaneously destroyed a whole world outlook, he performed a creative act that cannot be compared for a moment with the development of an insignificant piece of architectural equipment. The process, however, was the same in both cases. I can go further and say this—the Storagewall was preceded in time by a similar invention made by Serge Chermayeff when he was working in London. And doubtless others had arrived at similar solutions. Even this, however, did not invalidate what Henry Wright and I had done, for we too had produced our solution independently, and under our own power. It is only the pressure of a society dominated almost completely by false values that has made people consider results or "originality" more important than the creative act itself.

If I were to set down a third means for the designer—assuming that he is concerned with realizing his potential as an artist—I should describe it as the emotional capacity for performing destructive action. I think that if anyone reviews what has just been said in the light of his own experience, he will find that the creation-destruction polarity is at the core of the whole design process. Seen in this way, the familiar notion that creation is "good" while destruction is "bad" turns out to have no meaning whatever, while the pious platitude "evolution is preferable to revolution" appears as the most stupid kind of nonsense. Evolution and revolution, creation and destruction, are different names for the same thing. We use one or the other depending on our choice of a frame of reference. The designer who fails to realize this lacks one of the basic tools of his trade.

GOOD DESIGN CAN BE CREATED UNDER ANY CONDITIONS

If we take a chalk drawing of a mastodon, a nude by Renoir, say, and a fresco by Giotto, we can arrive at the most fascinating ideas by comparing them, but it is absolutely impossible to work out a satisfactory evaluation of their relative esthetic merits. You can run all over the lot looking for the answers. It is possible to say that Giotto had more technical facilities at his disposal than the Cro-Magnon who scratched up the wall of his cave dwelling, or that you prefer the luminosity of Renoir's figures to the stiff draperies of Giotto's saints, but in the end you are left with a residual conviction that each is a magnificent example of its kind, and that there is no way of saying that one kind is better than the others. If the example of painting seems remote, we can put ourselves into the same state of indecision by taking a chair. Can anyone convince himself that the Thonet bentwood chair is not a valid design solution because Breuer made a beautiful chair of tubular steel? Or that the Windsor chair is less wonderful because the Eames chair uses cycle-welded shockmounts? What I am saying is that a work of art can be created at any technical and social level. Once created, its validity does not diminish with the passage of time or with technological change for it possesses its own inner, indestructible life. This point is valuable for designers, and particularly for students, because it helps clear one of the psychological obstacles to creative activity. Students, for instance, are frequently bothered a great deal by feelings of fear and helplessness connected with getting out of school and launching a career. There is justification for the feeling, but not for some of the external manifestations that accompany it. I taught in the design class at Columbia for three years, and found that the students were intensely critical of everything they saw published in the magazines. So far, so good. But with this critical expression was mixed in another attitude, one of bitter frustration and helplessness. Its familiar form was, "Well, if you work for Sears Roebuck—or Metropolitan Life or the Pennsylvania Railroad—how can you do good design? All they are interested in is the money." This critique was then expanded to include the entire capitalist system. The implication was always the same: *if* we didn't have to satisfy these greedy clients, *if* we were going out into a world that was socialist, communist, or whatever you like, *then* we could really do wonderful things. Perhaps this chain of attitudes is familiar. It seems to me that this was what was wrong with what I heard at Columbia: in the first place, I was not at all convinced that the students would do wonderful work even under Utopian conditions. Certainly the work turned out in school was unimaginative and imitative. In the second place, the world they were getting ready to enter was not a Utopia, and they were wasting energy and fooling themselves by blaming their own inadequacies on the system.

If this sounds like a preliminary to loud praise of the status quo, I am going to have to disappoint you. It seems entirely likely that the system is always bad. The cave artist was in constant danger from his lawless neighbors; for Giotto there were the plagues and murderous brigands on unlighted streets; Renoir had as the background of his activity a society dominated by a distinctly putrescent bourgeois class. Yet each found an area within which he could be enormously productive. So if you would add to the other means at the disposal of the designer, a conviction that there is no combination of circumstances that can keep a man from some form of genuinely creative activity, you will find plenty of confirmation in what has been happening over the past ten or fifteen thousand years.

Historical perspective has another value. We have seen that the most an artist can do is produce a work of art. We have also seen that he is able to do this under a total variety of conditions. If this means anything it means that new technological developments, whether in process or materials, are irrelevant *as far as the problem of producing a work of art is concerned.* It is true that the designer is endlessly compelled to solve the same problems over and over again as new industrial developments take place—with every invention the designer's entire frame of reference is imperceptibly shifted and the world looks slightly different. But this compulsion is a different matter from grabbing on to the latest in products and materials as a means of remedying one's deficiencies as a designer. Architecture was architecture before glass block came in, and it will still be architecture after glass block goes out.

THE AMERICAN MYTH OF THE BUSINESSMAN — THREE VERSIONS

In a society as contemptuous of human values as our own, the designer can be a force of incalculable potency. Operation on the basis of principle has always shown greater staying power, in an historical sense, than any other kind of behavior. Now the designer who is deeply committed to a set of principles is in exactly the same spot as the designer whose activity is opportunistic: he has to work for business and business men. I think, therefore, that it would be well to examine the business man to see if he can be detached from some of the myths that have surrounded him.

Constant newspaper readers are familiar with the myth of the business man as the socially conscious individual whose efforts to do good are endlessly frustrated by the non-businessmen who run the Government. The picture of him as the purest flower of a great culture is also well known. To these we can add Sinclair Lewis' monumental portrait of the eternal Rotarian, and the horns and cloven feet attached to him by the left wing press. The designer, however, rarely encounters any of these types in pure form.

The business man, as I see him, is the instigator of a process that is now turning him into its victim. He began as the maker of a product whose qualities he doubtless believed in, and at any rate understood, and he is ending as a maker of abstractions in which only two colors—black and red—are used. Like other people, he behaves in response to outside stimuli whose nature he doesn't always understand, and today the intensity and variety of these stimuli have left him a pretty unstimulated character. Some of his problems include labor difficulties, tax difficulties, material shortages, diminishing margins of profit, endlessly shifting competition, the prospects of another war, and so on. That he should find time and energy to think about his product at all I sometimes find remarkable. Nevertheless, think about his product he does, and sometimes this involves finding a designer.

What the business man wants from his designer is a product that will do whatever a product can to minimize his worries. If the design can stimulate sales, fine; if it can reduce costs, better; if it can eliminate competition, this is the best of all. It would be easy to look down one's nose at the business man for this attitude but I am unable to. For one thing, the attitude is not a personal one, but an overlay that has been powerfully conditioned by social forces. And for another, I do not see why any businessman should share my attitude, which was formed largely by a personal craving to shape things so that I like to look at them and use them. But it is clear that there is inevitably difficulty in reconciling these opposed attitudes so that both the businessman and his designer are satisfied. Some designers have resolved the problem by becoming businessmen themselves.

Both Hegel and Marx dealt with the problem of what happens when a man is alienated from the products of his labor, when the aim of production shifts from things to profits, and Erich Fromm, among the modern social psychologists, has pointed out some of the effects on people of this shift of emphasis. For our purposes it is enough to say that the more effectively the business man is divorced from his product, the less sure of himself he becomes. Not knowing his product, he lacks the confidence that a good handicraftsman always has, and he hires consumer research people, color specialists, industrial designers and others to see to it that all risk in making the product acceptable to the public is eliminated. Not all businessmen conform to this stereotype either, but most of them are inevitably affected in large degree or small by the consequences of corporate management.

UNITED IN FRUSTRATION

Faced as he is with a Frankenstein of his own making, the businessman today is not a particularly happy character, and at the root of much of his unhappiness is the feeling that he is so hemmed in on all sides by obstacles that there is no room left for creative action. He may turn to drink or model railroading, he may become bored or filled with an insatiable craving for more power—whatever he does, his problem of how to function creatively still requires an answer, for the urge is not the monopoly of artists and designers, but is standard equipment for the human race. At this point we have an interesting parallel: many designers feel frustrated because their aims are not compatible with those of business, and many businessmen feel frustrated because their inner aims are not compatible with those of business either. The only important difference I can see is that the designer is far more conscious of his difficulties and is usually more articulate about them than the businessman.

If there is any truth in this analysis, it would seem reasonable for designer and businessman to pool their miseries for each has in his grasp a solution for the troubles of the other. The businessman has the power to give the designer the freedom he needs in approaching and solving problems, while the designer, by achieving progressively more interesting solutions, can give his client the excitement of exploring a whole series of new business frontiers. My own opinion is that the place where these two people should get together is at top policy level. Stated somewhat differently, one of the means of the designer is a voice in management decisions that affect design.

A DESIGNER'S CLIENTS ARE AS GOOD AS HE DESERVES

I do not mean by this that the designer will be called into the upper councils of industry because the board of directors will have decided that they need some visual expression of their faith in mankind. The changes that really shift a society around are never expressed in such grandiloquent terms. The reasons are all quite hardboiled. For instance, a small company will wake up to discover that the only way it can compete with the big producers is on a design basis. Or a recession will frighten the sales manager and he will decide that some products need face-lifting. What happens from here on is up to the designer, for he is in a perfect position to expose his client to the potentialities of his own business. For this reason I am inclined to believe that a designer's clients are as good as he deserves. The big industrial designer who says that not one of his 47 clients is any good is pronouncing a damning judgment on himself.

Another item one might add to the list of means of the designer is the fact of almost total specialization. This is a very important fact. It is important because it opens up a kind of activity that artists have not enjoyed since the Renaissance, when a man thought nothing of being a portrait painter, architect, and military engineer at the same time. Today this great variety of experience is again open, not because one man is capable of embracing all of the detailed knowledge in a half dozen separate fields, but because there are so many specialists in each *that he can refuse to specialize.* Many design offices, small as well as large, cover the entire field of design activity, from architecture and planning through products to graphic work. The comment of "jack of all trades" sometimes applied by the specialized professionals does not really apply because only one trade—design—is

involved. If trends interest you, I would say that this development is part of a very large and still imperfectly outlined process of social evolution that may again produce the "universal man," but at a new level. This is a very big picture, for it embraces the merging of the sciences, the impact of nuclear physics, the diversification of innumerable once-specialized industries, regional planning and other fields. The designer who finds himself moving in the same general direction should not be surprised or disturbed, for his impulse is based on a very deep-seated social transformation that is taking place everywhere.

AN INTENSELY PERSONAL MATTER

The last—and most fundamental—of the means of the designer I would call integrity, and by this I do not mean the professional codes of ethics that urges you not to steal jobs from competitors, or the common sense that keeps you from picking your clients' pockets. By integrity I mean the ability of a man to decide what is good for him and what is bad. It is an intensely personal matter, and it cannot be rationalized intellectually. It rarely involves big decisions, but in shaping a multitude of small ones it gives direction to the designer as a person and as an artist. Integrity, in the sense I am giving the word, has nothing to do with being right or wrong. A few months ago my office turned down a job to design floor lamps, simply because I felt that using a five-foot pole to support a 100-watt lamp was no solution to a lighting problem. It could be that this conclusion was entirely wrong—but it would have been worse to accept such an assignment as long as we felt the way we did. Right or wrong, the incident was an insignificant one, but I think it probably illustrates the kind of small, undramatic decisions the design office constantly has to make.

Many designers to whom I have listened consider attitudes of this kind an expensive luxury. Perhaps they are a luxury. It all depends on what you consider the responsibility of the designer—not to the "people" or any of the other silly abstractions we are so fond of using, but to himself. And I know that until a man becomes clear in his mind about what is good for him and what is not, he will suffer from the same confusion in every other area of his activity. Yet the one luxury the designer cannot afford today is confusion. In the momentous events whose rate of acceleration is increasing from one day to the next we can get a picture (if we look for it) of an old world in the process of destroying itself and a new one being created. Whether the actual birth will be accelerated by loud noises resembling those made by an atomic bomb is, in an evolutionary sense, irrelevant. What is relevant is that all the atomic bombs now in existence can do nothing more than hasten the immense social and moral transformations now taking place all over the world. The choice open to the designer is the part he wishes to play in bringing about what *he personally considers a desirable transformation.* Actually, this choice is the same one that has been available to him under a variety of disguises since the beginning of time.

People do change . . . Ten years ago this point of view would have been completely unacceptable to me. Quite a few still found it so, recently, when "Industrial Design" published it.

OBSOLESCENCE

Have you heard of the wonderful one hoss shay,
That was built in such a logical way
It ran a hundred years to a day.
It went to pieces all at once
All at once, and nothing first
Just as bubbles do when they burst . . .

  The Deacon's Masterpiece by Oliver Wendell Holmes

Is this what we mean by obsolescence?

We have bombs, and we have disposable tissue, but in our total industrial inventory there appear to be very few other products that can match the perfectly planned disintegration of Dr. Holmes' little fantasy.

Yet we believe in obsolescence. We support it the way we support the multi-party system, pasteurized milk, and a free press. We also talk quite a lot about "planned" obsolescence. At the same time, the implications of the word make us uneasy; they even provoke some people to equate obsolescence to commercial conspiracy and social degeneracy.

The way our practices impress visitors from abroad tends to reinforce the discomfort of this conflict. Recently a British designer observed that if present trends here should continue, manufacturers would presently be issuing certificates guaranteeing that if by a certain date the article purchased had not fallen apart, the customer would get his money back.

Spoofing in the standard British manner, of course, but is this what we mean by obsolescence?

A dozen years ago the air used to be full of tales about products deliberately made so that they would become useless after a predetermined period of time; razors which lost their edge after a single shave, light bulbs designed to flicker out after too few hours, stockings treated to encourage fatal runs after a couple of wearings. One hears little of this kind of talk any more. It appears to be generally agreed today that whatever we may mean by obsolescence, the customer's interests are also supposed to be served by the process.

What Oliver Wendell Holmes meant by obsolescence was that the product be so perfectly designed that its utility within a given time-span approached 100 per cent. Dr. Holmes was a pretty good representative of the 19th Century in America, a time and place responsible for a number of optimistic ideas.

The fact, alas, is that with a technology beyond any possible imagining of Holmes and his contemporaries, we are still a long way from being able to contrive a product so delicately that the almost infinite number of variables involved in its use can be balanced out to produce an equal rate of wear on all its parts. Nor does it seem likely that we will ever be able to do so.

Perhaps we can agree that this bubble that bursts perfectly is *not* what is meant when we talk about obsolescence.

The truth of the matter is the question is not as simple as it looks. This is not to say that it is impossibly difficult to cope with, but rather that it is complex. What an exploration of this kind appears to turn up is a rich and interesting variety of implications and concepts, all of which have an intimate connection with the attitudes of manufacturers and the behavior of designers.

Two years ago a small group of Americans, in Germany on the invitation of the Bonn Government, sat down to a lunch given by the Mayor of Frankfort. The guests consisted of artists, architects and designers, and they were mixed in with Germans whose English was impeccable and whose knowledge of things American was remarkable. Inevitably, as the lunch progressed, the talk veered to the phenomena which seem to fascinae all Europeans: U. S. production, superhighways, jazz, automobile design—and the incredibly wasteful behavior of Americans. Especially the wasteful behavior of Americans.

The European attitude towards our habits, especially where the use of products and services is concerned, is a blend of appalled curiosity, downright disbelief, righteous indignation and envy. How can a people have so little interest in the permanence of possessions? On what comprehensible basis does a nation throw away its cars when the ashtrays are full and trade in its TV sets before the tubes are fully warmed?

In middle-class European hotels and apartment houses the hall lights are on time-switches: you have to keep moving to make the top of the stairs before total blackness descends. European cars have reserve fuel tanks because practically no one can bring himself to buy gas until the last possible moment. Anyone who shops for food has to come prepared with her own bag: string, wrapping paper and paper bags are not willingly dispensed to the customer. To anyone conditioned in this atmosphere, American behavior ranges from incomprehensible to immoral. I had heard these expressions of exasperated wonder so many times in Europe that they had become part of the scenery, so to speak, rather like the cathedrals. Yet the attitude reinforced a vague sense of guilt about the impermanence and wastefulness of the American system.

Then at the Lord Mayor's excellent lunch, for some reason, a question suddenly suggested itself:

Let us assume that all Europeans are totally efficient in their thrifty use of products and services.

Let us further assume that all Americans are utterly wasteful in these matters.

Question: Then why is America so rich?

The point of the story is not the triumph of Waste over Thrift, or of Us over Them. The point is a question. Why do we seem to get richer as we get more "Wasteful?"

Which, of course, leads to other questions. Is it possible that what our transatlantic neighbors describe as "waste" may actually be something else? In nature there are certain procedures which could easily (though incorrectly) be described as wasteful: a fish lays immense numbers of eggs, few of which reach maturity; an oak tree drops a prodigious quantity of acorns, but only a minute percentage develop into trees. Is it possible that in a highly developed industrial society a rapid rate of obsolescence plays a somewhat similar role in furthering the society's unconscious aims? Evolution in nature has involved immense destruction, in terms of entire species, and to a dinosaur no doubt the process must have seemed "wasteful." Is there an analogy here? Rapid, large-scale consumption certainly accelerates the replacement of plant and tools, and this renewal is always at a higher technological level. Does an industry-based society reach a point where the highest efficiency is reached through what superficially appears to be waste?

It certainly seems likely that we can become unduly—and quite unnecessarily—concerned with what the rest of the world arbitrarily describes as waste. It also seems desirable to recognize that our present pattern of obsolescence is by no means uniform. We do trade in cars after a relatively short period of use, but cars, while perhaps our most conspicuous product, are still only one product. We do not consider a 15-year-old refrigerator obsolete. Watches are worn as long or longer. We do not trade in the furnace every three years. And as far as cars are concerned, trading in does not mean throwing them away. As the economist Peter Drucker points out, "In the automobile industry the annual model is our vehicle for making it possible for everybody in the country to have a car. Without it we would simply not have a national car market but would, like European countries, have only a new-car market confined to a very small upper income group which then hangs on to a car forever. What we actually have is a system under which the purchaser of a new car, by taking an immediate major loss on 'planned obsolescence' subsidizes the car purchasers of the lower income groups and ensures that even the sharecropper still gets a fairly serviceable car at an amazingly low price, both absolutely and in relation to the sharecropper's annual income. This is not 'waste'."

It is too easy to observe the procedures we have developed and to dismiss them as "American," as if this were somehow an explanation. Up to World War I there was relatively little difference between consumer behavior in the U. S. and abroad. Thrift was a major virtue here, also, not merely because of a Puritan inheritance, but because the country needed every spare nickel for investment in capital goods. In other words, "thrift" and "waste" are not absolutes by definition, and they are less a reflection of national temperament and resources than a logical consequence of the prevailing industrial level. The U.S.S.R., larger than we and possibly even more richly endowed with natural resources, has beggared itself for thirty years, not because Communists object to seeing people walk around in shoes, but because there was no way other than extreme "thrift" to create a huge industrial base in a hurry

The U. S. is unique at the moment because of the scale on which it can make and sell consumer products while at the same time investing between $20 and $30 billions annually in capital goods and even more in the military establishment. Most of our attitudes regarding obsolescence rates in consumer products stem from this unprecedented situation. The attitudes are "American" only in a relatively temporary and accidental sense. As other societies reach a comparable level, similar attitudes will emerge.

In any discussion of obsolescence, therefore, it would seem that the problem is not so much a matter of comparing our practices with those of our neighbors as of isolating those factors which are real.

WHAT DOES OBSOLESCENSE ELIMINATE?

A product or procedure is obsolete, presumably, when something emerges which is better. Admittedly, "better" is not always easy to define. The clearest examples are more often to be found in capital goods than in consumer products. The diesel locomotive obsoleted the steam locomotive in a thoroughly unambiguous way. Turbines are driving the internal combustion engine out of the air and may presently do the same on the ground. Automation has superseded manual operation in oil refineries. These examples are widely known and admit of no argument.

Obsoleting a product does not necessarily eliminate it. It may, and it may not. In a great number of instances it seems merely a way of extending the number of available tools. The carpet sweeper, for example, introduced a kind of performance the broom could not match, and it in turn was "obsoleted" by the vacuum cleaner. All three products, however, are still to be found in the average household. Housing offers a somewhat different kind of example. Most U. S. dwellings could be described as "obsolete" by any reasonable standard, but this does not mean they are uninhabitable.

The automobile is so frequently taken as a case in point that it might be treated as a special example. Actually, however, it is more conspicuous than unique; the industry brags more about its "planned obsolescence" than it really does. The advent of a 1957 car *is* supposed to make possession of a 1956 model less gratifying, but it does not obsolete it. In fact, it is part of the industry's scheme of things *not* to obsolete it, for this would raise hob with the existing trade-in procedure, infuriate all 1956 customers, and so on. Annual styling and mechanical changes are designed to create a gradual increase of discontent in the customer until, after two, three or four years, he becomes willing to accept the loss involved in a trade. This annual piling up of changes will undoubtedly sometime render obsolete a car of a given vintage, but the date is hard to pin down. There are still 1935 automobiles on the road.

It is just possible that the established trade-in process works so well for cars simply because they have wheels. There is a minimum of difficulty involved in taking the old car to your dealer and driving off in a new one. Major appliances, the producers of which look to Detroit with such envious admiration, enjoy no such facility of exchange. If an increase in the rate of obsolescence is part of the policy of these manufacturers, one would think they would be less active in fostering the current trend towards more built-ins.

WHAT MAKES A PRODUCT BETTER?
Actually, it takes more than ease of exchange to establish a pattern of rapid obsolescence. The fact that certain products combine high cost with a high degree of conspicuousness also leads to their acceptance as status symbols, and a desire to look well in the eyes of one's neighbors can constitute a more powerful pressure than either economics or technology. The rapid increase in the acceptable size of a television screen is a good illustration of this. One might have assumed, from the sales curves, that the larger screen was more desirable because of greater ease in viewing, but the phenomenal success of portables in 14- and 17-inch sizes suggests that many purchasers of consoles were ashamed to be found with less than the largest. Portables, on the other hand, are supposed to be small. Ownership of a 14-inch screen (in a portable) therefore

does not diminish the owner's stature. An 8½" screen may even enhance it.

Thus it is possible to evaluate the obsolescence process in terms of pressures. All of these pressures have to do with wants and/or needs. These, however, are of many kinds, some economic, others quite irrational and difficult to measure. The most significant of all pressures is performance.

If performance were always measurable and demonstrable, obsolescence rates would be higher than they are now. The classic example, as we all know, is the military, where the latest technological miracle is usually presented with the comment that it is already obsolete—obsolete because what was learned in building it provided the knowledge needed to build a better one.

In the military area, what is "better" can usually be defined with a minimum of confusion. A bomb has a force of a megaton, or less, or more: "more" equals "better." A ceiling of 60,000 feet is better than 50,000. When performance can be evaluated so directly, product design becomes very pure and the appearance of the product, highly satisfying esthetically.

But performance cannot always be so evaluated. When the long-playing record came out it showed so many obvious advantages over the older types that these were quickly obsoleted. However, the machines on which these words are played do not compete entirely on performance, because people vary in their ability to judge the quality of sound.

One might state as a rule that *the more accurately performance can be measured, the higher the rate of obsolescence*. Like all rules, this one has its exceptions, but it is important because of our uneasiness about the increasingly rapid rate at which we change things. It happens to be my opinion that this is nothing to feel guilty about.

Imagine a theoretical situation in which the entire population was committed to the idea that the best was none too good for the consumer. Imagine that no manufacturer had any other motive for making things and that all tax legislation was designed to further this concept. The result would then be much as it is in the military: great beauty and perfection of product combined with a very fast rate of obsolescence. If rapid change comes from a continuing demand for the best possible product, then why do we look on accelerating obsolescence as if it were fostered by a conspiracy of stupid consumers and irresponsible manufacturers?

It seems probable that we will reach this theoretical situation about the same time we learn how to build the one-hoss shay, but it does no harm to realize that what we are doing with our technology is not entirely stupid or wasteful.

There is one very special aspect of performance which does provide a very handy yardstick for both designer and manufacturer. It has to do with an interesting characteristic of people in our time: we tend to accept without question *anything that will do more with less*. We find suspension bridges more satisfying than truss bridges. The transistor moves in to replace the vacuum tube and we react favorably to the idea of smaller radios. The slim turbines on the Viscount suddenly make piston engines look old fashioned. And so on. Again, there are exceptions, and important ones, but designs which result in reduced weight, bulk, or both, tend to have a significant effect in speeding up obsolescence. For a manufacturer, "speeding up obsolescence" can be translated as "strengthening the competitive position."

WHAT A SURVEY REVEALED ABOUT OBSOLESCENCE

Business competition is perhaps the most obvious of the pressures affecting the process of obsolescence, but how it operates is anything but obvious. It is in this area that one begins to hear about "artificial" obsolescence and a variety of other brands; all, by the way, being described as "bad" in one way or another. It is here, too, that the accusations of "waste" can most easily be made. Recently the magazine, INDUSTRIAL DESIGN, undertook an informal survey to explore some of the current business practices and attitudes toward obsolescence. One fact that the survey indicated was that this element of competition that spurs obsolescence also ties in closely with performance as a factor. For instance, the sharp increase in industrial budgets

HOW FAR AHEAD DO YOU WORK ON NEW PRODUCTS?

Now	1946	1936	Manufacturer replying
3 yrs.	1 yr.	6 mos.	Appliances
5 yrs.	5 yrs.	1 yr.	Watches
3 yrs.	1 yr.	1 yr.	Carpet sweeper
3 yrs.	2 yrs.	2 yrs.	Vending machines
3-5 yrs.	3-5 yrs.	3-5 yrs.	Cameras

for research is a reflection of intensified competition, but the objective of research is generally some kind of improvement in performance. The survey also indicates that advance planning for product development looks considerably farther ahead than was the case only a few years back. (See box, p. ?.)

The same survey contained questions about the factors leading to major tool changes, and the answers indicate with a high degree of unanimity that sales requirements have much more to do with tool life than does the condition of the tool.

IF A BASIC CHANGE OR INVENTION WERE AVAILABLE IN YOUR FIELD, HOW WOULD YOU DECIDE WHETHER TO ALTER YOUR PRODUCTION? GIVE RELATIVE WEIGHTS:

Factor	Furniture	Radios	Carpet Sweepers	Appliances	Watches
Saleability of features	1st (100%)	1st	1st	1st (80%)	1st (75%)
Investment in current stocks			2nd	5th	4th
Fear of lagging behind competition		4th	2nd	2nd (20%)	3rd
Cost of tool change			3rd	3rd	2nd
Advertising cost			5th	4th	5th

For instance, in a number of product categories the life of a major tool averages out at around 1,000,000 pieces. One might assume that when the tool becomes "obsolete"—that is, wears out—a major design change might be expected. This does not appear to be the case at all. Tools are not obsoleted by normal wear, necessarily, but by the sales department's picture of the condition of its market. In a strict sense, scrapping a tool before it wears out is a waste of capital goods, but whether this adds up to waste in a broad social sense is a question that could hardly be answered without an immense amount of economic data.

What this adds up to is that somewhere outside the producing plant itself there is pressure to change—not necessarily to change for the better,

47

but simply to change. This pressure can be generated by the sluggish response of the customers, by the complaints of dealers, by a styling spurt in competitive lines. Such pressure is extremely difficult to isolate and measure, and the need to do so keeps a great many marketing organizations busy.

Now the problem of how to change a product which seems to be perfectly good as it is, is quite a problem. It is one thing to demand that a plane's speed, range of ceiling be increased by so many units; such a problem can be broken down into its components and solved. But it is a very different matter merely to say "make it different." It is this demand which keeps so many designers occupied, and it is this aspect of our social behavior which baffles or irritates so many foreigners. And yet it is not easy to dismiss the obsolescence which occurs as a result of this pressure as "artificial." At least two factors complicate matters.

Every society lives out its span in the grip of certain ideas which are so powerful and so widely held that people are scarcely aware of them. These ideas come to a focus in what might be described as a "master area" and they spread out from there to give the entire community its character. Such an area, in the 13th Century, was the church. Today, in America, it is business. Business is based on a gigantic industrial complex, and the heart of industry is in the area of capital goods. Science and technology exist to service this complex, and they are supported by it. In this whole area the idea of change is dominant. Progress, improved techniques, all the things we are striving for come through change. Change, in this area, is always acceptable. Its benefits can always be demonstrated.

The idea of change as something beneficial, something desirable, has moved out from the "master area" to color the thinking of the whole society. It is absolutely inevitable that we should succumb so easily to the lure of "the new" in many areas where the fact of change could not possibly matter less. The power of the concept—completely valid in capital goods—is so great that we tend to apply it all the way across the board. It seems perfectly reasonable that this should be so, but for a number of people in industry, including the designer, this creates the first area of complicating problems. These all have to do

with the acceleration of obsolescence at secondary levels, that is, levels at which basic pressures are not operative.

The second complicating factor is fashion. Fashion is an expression of people's habit of getting tired of things, and it constantly obsoletes things (jewelry, clothing, etc., etc.) long before they are worn out. In a society so subject to fundamental change as our own (and so well equipped to disseminate information rapidly) fashions change swiftly. The essential characteristic of fashion is that it is cyclical, and it therefore has little to do with obsolescence of a basic kind. The newly old is always unfashionable, but let enough time pass and the old seems new again.

True obsolescence is a process put in motion by genuine improvement. The direction, generally speaking, is one way. It is not likely that it will ever again be fashionable to believe that the earth is flat. The active element in the process is design. That is, someone restates the problem at hand using new information, and comes up with a better answer. Design, to put it a little differently, is an attempt to make a contribution through change. When no contribution is made or can be made, the only process available for giving the illusion of change is "styling."

Styling is what most designers have to do most of the time. In a society so totally committed to change as our own the illusion must be provided for the customers if the reality is not available. This emphasis on the distinction between styling and design is not made to suggest that one is nice and the other nasty. For industry they represent two entirely different tools, and there is considerable practical value in being able to distinguish one from the other.

Consider, a firm making prefabricated houses. The aim of such a company today is to turn out a product which cannot be identified as a factory-made house. Now an industrial product which has to be indistinguishable from the handmade product cannot pass on many of the benefits of industrialization. In other words, there is no design problem. Design involves a contribution. Styling, therefore, is what has to be done. Roofs, wall textures, door knockers, shutters and all the rest have to be diddled with to produce an appetizing ensemble that looks "different" but not different enough to frighten the customers.

Prefabrication today is a large business, but not an industry—not, at least, in any developed technical sense. Yet it has to become an industry, and it can only do this by obsoleting the hand-made product. It can only obsolete the hand-made product (to which the general public is deeply attached) by using industrial techniques to step up the performance of the product (for instance, it would be a distinct step-up in performance if houses didn't burn down quite so readily). And it can do all these things only if it resorts to design rather than styling. In such a situation, the ability to distinguish clearly between these two types of activity can have a profound effect on company planning.

Design implies a designer. The designer does not have to be an identifiable professional. Anyone who plays a key role in product creation and development has a design function. The designer has a good bit more to do with obsolescence rates than one might at first think, because he is temperamentally unable to leave things alone. In the survey mentioned earlier, a question given to both manufacturers and designers was, "Do you consider your present product obsolete?" The manufacturers, almost to a man, rejected the suggestion. But not the designers.

IN TERMS OF NEW POSSIBILITIES OF WHICH YOU ARE AWARE, DO YOU CONSIDER YOUR CURRENT PRODUCT OBSOLETE TODAY?

All products in use today are obsolete. The only question is when they can be replaced economically and satisfactorily to both the consumer and the manufacturer. *Raymond Spilman*
Most products are to some extent "obsolete" within months after they have gone into production, because of the time between "locking up" and market release. Technology catches up and so does design during tooling-time—and often it passes a dated product development. *James Balmer*
There are always opportunities to increase value, add features and reduce costs in the redesign of most products. . . . *Jean Reinecke*
. . . The ranch-type home, the utility room, the kitchen of tomorrow, the built-in washer-dryer, the wall refrigerator, and the central cooking center appear at first to be the ultimates in modern living. However, in 1902 Ransom E. Olds, designer and builder of the fabulous Oldsmobile car, formed a new company and produced the Reo car, his initials making up the name. He announced it to the American public and to the world as the greatest accomplishment in automotive engineering and design that could ever be attained. He called it "My Farewell Car." . . . *Brooks Stevens*

To a designer, anything that is, is obsolete.

This attitude, of course, is part and parcel of the makeup of the creative individual, but it has been greatly enhanced by the American tradition, just as the entire process of obsolescence has been accelerated by it. Couple a deeply-ingrained social attitude that the best is good enough until something better comes along, with the rapid increase in competitive business behavior, and the influeuce of the designer is not hard to see. When the design process takes place within the framework of a furiously expanding technology, the results can be explosive.

It might be stated as a general rule that *the rate of change in any area of activity is directly proportional to the number of possibilities.* There was a time when the only way a man could light a fire was by rubbing two sticks together. The number of design opportunities, so to speak, was greatly limited by the technology. We have comparable situations today, and it is one of the major functions of research to enlarge the number of opportunities.

Dishwashing is a fairly good example. You can wash dishes by hand in a sink, using water with soap or a detergent, or you can put them in a dishwasher, where they are washed with water and a detergent. The rate of change in both sinks and dishwashers has been slow because the limited number of "washing options" has put a ceiling on the possibility of change.

"Planned obsolescence," a subject about which a great deal has been said, must of necessity include a plan for increasing the number of design opportunities. If you want to try out some planned obsolescence on dishwashers, for instance, you have to find ways of handling the dish problem other than by the use of soap and water. Otherwise, all you can do is make mechanical changes which may improve the product, but will hardly obsolete it rapidly. Planned obsolescence is not necessarily a problem in technology. One could "solve" the dishwashing problem by dumping the dishes into the garbage grinder along with the food.

IS OUR OBSOLESCENCE PLANNED?

Another way of describing planning for obsolescence is to call it "advance planning." It would seem evident that the farther ahead the designer can see, the better the chance that obsolescence will occur by intent rather than by chance. As such planning takes over, the problems of the designer increase, for information needs to grow geometrically. Extrapolation is one of the most useful methods for looking ahead, but it is not scientific and hence risky. The inspired "leaps" made from time to time in this way have to be buttressed by increasing quantities of information, not only technical, but scientific, metaphysical, economic, social, psychological. If we really want to plan our various kinds of obsolescence, it means a lot of work for somebody.

Actually, for all the talk about it, we have precious little to show that can be properly described as *planned* obsolescence. The traditional city has been obsoleted, in a very real way, by the automobile. But what has happened just happened: there was no planning.

This is where the real waste occurs and this is what we are gradually beginning to realize: obsolescence as a process is wealth-producing, not wasteful. It leads to constant renewal of the industrial establishment at higher and higher levels, and it provides a way of getting a maximum of good to a maximum of people. We have learned how to handle obsolescence as a prodigious tool for social betterment in those areas where we have both knowledge and control. The waste occurs where obsolescence is both too slow and too haphazard, where adequate information and adequate controls and systematic elimination are lacking. We do not need fresh technologies to show us how to upgrade housing—but we do need a continuing method for getting rid of the production we have outmoded. The same holds for the cities.

What we need is more obsolescence, not less.

Our acceptance of change as a dynamic method of achieving security has to be extended beyond the limits of industry.

The question was more timely in 1949 *than it is now, but the content, I think, still applies. The lecture was given in an astonishing hall of Spanish-American War vintage for a group of architects and engineers.*

A NEW PROFESSION?

Industrial Design differs from architecture and engineering in one interesting way—it is the only profession that became a myth before it reached maturity.

You are all familiar with the picture created by publicity for industrial design. According to this glamorous portrayal, the designer combines the talents of Archimedes, Thomas Edison and Michelangelo. This superior character has re-modeled all the familiar adjuncts to civilized living, creating power mowers that will cut the grass but leave the puppy undamaged, truck cabs with more comforts than first class on a luxury liner and refrigerators that practically order the groceries. This happy individual has a problem too—having created these merchandising mira-cles, he is then supposed to make new designs so much more appetizing that the consumer will do nothing but junk what he has bought to make room for the improved models.

Exaggeration has always been part of the American tradition, and the making of myths is as old as the human race. And while the legend of a super-professional whose fabulous talents are matched only by his fabulous income is already over life size, there is plenty of evidence that designers have produced impressive results in terms of business.

Before we get to the basic concerns, there are some immediate ones that may interest you. Industrial design as a recognizable professional activity is about thirty years old. This means, of course, that the group which practices it has neither the stability nor the academic standing attached to architecture and engineering. You might therefore expect to find a certain nouveau riche attitude in the profession and perhaps more than a hint of an inferiority complex. You do. Because the industrial designer's work is rarely concerned directly with matters affecting public safety, there is no legal method for con-trolling entrance into the field. You might there-fore expect to find quacks and shysters in it, and you do. Industrial design is by its very nature connected with an industry that is frequently concerned more with sales than with integrity of design. You might therefore expect to find in this profession people who are frustrated or defeated, and you do.

One of the successfully established designers remarked to me, "It's perfectly true that as a group we are barely twenty years old, but there are times when I feel like a member of the world's oldest profession." This judgment is unnecessarily harsh, but there is a basis for it. The industrial designer is under greater compulsion to compromise than any other practitioner in the arts. By "compromise" I do not mean the adjustments made to simplify manufacture or reduce costs. I am referring to the perversions of a good design solution in an effort to please the consumer. It is here, I think, that the problems of the industrial designer differ sharply from those of architect or engineer. Because his effort is almost never directed towards a unique object, such as a building, but is expended upon something that will be repeated many times, he finds himself, whether he likes it or not, faced with a merchandising problem. The nature of the merchandising problem, as it is stated to the designer, is that the designer's personal tastes and convictions are of no importance as compared with those of the average consumer. The result is that most designers, if you question them on this point, will explain to you that they are not designing the "best" product, but the product that will sell. It is this factor of sales and merchandising that constitutes the main difference between the industrial designer and the architect, and the most formidable obstacle to the achievement of first-rate design solutions.

The industrial designer exists today because a growing segment of the population is finally beginning to realize that a machine product can look like a machine product and still be beautiful. And it happens that except for very exceptional fields such as aircraft, the manufacturer is rarely able to shape his product so that it is beautiful—he lacks the training and understanding for the job. The designer, therefore, comes in to fill a gap which must be filled if the product is to achieve a high degree of perfection. The fact that most design for industry is actually a very superficial kind of styling is beside the point—what I am trying to say is simply that the presence of an artist in the production process is desirable.

It is only during the past century and a half that the notion of associating an artist with manufacture has come to seem strange—before the Industrial Revolution there was a great tradition of design for production that extends all the way back to the Stone Age. One has only to visit a museum to realize this. Setting aside the painting and sculpture, virtually everything on display is an object made for daily use—a lamp, mirror, bowl, vehicle, jar, plate or fork. Mankind has always devoted an enormous amount of energy to the beautification of things for common use. The difference between today and 600 B.C. is that formerly the artist was also the manufacturer—today the job is too complicated. The real contribution of the industrial designer, as I see it, is that he has revived an essentially healthy traditional way of doing things.

If one takes the time to review the state of the contemporary arts, it soon becomes apparent that many of them are in a state of decline. In architecture, for instance, we seem to have lost entirely our capacity to do monumental buildings—even in the U.N. group for New York, where the pick of the world's architects were assembled, all that was achieved after the huffing and puffing was a pleasant arrangement of rentable space. Our churches are nothing more than clubhouses. Painting and scultpure are the pastime of a small minority. The film, with all its promise, has been pegged at the emotional level of the comic strip. Against this background of impotence and indifference, one can project the excitement caused by the curve of a new fender or the shape of a kitchen sink. The industrial designer, in other words, appears to have become the instigator of a new kind of popular art.

The test of a popular art is not so much its diffusion, as the freedom and critical discrimination with which people will pass judgment on it. For example, the man who would be baffled and inarticulate before a sculpture by Henry Moore will speak his mind freely when confronted by a meat slicer, say, that may display similar forms. The case is even clearer with the motorcar, since consumers have long since stopped bothering about mechanical features and base their judgments largely on design.

It is curious that although the engineer, the architect and the painter set the stage for the industrial designer, almost none of these took over his role. It is my guess that they failed to grasp the opportunity because they did not understand what was happening. The architects, twenty years ago, were busy turning out gentlemanly forgeries of European buildings. Engineers, when detached from their slide rules, tend to become self-consciously arty in an oddly spinsterish fashion. The painters had no interest in acquiring the necessary technical knowledge. So the designers, when they appeared, came from such improbable sources as the theater, museums, advertising and publishing. The reason, I think, lay in the connection between design and sales. The discovery that one could actually sell more of a product through some sort of cosmetic treatment had to be made—in this country at least— by people in contact with the problems of sales and display.

The stories one hears about the first design jobs tend to bear out this conclusion. One of the designers, for instance, had been manager of a theater in a farm community. He noticed that most of his customers came to town with boots heavily caked with mud. On the basis of this observation he replaced the theater's plush carpeting with rubber mats and business improved immediately. The same man as a designer observed that people hefted alarm clocks before they made a choice. He induced his client to add some weight in the base and watched sales skyrocket. This kind of behavior is most intelligent and observant, but not what one would normally consider part of the design process. The success of the first designers was based not so much on professional skill or knowledge but on the kind of imaginative common sense one would expect from a first-class salesman.

The work you see coming out of the majority of the design offices today is also what you would expect from a first-class salesman, and while part of the profession has made a great deal of money, it is probably one of the reasons the designers as a whole are not accepted by, say, architects and engineers as equals in a professional sense. The average design office is too close in outlook and output to the advertising agency to be taken seriously by those men whose lives have been spent in one of the more firmly established traditional disciplines.

An interesting situation, I think, is revealed by examining the nature of a designer's work.

Let us assume that a young man has designed a group of printed fabrics and that these fabrics have been so successful that he decides to take the plunge and open his own office. Now fabric design is exacting work requiring little technical knowledge but considerable understanding of two-dimensional composition. Let us now imagine that a brother-in-law of his client makes wrist watches, and that he is so impressed by the performance with fabrics that he hires our man to design watches. Let us further imagine that the work on watches leads to an instrument account which in turn brings in the job of styling a plane. There is no point in extending this hypothetical success story because it is clear that the designer is already working in a wide variety of fields which, from the viewpoint of technique and production have very little to do with each other. Now it is very easy indeed to make too much of this point—the designer does not have to know as much as you might think to work effectively in a variety of fields, and he certainly does not have to become a specialist in each. Nonetheless, the demands made upon him are different from those made upon the architect who, in the end, always turns out one product— a building. The fact that one building may be a hospital and another a guest house on an estate does not change the fact that the same technical personnel, with only slight modifications, can handle either problem.

It seems to make relatively little difference whether an industrial design office is large or small or whether it appears to specialize in one field or another. The characteristic fact remains that its operations cover a greater diversity of problems of techniques and uses than is encountered in architecture or engineering. As a matter of fact, a number of big offices have periodically included architecture and engineering within the scope of their over-all activities.

As I see it, the main difference between one design office and another has to do with size as an expression of a working philosophy. It is true for the industrial designer as it is for the architect or engineer that once his work gets beyond a certain volume, it is not possible for the principal to exert a creative function with respect to each job. An organization consequently takes the place of the individual and it has both strength and weakness. Its strength is the ability to turn out a quantity and variety of work, presumably with competence. Its weakness is the danger of deadening the creative process through increasing emphasis on efficiency and business volume.

Most of the younger people show a distaste for the large organization, but this may merely reflect their own situation. My own feeling is that in industrial design, just as in the other professions, the underlying attitude of the office is more important than the number of people in it. A concern for one's integrity as a designer seems to me the crucial factor in the work an office will turn out, but I also suspect that this concern tends to diminish as the enterprise becomes bigger.

In one special respect, the designer differs notably from both architect and engineer. Functioning as a kind of arbiter between the manufacturer and a buying public which has the manufacturer constantly worried, the designer cannot avoid being concerned with his work as it relates to sales. As a result, he becomes preoccupied with the whole subject of mass production. In this respect, of course, he differs almost totally from the architect whose products are largely handicraft objects produced on the basis of one-of-a-kind. The subject of mass production and mass distribution, however, can be and frequently is over-stressed by the designer. It seems to be rather difficult for the members of this profession to realize that if the profession is going to attain a position comparable to architecture, painting or sculpture, the basic preoccupation must be with design. It has to be realized that the same process of creation is demanded whether the designer turns out something which will be made only once or duplicated a hundred

thousand times. The only difference between large scale and handicraft production lies in the size and complexity of the tools and the productive establishment as a whole. One might add that to some extent the very idea of mass production and mass distribution is more of a myth than a fact. Even at the level of the motorcar manufacturer who may turn out a million units in a year, the product still reaches less than three per cent of the nation's families. The danger in the designer's concentrating too long on the problem of mass production is that he inevitably finds himself designing, not for the three per cent or the tenth of one per cent who will actually buy his product, but all the 140 million who supposedly constitute his market. The only possible result is a scaling down of any work done to the lowest possible denominator of taste and it is this, I think, that constitutes the most serious indictment of the profession and its work.

Back in 1935, Walter Gropius of Harvard's School of Architecture wrote of the importance of establishing what he described as, "A modern architectonic art which, like human nature, should be all-embracing in its scope." The art to which Dr. Gropius referred is nothing more or less than the practice of industrial design. Starting with relatively simple consumer items, the design profession has broadened its range to include transportation in all its forms, buildings, typography, packaging, magazine layouts, heavy machinery and even cities. I do not think it is necessary to conclude from this that the designer is going to take over architecture or city planning. What should be perfectly clear, however, is that the lines between the arts today are breaking down precisely as they have in the sciences. Whether the man now labeled as an industrial designer was trained as an architect, engineer or typographer is of comparatively little importance.

When one looks at this astonishing expansion of creative activity, the temptation to draw a parallel with the Italian Renaissance is almost irresistible. Then too the lines were blurred: your portrait painter might have been a sculptor, stage designer, goldsmith, architect and military engineer in one. But this analogy cannot be stretched too far, because the Renaissance artist worked as an individual whereas today's designer is almost certain to be a group of collaborators. Nevertheless, as an individual he is supposed to give creative direction to work in a great number of different fields.

Now I say that everything the industrial designer does—everything which is outside his function as an artist working in industry—is a secondary or subsidiary activity. He may have a staff of 500 and a complete assortment of specialists of all kinds—ultimately he will be judged by the appropriateness with which he shaped the things that were handed to him. Until this basic criterion is accepted and acted upon, the profession will never succeed in producing the great figures, such as Wright, LeCorbusier, Henry Moore and Picasso, who are to be found in the related fields of architecture, sculpture and painting. The best that industrial design has done to date is produce some highly talented and successful men.

So in the end, even this most prosperous and glamorous of professions comes down to a thing that is very old and very simple: one man's integrity against another's—one man's capacity as a working artist against another's—the vision with which he establishes his standards and the courage with which he sticks by them.

STRUCTURE AND FABRIC

*A statement promised to American Fabrics and then
forgotten. As a result, it had to be dictated in twenty minutes. It would have been
less to the point had there been sixty.*

A fabric is a structure.

When the poetically inclined talk about "the fabric of the universe" they are talking about a structure. Its components consisting of tension lines stretching for light years are largely invisible, but it is a structure nonetheless.

I happen to be interested in structures, both visible and invisible, and therefore tend to look at fabrics in the same way. It may seem strange to define a fabric in these terms, but there are good reasons for doing so.

We belong to a society which has been busily revising its concept of structure, and the whole idea of compression (stone on stone, stick on stick) is being replaced by the newer idea of tension. The shift in terms of examples is from the Pyramids to the Golden Gate Bridge.

The idea of structures in tension excites us because it represents an advance in our control over nature. A nylon thread a mile long can hold up a weight; a granite column a mile high could not even hold up itself.

With these rapidly developing shifts in concept, fabrics take on an entirely new kind of interest.

In some instances the traditional uses of fabrics have been outmoded by technology. A man who wakes up in a heated house, drives to work in a heated car and arrives to work in a heated office building, does not wear long underwear. A vacuum formed plastic sheet in the Plymouth station wagon looks better and delivers better performance than the fabric ceiling it obsoleted.

In dealing with so basic a structure as fabric, obsolescence is a two-way street. In the modern interior with its emphasis on open planning what has become obsolete is the heavy wall of wood or masonry, to be replaced at times by screens weighing ounces.

To us, anything that exhibits unnecessary bulk or weight has become offensive. It is our function as a society and as a period to do the most with the least.

So many of us are beginning to look at fabrics —those wonderfully varied, colorful, warm, decorative, pliable structures with which we are so familiar—and we are beginning to see them as new things for which we may presently have unexpected uses in our continuing struggle to do more with less. Out of this changing vision, not yet sharply focussed, new areas of activity will develop.

*This began as a collection of slides and then became
a lecture in which unexpected similarities serve as
a jumping-off-point. A few of the pictures are here
with most of the lecture.*

The most interesting single question about design that has occurred to me in a long time is: How does it happen? What really takes place in the process during which isolated and unrelated factors are made to come together into something which has coherence, unity and perhaps beauty?

I do not propose to answer this question; I doubt if the present state of the non-physical sciences would enable anyone to do so. But exposing a problem frequently has as much unexpected value as answering it, and I believe that in this question there is concealed a good bit of material with an important bearing on both the practice of the arts and the training for them.

We learn from daily work at our trade that the design process usually begins with a specific problem—a client wants a room, a building, a lamp, a locomotive, a fountain, a mural. At this point the designer (I am using the word interchangeably with "artist") brings to the problem his own private baggage, his personal collection of images and the individual philosophy he holds whether he is aware of it or not.

No matter how objectively the designer attempts to view his problem, he is conditioned at every step in the design process by his accumulated notions of workable solutions, appropriate shapes and forms, and so on. Regarding the workable solutions, we approach the method of science, for solutions have been tried before, and thus tested. Selecting "appropriate" shapes and forms is more mysterious, for it involves intellectual and emotional processes not yet understood in their entirety.

We do know this, however: the only place from which the designer or artist can derive these notions is from the world around him. This too is no answer, for it leads to another complex question: What is this world really like? And also: What do we really see when we look at the world?

This much we do know—the range of vision, both inner and outer, varies enormously with individuals, occupational groups, and social groups. In areas such as modern art the difference in vision between artist and onlooker leads to great confusion. The "private baggage" brought by a Picasso to his problem (his view of the world as it is) must be vastly different from the vision of Joe Doakes, who finds the picture resulting from Picasso's view incomprehensible. And, one suspects, it is probably a much bigger and truer view than Doakes'.

What I am getting at is simply this—if in its broadest sense, design is the result of a personal

59

totality of experience, and is expressed as vision focused on a problem, then the crucial problem for the designer is the enlargement of his vision. It is crucial, I think, because it relates to one of the oldest questions that have confronted the arts—how does the artist achieve the greatest depth of meaning? It seems fairly obvious that you cannot create in a bigger way than you can see. The special problem today is how to find meaning within the framework of a society which is going through a transformaiton of extraordinary dimensions, a change so drastic that it tends to assume more and more the appearance of a crack-up; physical, economic, moral, and esthetic.

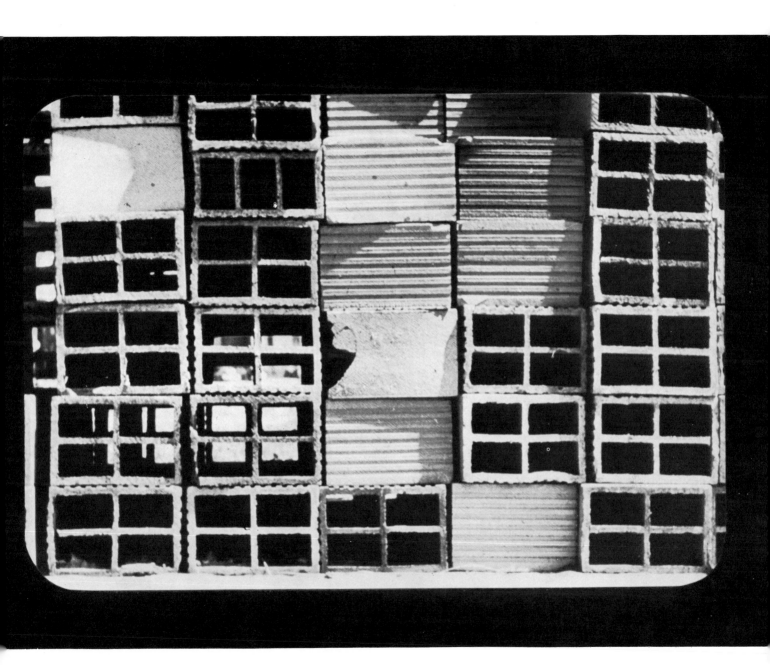

Historically, when societies have disintegrated, we generally point to evidence of internal corruption. In one's own time this approach is generally unfashionable and frowned upon.

Words are difficult things to handle, and in expounding an idea as unpopular as the one I have just outlined, words become particularly tricky. When I talk about a "society," I do not mean the U. S. alone, nor do I mean by "crackup" that our battleships are going to fall apart. What I do mean is that the institutions at the society's base are losing their original force and validity. To cite a single example, within the past year two thoroughly conservative reports

61

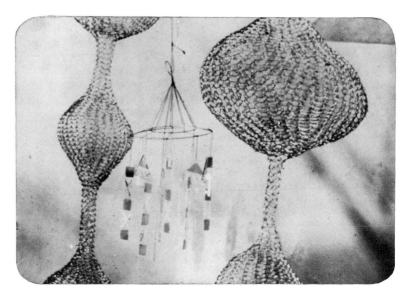

The camera eye requires only a change of focus in order

to see what appears to be an entirely different image.

have stated that the two-party system—one of the cornerstones of our particular kind of democracy—has almost completely gone to pieces. And in referring to "internal corruption" I am not thinking of the sensational investigations of racketeering now going on but that our social values have become predominantly materialistic. Man does not live by bread alone, nor, for that matter, by television screens or automatic washers, useful as these things are.

If you are wondering what all this may have to do with architecture, consider almost any housing project and recall what happens when the tenant is reduced from a human being to a statistical unit—when the calculations of the real estate mind cancel out the vision of the architect.

Christopher Fry's recent play, "The Lady's Not For Burning," deals with a young woman accused of witchcraft. Behind the accusation lie the usual motives of fear, greed and hate for anyone whose behavior deviates from the conventional. Horrified by the network of lies and suspicion thrown around her, she turns to the mayor and cries, "If, as a living creature, I wish in all good faith to continue living, where do you suggest I should lodge my application?" Where indeed? Is there anyone among us who would not like to know the answer?

The fear of sudden annihilation all of us have carried since Hiroshima is not entirely new. Mankind in its short history has lived out most of its days in jeopardy; and jeopardy, if you are exposed to it—or think you are—feels total, regardless of its specific nature. But today's fear is different in one sense: we created it. The Black Death which destroyed something between one-quarter and three-quarters of the populations where it struck had no known cause or cure in the medical science of the 14th Century. The Bomb was programmed, designed, built, and exploded by people who presumably knew exactly what they were doing. It is, I think, this new sense of intellectual mastery over the physical world that is making us so acutely and unhappily aware of the world over which seemingly we have no mastery at all.

It is here that I want to introduce the problem chosen for discussion. I believe that it is of crucial importance for the design professions and for the influence they have on human development. The problem I described as "enlargement of vision." Outer vision and inner vision. To

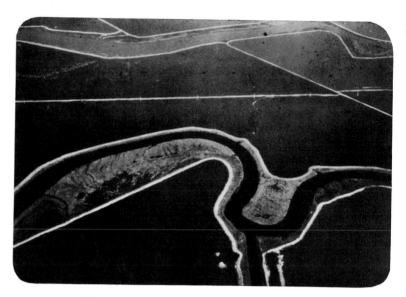

The airborne eye can see again, in an entirely new

context, the lines traced on prehistoric Peruvian pottery.

put the question another way, how can one learn to see the world?

At first blush this question may seem unnecessary or even downright silly. After all, it is the world we are living in, and we look at it all the time. I submit, however, that the central events of our time indicate with painful clarity that what we see is not the world of the mid-20th Century, but a series of out-dated inherited images of earlier periods. I am quite sure that "the world over which seemingly we have no mastery at all" is a world we scarcely see at all. Our vision is cluttered with retained images and it is too narrow.

It has been my own experience that to begin to approach an awareness of the shapes of our time requires an extraordinary intellectual and emotional effort. Enlargement of his vision is one of the most difficult assignments an individual can assume and the revision of habitual modes of thinking is no easier. Perhaps it is only the isolated genius who can ever see past the bare outlines of the age in which he lives; nevertheless, the effort is necessary for the common man, not only for survival, but for creation. "Without vision we the people perish." This well-worn platitude is true spiritually and materially. In architecture, specifically, we can build only up to the limits of our vision. You cannot design something you are unable to grasp in your thinking and feeling. The architects of the zoning-law skyscrapers were unable to visualize the slab type of tall structure, and they used setbacks even where they were not required.

Our habitual way of thinking and seeing, the result not only of schooling but of our total education, can be described as "atomistic." That is, everything is seen as a separate, static object or idea, not related in any important way to anything else. This way of seeing was once perfectly workable. It has relatively little usefulness in a world where people have learned how to convert mass into energy, which is an exceedingly nonstatic kind of operation. Most of our political thinking is atomistic. A conscientious reader of the papers and magazines soon learns, for instance, that the U. S. A. is a good country and the U.S.S.R. is very bad. The Soviet citizen, of course, learns just the reverse. It is possible that one or another of these propositions is actually true, but the kind of thinking that sets them up no longer provides a basis for practical action.

The modern eye sees nature directly sometimes, and sometimes

through glasses provided by the artists — which clarify.

Modern relationships are an expanding network that links even enemies like Siamese twins. Beating the other man to the draw was once a workable technique for survival, but for Siamese twins it is not. We defeated Japan and Germany and since have been unable to leave them to their defeat or to detach ourselves from them. Nobody can get detached any more.

The modern way of seeing things starts with the assumption of a dynamic rather than a static situation, and it proceeds from this assumption to a growing understanding that relationships can take us closer to the truth about things than the things themselves. It also includes the idea that the path to truth can contain a number of contradictions. We were brought up to believe that if X is true, Y must therefore be false. The contemporary physicist would be in a difficult spot if he had to work on this basis—for he has to operate with both the wave and quantum theories, which seem contradictory in their explanations of how light is transmitted.

City development at this point demonstrates one active contradiction: as streets and parking lots become congested to the point of standstill we build more skyscraper offices and make automobiles larger. Or to revert to the political area: the U. S. as a so-called Christian nation presumably subscribes to the morality taught in the Old and New Testaments; recently when thousands of Chinese and Korean Reds were roasted alive by jellied gasoline bombs, the press indulged in an orgy of gloating that would have embarrassed a cannibal community. Are we Christians or barbarians? I suspect that the "either—or" method will get us nowhere. At the Museum of Modern Art of few years back there was a symposium on the "International Style versus the Bay Region Style." Aside from Marcel Breuer's comment, "This would have been fascinating twenty-five years ago," the whole evening was fruitless nonsense and had to be, because the modern house is a contradiction and not to be solved by grammar school logic. The modern house is a contradiction because though its design implies the existence of industrial methods it is actually not particularly different in construction, materials, finishes, or services from a contemporary "colonial" house. Both are handicraft products. What really makes today's modern house "modern" is not its technique but the form of the architect's response to the contemporary world. In this

Vision acknowledges only what it is looking for: here the rhythmic order of parallel lines.

But it can also learn to accept

other expressions.
"Chaos" in this detail of a Pollock painting becomes "order" in a microphotograph.

When articulation becomes
meaningful

its expressions
become visible everywhere.

The same thing happens with
awareness

of enveloping forms.

IMPOR'

In the event of enemy attac
York State, **NO** private veh
vithin the boundaries of the

Literary content
destroys awareness of forms. Forms must first be made "illegible," in
order to be "seen."

The suprematist painters taught us to see the plane in new perspective.

sense it is like modern painting which more often than not uses the same oils, brushes, and canvas as Rembrandt, or like modern sculpture, which may achieve its aims with the processes and materials of the Stone Age. There can be modern houses which employ the resources of an advanced technology, just as there may be sculpture made of high tensile strength alloys with welding equipment, but the vision of the artist—the extent to which he has perceived the shape of the world today—is the crucial factor.

When viewed in this light, the mixture of incomprehension, ridicule, and hostility with which modern art is still received, is not entirely surprising. If it is correct that the picture of the world carried in the mind of the average citizen is largely a preconceived and a preconditioned image, then the insights of today's greatest painters and sculptors cannot be other than profoundly disturbing. I also suspect that the resistance to modern design in houses, furniture, churches, and public buildings which still exists can be explained on the same basis.

One of the things that helps to broaden the visual horizon is an understanding that the tremendous changes that have been occurring since 1914 at a geometrically increasing rate of speed do not just "happen." Except for relatively inconsequential details they really cannot be blamed on that man in the White House or even that man in the Kremlin. The complex of events and atmospheres in which we struggle today has an evolutionary history just like anything else. Let me pick up one small thread to illustrate what I mean. It is only since the early Renaissance—say 500 years—that Western man has learned to think of himself as an individual. Before that he was an anonymous member of a flock whose shepherd was God, whose shelter was the cathedral and whose ultimate destination was Heaven or Hell.

Since the beginning of the Renaissance, the individual's consciousness of himself as an entity has grown. It found its expression in private palaces, in the development of portraiture as an activity for artists, in the French and American Revolutions with their Declarations of the Rights of Man and the Bill of Rights. And it found an extraordinary radical and contemporary twist in the discoveries of Dr. Freud, who succeeded in demonstrating that the "entity" the individual considered himself was actually not an entity at all, but an entire constellation, within which childhood experiences, the sexual drive, religious taboos, and social influences operated in as mysterious but as powerful a manner as the force of gravity. At roughly the same time the physicists were demonstrating that other material "entities" —say solid objects such as tables or chairs—were really complicated series of electrical tensions. It was no coincidence that at the peak of his self-consciousness the individual dissolved into an almost incomprehensibly abstract network of relationships and that the same thing happened to his concept of inanimate matter. Both developments, you will note, tended to substitute transparency, in a sense, for solidity, relationships for dissociated entities, and tension or energy for mass.

It should not be necessary to go into detail to link up these remarkable developments with what has been happening in painting and sculpture. In architecture it is obvious that transparency has become a functional and esthetic factor, that building is becoming less of a traditional art and more an integrated, sheltered network of "nervous systems" for communication, illumination, air conditioning, and that strength in tension is constantly increasing its advantage over strength in compression. Furniture very naturally tends to find its organic place in this highly organized complex as one of the built-in services. Today furniture design is prominently featured as a vehicle for individual expression. I think it will unquestionably lose this position and tend to recede into a serviceable anonymity in much the same way as lighting and heating and plumbing.

Another point about modern architecture, in passing. In school it was a standard joke, if the construction details had not been clearly thought out, to suggest that the building could always be held up on "sky hooks." Such buildings are not any longer a joke. Space platforms outside the earth's atmosphere are already a theoretical possibility and only time and work stand between the theory and its realization. One interesting way to apprehend the nature of the contemporary world is to meditate at length on the implications of a structure whose "foundations" are the invisible lines of tension which can transmit the "load" at 186,000 miles per second for distances approaching infinity.

So far, this picture of the world, sketchy and

  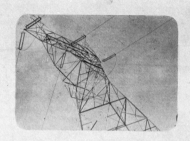

For the modern eye: old and new faces . . .   *. . . new and old . . .*

  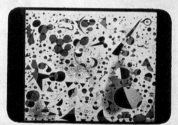

. . . designs in tension . . .   *. . . and complex organizations of form.*

fragmentary as it has to be, consistently suggests the existence of a kind of dissolving transformation in areas seemingly as unrelated as art, technology, politics, psychology, and physics. The destructive aspects of this change might indicate reason for profound pessimism, were it not for the fact that destruction and creation—here we have another example of the contradiction in action—are only two sides of the same coin. One therefore has the free choice of identifying himself with either the decaying or the new and growing elements in the process and then basing his personal philosophy and actions on this choice.

There is probably no better or more familiar example of the simultaneous operation of the destruction-creation cycle in our society than industry. On the part industry has played in the transformation of the world there have been many books written, notably Mumford's *Technics and Civilization* and Giedion's *Mechanization Takes Command.* The detail on which I propose to concentrate is industry's role in widening the split which has shattered Western culture. This split has been described in a number of ways. Dr. Giedion, for example, writes about "a period in which thinking and feeling were separated," and observes that "mentally trained people are capable today of following the most difficult scientific research . . . but are lost when faced with new artistic means which force them to an enlargement of their inner natures." John Dewey, in *Art as Experience,* refers to the "compartmentalization of occupations," and points to the "separation of that mode of activity commonly called 'practice' from insight, of imagination from executive doing, of significant purpose from work. . . ."

Industry was largely responsible for this separation of "significant purpose from work," and the way in which this happened seems fairly clear. If you take a man away from work where he has full knowledge and control of materials and processes (say the making of handmade shoes) and put him into a factory, where he knows only a small part of the process and controls none of it, he will become a different kind of man. Alienation of the man from his work produces a split in his personality and he becomes emotionally deranged. Since we all have the sickness to a greater or lesser degree, we describe this state as "normal." In terms of behavior this man becomes dependent rather than independent, less responsible, less decisive where choices are involved, and he will finally consider work not a discipline for building character and developing creativity, but as a thing to be avoided if possible. Hence the popularity of the insurance plans for retiring on $200 per month at age 55. Politically he tends to move in the totalitarian direction, for the implications of freedom become frightening, and he takes to mass-produced entertainment in a way that would have horrified his pioneer forebears.

This man is not my invention. Let me read to you what Henry Steele Commager writes in *The American Mind.* "Recreation came to be enjoyed vicariously. From playing games Americans took to watching them and then to listening to them on the radio. Even enthusiasm ceased to be spontaneous and was artificially organized by cheer leaders. Men who enjoyed artificial adventures in the pages of mysteries or westerns, and women who acquired artificial complexions, found little difficulty in adopting artificial emotions: they turned to the radio and the movies for excitement and sensation, laughter and tears and learned about love from the magazines. There seemed to be, in short, a progressive atrophy of the creative instinct of the average American."

It is much less than a generation since Huxley's *Brave New World* was read as an outrageous fantasy. But here we have the same picture in a sober report. It applies not only to America, but to the average world citizen wherever industry has taken over in a competitive society.

When work ceases to have significance, not only do people in all social groups become restless and unhappy, but the capacity to find meaning in other areas also tends to disappear. Our cities are excellent demonstrations of this. It is almost impossible to find a U. S. city where there is visible evidence of a genuine concern for human values. In the remaining colonial villages, yes, but not in anything built since the Civil War. In those metropolitan centers where we have installed subways, we put the people underground and let the trucks ride in the sun. I do not know a single U. S. city which, if destroyed in a bombing attack, would be regretted by posterity. With all of our horsepower, we haven't produced a community remotely comparable to Athens, Florence, Venice, Rome or

Paris. Even New York would probably be more picturesque as a quiet rusting ruin than as it now is.

No society, as I said before, can build beyond the range of its vision. The vision of a materialistic society is a materialistic vision. Its creative potential in building extends to roads, dams, powerhouses, and factories. In this respect we are not unlike Rome; and Rome as an example to follow, hardly seems good enough.

A little earlier I cited the industrial process as an example of a contradiction in that it simultaneously threw off destructive and creative effects. The individual so devastatingly described by Mr. Commager is real enough, but we do not yet have his whole story. He has other characteristics acquired through daily immersion in. the modern world.

Our conditioned man, for example, is learning to cooperate. Not through persuasion or fear of damnation, as the dictators do it, but through the natural discipline of the process itself. In other words, this man of ours, while degenerating badly in many respects, is at the same time becoming a social being operating at a new level.

He is beginning to understand that much of the "individuality" attributed to him has become a myth and that he is as expendable as a machine tool part. But he also knows that the large organism within which he moves needs him to function properly. He accepts his role as a member of a synchronized, cooperative group and one of these days he will arrive at a new comprehension of the many possible constructive relationships between the individual and the group.

He is, in other words, a prototype of the non-competitive man about whom the religious teachers have been talking since 2500 B.C. He is one of the meek who will inherit the earth. He has as little in common with the Victorian robber baron or the rugged individualist as with a man from Mars. He may have barely squeaked through grammar school, but when he runs a machine or drives an automobile, he becomes his brother's keeper. Not because of what was said in Sunday School, but because *his* life is entrusted to the driver of the car ahead of him. He is also, as I suggested before, a thoroughly non-national character and is being produced as surely in Soviet Russia as here. Idealogically he may be taken in by the propaganda pumped into him so persistently wherever he lives, for he is still a bit green, but every major development in his very dynamic world, whether under capitalism or communism, in peace or war will act to foster him as a type.

The reason I find this man so fascinating is very simple: one of these days he is going to be our client. Not in our lifetime, perhaps, but certainly in that of our profession. I think that the outcome will be non-competitive architecture and non-competitive cities. With this kind of client at full maturity we could again discover and express the human values which fostered the Acropolis and the Gothic cathedrals. It is because this magnificent possibility seems to me to fit so clearly in the picture of the unfamiliar world that is taking shape that it is essential that we learn how to see it. This is why I believe enlargement of our vision to be the most significant problem in architecture and design.

THE DESIGNER IN THE MODERN WORLD

The designer lives in the modern world. For him and his work it acts like a target, establishing the direction of his efforts and setting up a boundary outside which these efforts become ineffective.

The modern world—any world in its own time —is always a complex. It contains not only material that is truly of the immediate moment, but also innumerable memories of past worlds. There is also a constantly developing sense of worlds still in the making.

Any individual engaged in the effort to cope with his world is enmeshed in a tangle of phenomena relating to a near-infinity of times and places. Education is a process designed to impose something resembling a common order on this mass of events, an attempt to provide the individual with methods for coping with quantities of seemingly unrelated information.

To serve its own purposes, education must be based on social agreement. Otherwise communication between groups in the society cannot take place. During periods of great change this agreement breaks down. Certain groups react to the changes more rapidly than others, and communication becomes difficult.

The designer sometimes appears to have problems different from those of his contemporaries, such as scientists or businessmen. This is because he gives visible form to objects, an activity traditionally attributed to the artist.

Western society, during the past century and a half, has had very little use for the artist, and the feeling that he was a man apart had its basis in actual fact. But with the social isolation of the artist the myth grew up that he was *in essence* a man apart.

In the eyes of a public that had no use for him, the artist was a man who worked from "inspiration" and hence did not process the common fund of information in the same manner as other men. He was "impractical," a "dreamer." For the hard work to which other men were subjected he substituted "talent" (a very mysterious thing) or sometimes "genius" (equally mysterious but more respectable because of the long-term publicity attached to it). Because of his isolation, and the consequent loss of communication channels to the rest of society, work with the painter's brush and the sculptor's tools ceased to look like work, and it became suspect.

When Santayana said that the artist was not a special kind of man, but that every man was a special kind of artist, he was not announcing a discovery, but a re-discovery.

The industrial designer, as an identifiable category of professional, dates back barely thirty years. The importance of this phenomenon is not that the designer is anything remarkable, but that he is a conspicuous part of the new process of reintegrating the artist with society.

Two things make it hard to see the industrial designer as an artist. His activity has to do with common articles of use rather than the traditional media of painting and sculpture. And even more confusing to anyone who persists in visualizing the artist as a solitary character in a garret, is the fact that the designer is far more commonly an *organization* than an individual.

One of the most significant facts of our time is the predominance of the organization. Quite possibly it is the most significant. It will take time to realize its full effects on the thinking and behavior of individuals. In this conditioning process, few escape its influence. Even driving a car becomes part of a shifting but organized activity in which speed with safety are the result of voluntary cooperation by thousands of highly disciplined individuals.

The existence of the industrial designer marks one phase of the reassimilation of the artist into society. But because he is accepted (the criterion is very simple: people pay him money because they need what he does) he in turn must accept the beliefs of the society, and among these is the conviction that the organization is the proper form for important activities.

The existence of the organization as a dominant social form is a social response to a social problem. The problem is how to cope effectively with increasing quantities of information. A ten-year-old boy today has more information than

Erasmus had at his prime. A small business or industry is already too complex to be handled by a single individual. So the specialist appears. The specialist, however, cannot exist without the organization because his particular package of information is useless unless coordinated with many others. And since this cannot be done without effective two-way communication, there arises a problem in education.

I have already described education as a method of imposing a common order on a mass of events. Specialists can communicate only if they agree on something. If I believe that fire is the expression of a particular god's wrath and you are equally convinced that it is a process of rapid oxidation, we cannot communicate, at least where fire is concerned.

The quantity of information now available has become so large that it can no longer be processed by traditional methods. This is the reason for the crisis in education and the many controversies about possible solutions. Finding workable answers is crucial, because science, business, industry and political institutions cannot continue to develop unless many people acquire a greater capacity to process information and learn better methods of communicating with each other. The industrial designer is subject to these pressures as much as everyone else.

The cultivated individual of the 18th century had a common ground with others in his class: all had studied Greek and Latin and had made the grand tour of the Continent. We enjoy no such unanimity today.

It is possible that agreement on a basic curriculum will never again be reached, that the new common ground will be found in *methods* of organizing and transmitting information.

One common element with interesting possibilities is the widespread use of abstractions. A man trained for management learns to deal with abstractions consisting of some two dozen alphabetical symbols, a handful of Arabic numerals and special kinds of pictures called charts or graphs. He does not as a rule think of these as abstraction, just as Moliere's bourgeois gentilhome did not realize that he had been speaking prose all his life. Yet it is true that the powerful images used by management have no visible resemblance to the physical world and might correctly be described as abstractions.

The artist deals with other sets of symbols in two or three dimensions, most of which relate in some visible way to the world around him. *His* abstractions, however, are generally considered meaningless by the men who deal with letters, numbers and graphs.

Both groups, then, deal with constellations of abstract symbols that appear to have nothing in common. Yet the processing methods employed by each are not too dissimilar. And an understanding of the nature of the abstracting process might make communication possible.

When I was a student of architecture in Europe in the mid-30s, I was struck by the observation that the weights of government buildings in various countries differed greatly. Those built in Italy during the early years of the Mussolini regime were relatively light and open, but as the Italian position deteriorated in relation to Germany, the new buildings acquired thicker walls, heavier details and a generally more massive appearance. In Germany, under Hitler, the official structures from the beginning were extreme in mass and weight, and modern architecture, which is very light in structure and appearance, was forbidden by edict. In Scandinavia on the other hand, where it was not unheard-of for the King and other ruling personages to be seen on street cars, government architecture had reached an unprecedented stage of apparent fragility.

So much for the observation. Now for the conclusion. After much perplexed pondering I finally decided that *the greater the internal stability of a modern regime, the lighter its buildings.* This conclusion, as it happened, was borne out by events of the next ten years, but what is important about this example is the fact that a set of esthetic symbols had been processed in precisely the same way an accountant might examine a company's balance sheet.

I believe that it is crucial for education today to explore such similarities in the greatest possible variety of activities. From these similarities we can build the bridges needed for communication.

Using such bridges, one becomes capable of exploring almost any combination of specialized activities. As an example one might say that what Joyce's "Ulysses" does to a space framework (Dublin) and to a time span (24 hours) is not unlike what the nuclear physicists did to the 19th century atom. Or what a movie director, using such devices as montage, might do with something called "boy-meets-girl." Or what the super high-speed camera does with a flame at the instant it is snuffed out. Or what Picasso does when he compresses into a single two-dimensional frame a variety of events in time and space.

Obviously these are the most loose of analogies and the comparisons could not be pushed very far. Nevertheless the space-time manipulations in each have a common—and thoroughly contemporary—character. Equally obviously, all of this activity of relating or "bridge-building" has a great deal to do with the industrial designer, who is the least specialized of all possible specialists and who must, therefore, think in terms of increasingly complex networks of problems.

In such observations as these, it seems possible that there may lie a very significant and productive concept:

The unity being sought throughout the modern world (seen from this point of view the conflicts spread over the morning paper are gropings in this direction) is not to be achieved through the reduction of complexity to simplicity, for this avenue does not exist even as a remote possibility.

It can be achieved only through the *acceptance of increasing complexity* and the establishment of a common framework within which phenomena can be related and evaluated.

The educated individual in this time does not set out to acquire more information—he enlarges his capacity to process (i.e., relate) the vast quantities he already possesses.

The industrial designer does not differ from other categories of individuals in this respect.

Because of the extreme diversity of the problems to which he is exposed, the modern designer has been compared to the artist of the Renaissance, a man who might take a commission for a portrait one day, carve a tomb the next, design a palace or work out a problem in military engineering. The similarity exists, but it is superficial. A superior individual in the Renaissance could assemble in his own head all the significant information of his time. A superior individual in the 20th Century could not possibly begin to do this. His role in this respect has had to be taken over by the organization.

For over ten thousand years the artist has been a visible landmark in the human landscape. Today is the first time in his history he has found it necessary to take out incorporation papers.

HIGH TIME TO EXPERIMENT

More on the problem of education . . .

One year ago, almost to the day, I was standing on a station platform in Stuttgart waiting for a train. Also waiting were some two or three dozen GIs, each seated comfortably on his suitcase, each absorbed in a book. Every book—I checked, and there were no exceptions—was a comic. At the time postwar Germany was new to me, and I was unacquainted with the drafted defenders of our ideals and culture. So I was shocked, and the vision of these boys growing up to be latter-day versions of Senator Knowland was not happy-making. Later on, recollection of the scene created an entirely different impression: they all had shoes and, with the aid of simple cartoons, they were able to read. We, the richest and most advanced nation in existence, had achieved this. You cannot say as much for the majority of the world's population.

I tell this story because I have a deep distrust of discussions of education that fail to find a connection with the world as it is. I have listened to too many "educators" whose idea of proper barber shop reading is Petronius in the original. And to others whose concept of education is a carefully winnowed selection of unusable facts. I happen to believe that the knowledge of languages—even Latin—is a good thing, and that if it entertains a man to know the date of the Council of Nicea, it does neither him nor his neighbors any harm. But I also happen to believe that the problem of education is always a contemporary problem and that if it is to be solved at all, it will be solved in contemporary terms. Speaking of it in contemporary terms, I can tell you what it is *not*: the problem is no longer one of piling up information. My youngest son, aged ten, contains more information—ten times more informtaion—than did Erasmus in his prime. The same holds for his playmates. But they are not educated people any more than the soldiers on the railway platform were educated people.

Up until fairly recently, our society has not been especially interested in education. There has been a lot of talk, and many a well-heeled alumnus has gratefully endowed the old alma mater. In actuality, however, the main focus of interest has been *training*. The difference between *training* and education seems simple to me, although in my layman's way I may be greatly oversimplifying matters. In any event, training as I see it is a procedure for developing special competence. Thus one might describe the first ten grades of school as training—primarily—in the recognition and use of words, the manipulation of numbers, the memorizing of useful facts. The college student who begins professional specialization in sophomore year is clearly concentrating on training. This is one of the things that so frustrates faculties in the humanities.

There is nothing wrong with training. Every society needs skills, and our own demands in this respect are enormous. During the period of our growth, we had a desperate need for trained people in order to establish a technological base for industry and agriculture, and that need continues. But along with this is developing, for the first time in our history, a mass demand for education.

Training is not a difficult matter. If we, the world's melting pot, could achieve our dazzling technology, if the Russians with a mass of illiterate peasants could build a powerful industry in a generation, then it *cannot* be difficult. Even those uniformed blobs in Stuttgart, so absorbed in their bubble gum and comics, probably represented a rather imposing collection of technical skills. Education is a horse of an entirely different color and there is nothing simple about it.

EDUCATION IS A HANDICRAFT ACTIVITY

The aim of education, as far as I can make out, is no less than the total integration of a man's capacities. It has little to do with the particular facts or skills at his disposal. That is why we can still regard Erasmus as a model of the educated man. Erasmus was an authority on Athanasius (an individual of little contemporary interest) and he believed as fact many things since discovered to be nonsense. What established his position as an extraordinarily cultivated individual was his ability to take such knowledge as his time offered, and make from it a new picture of the world. The educated man collects information primarily for the purpose of establishing new relationships—after all, he is a man and not a magpie. He also has some understanding of who he is and how he relates to society. He understands the meaning of tradition, relating himself to the past rather than worshipping it. His equipment includes a concept of morality. His orientation is essentially creative. Finally, his picture of society is the result of critical evaluation, which takes courage since he may find himself in opposition to it. All this adds up to quite an order, and I suspect that existing educational procedures are not capable of handling it. The reason: no handicraft activity (education is a handicraft activity) can function effectively in an industrial society. If there is any truth at all in this dismal view of education, then it is high time we began to experiment.

What evidence indicates a developing demand for education? For me it lies in the many indications of a new social need. Consider, for instance, the widespread uneasiness after Hiroshima—not only the natural fear, but the feeling that so much power in the hands of scientists and technicians was uncomfortably like handing a child a large firecracker and a Zippo lighter. The feeling had to do with the possible *lack of education* in intelligent, highly trained people. Now the fear has spread to include the politicians. The world heaved an audible sigh of relief when at Geneva both Eisenhower and Bulganin showed that they understood the consequences of speeches and actions. Life has always been the prime educational force, and developments of the past ten years have accelerated our stumbling progress towards maturity.

The change in industry has had a lot to do with our shift in attitudes. Initially industry needed labor; as machines and processes became more complex, semi-skilled labor was required; today, with automation coming fast, the prospect is *no labor,* but a vast reserve of skilled professionals. At management level the need for broad vision and independent thinking becomes ever more acute, and since these qualities are among the attributes of the educated man, business and industry have discovered a pressing need for education. In this connection the experiment of Pennsylvania Bell Telephone and the University of Pennsylvania is revealing. Over a five-year period some ninety-odd middle rank executives will be run through an intensive one-year course in the humanities. Since the cost of this venture could easily run to two million dollars, one presumes that the company's interest involves more than lip service.

The problem presented by this increasing interest could be gauged in numbers: take the 3,500,000 currently in college and plot the growth curve, add a swelling number from business and industry, add the adults who are discovering an itch for knowledge, and you have a very large number. The only flaw in the picture is that education was originally designed for a very small elite, and its basic methods have not changed.

What interests me about this problem, since my work is mainly with industry, is that manufacturing once had it too. To set up an absurd but perhaps revealing comparison, imagine the 1955 output of cars made by hand, and assume that three skilled craftsmen could make a car per year. We would then need 20,000,000 such people in the automobile industry. Obviously no such number is available, but equally obviously there is no shortage of cars. The reason, as any child knows, is that the central concept of industry is that a production tool can turn out large quantities of something—inexpensively, at a high level of quality, and in short order.

Today in education we have a shortage of teachers—not good teachers, but any kind of teacher. How does one quickly correct the shortage of an important social commodity? Is there any way of converting the good teacher into a "production tool," thus multiplying his effectiveness? It may sound absurd to compare industry and education, but is it really? Education is still wedded to the handicraft idea—that is, one teacher can turn out twenty or two hundred students and that is the end of it. All evidence at hand strongly suggests that handicraft production is meaningless in an industrial society except as a hobby or therapy. There is another fact to toss in the hopper: mass production has come to mean quality levels incomparably higher than those afforded by handicraft. Not everyone realizes this, but I have yet to see anything out of the Periclean age that can match, say, a Rolleiflex (I am talking about craftsmanship, not art). Could the application of the methods of industry achieve anything in this respect with regard to education? I submit that a most fruitful area of experimentation lies right here.

TWEEDY RAMBLINGS AND PRODUCTION TOOLS

Such talk may not go too well with tweedy ramblings on quiet campuses, but campuses are not so quiet any more. It may also help to remember that education has relied heavily on one mass production tool for a long time now. It is called a book.

Since the book was invented (a lot of people were pretty upset when this happened) a number of devices have appeared which increase the speed and accuracy of communication. They include photography, printing methods, records, radio, magnetic tape, television, movies. Virtually all of them have been used in training, and very successfully too. What remains is to test their effectiveness in education.

Let me try another set of assumptions: (1) There are very few great teachers; (2) it would be desirable if the small number now exposed to these people could be vastly expanded; (3) this can be done if a suitable medium, such as film, is employed. In other words, the teacher's message is "tooled" and then reproduced in any quantity desired.

Film is a remarkable medium. It can convey not only the message, but something of the personality of the transmitter. It can also take a message as delivered by an accomplished lecturer, and compress it into a fraction of the time, with improved clarity and impact. A particularly interesting characteristic of film is that it is better at dealing with relationships than with isolated facts. Actually, a film *is* a relationship—the picture strips of which it is composed have no meaning by themselves. This most modern of media happens to fit like a glove the most important of all problems in education: development of the individual's capacity to establish connections between isolated phenomena.

So there we have our experimental program: find the great teachers in every area, squeeze them to the last drop, pour the precious distillate through a Mitchell camera and put the results in a million cans. It certainly is an application of the industrial method. What, if anything, is wrong with it?

Since it is difficult to be ruthless with one's own pet ideas, I'll try first to indicate what isn't wrong with it. Educators who have criticized the proposal seem to be unanimous on one point: personal contact between student and teacher is destroyed in the "canning" process. This is true. The question is, is it important? How many teachers have anything worth transmitting, whether by personal contact or otherwise? I have the unhappy feeling that there are few who do. And is it the contact of *persons* or of *minds* that is significant? Literally billions of people who never met Buddha, Moses, Jesus, Mohammed or Lao Tze have been deeply affected by their teaching.

What I believe is wrong with the "tooling" concept as applied to education is not the lack of personal contact, but the fact that it is incomplete. It is too simple. A man is a complex affair, and he cannot be handled in the same summary fashion as a piece of material. For instance, when a factory produces a refrigerator we have a situation in which the tools are the active elements, impressing themselves on inert materials. The finished refrigerator has no response to the process which created it, no sense of relationship to the factory. There is no "feedback" from passive to active. Education is more involved. There is teaching, in which the teacher attempts to impress his message on the student, but there is also learning, in which the student, so to speak, "talks back." He argues, asks questions, reads books, writes papers, memorizes, forgets. Communication includes both message transmission and feedback. Furthermore, both transmitter and receiver are continuously modified by the process itself. The trouble with the tooling concept as a complete answer to problems of education is that you cannot *manufacture* an educated man—he has to do most of it himself.

The student can be greatly stimulated and perhaps enlightened by the teacher-on-film, but there is no provision for his response. This, by the way, is also the limitation of the book. Following this line of thought, one might re-define the school as "a device for organizing the student's response to the stimuli received from books and teachers." The advantage of the film is that to a somewhat greater degree than the book, it can discharge the function of both book and teacher. Its ability to bring outstanding teaching to millions cannot, I believe, be seriously questioned.

A short time back, in studying some research on the behavior of groups, I came across a statement that impressed me: *If a group wants to learn something, it can teach itself.* Needless to say, such a statement needs to be buttressed with reservations. The kernel of the idea is exciting, however, for it may offer the needed complement to the concept of "tooled" teaching. If a film presents a message, the group can deal with the processing of student responses. In a way, this is the idea of the seminar, but with a different orientation.

Taken as an interlocking unit, the concept of industry-based teaching plus the group as a device for handling feedback could have interesting effects on existing methods. For one thing, the quality of teaching could be up-graded in many areas with dramatic rapidity. There might also be an increase of student responsibility and a better understanding of the nature of the learning process. For adult education, and particularly for the new requirements of business and industry, it could be a tool with great mobility and flexibility. Incidentally, the method would not eliminate the teacher, any more than industry eliminated jobs. It would raise standards, however, and many teachers might privately find this objectionable.

The dangers inherent in this proposal, with its emphasis on standardization? They are considerable. Unfortunately life itself is dangerous, and getting born, particularly so. The human animal would still be peering out of holes in cliffs if the estimates of danger had always precluded the taking of risks.

SOMETHING COCKEYED INDEED

This particular bee flew into my bonnet a couple of years ago, when an experimental venture at the University of Georgia pushed me into an awareness of the industrial approach as a possible factor in education. The experiment, like so many things that leave a good feeling afterwards, was not planned. I had been invited to serve as a consultant to the University's Department of Fine Arts. Knowing little about education and less about art school curricula, I went

down for three days, visited classes, listened to faculty members and left, silently, but with an impression that there was indeed something cockeyed about the curriculum.

A second visit, in which Charles Eames joined me, revealed one thing that seemed very wrong; in certain classes *a very long time was being taken to teach things that could be learned in a hurry.* At the faculty meeting we expressed this as an opinion. Feelings were ruffled, there was indignation at the implication that time and motion study methods might have a place in the halls of learning, tempers flared, and suddenly people were talking quite frankly about problems of education. It wasn't like a faculty meeting at all, and before we quite knew what was happening, Eames and I had promised to return in five months with a demonstration of some of the ideas we were advocating.

The demonstration turned out to be quite a thing—a one hour "lecture," without a lecturer, for a non-existent course dubbed "Art X." It consisted of slides with taped narration and music, of simultaneous triple-slide projection, of movies (some made for the purpose, some borrowed).

The theme of the lecture: communication. Its objective: to show relationships between areas people normally considered separate. The show was exceedingly rich visually and it excited many people in many different ways. Later when shown at UCLA, by the sixth and last performance the hall was loaded to something close to three times its rated capacity. Apparently it was not necessary to have a live teacher on the lecture platform to get students to a high pitch of excitement.

What happened at Georgia was even more gratifying. A number of faculty members banded together and created a new kind of course. It merged "passive" learning (mechanized lectures produced by the faculty) with "active" (drawing, painting, modeling, carving, etc., etc.). The lectures supposedly have something to do with art theory, but the students are as likely to be subjected to a film on screw machine operation as a slide presentation of Picasso's painting (sometimes both are run simultaneously.) The classroom is the only one I have ever encountered that smells like a gymnasium and the amount of work turned out is unbelievable. And just to make the point to the students that they are supposed to be learning, not turning out minor art works, the instructors generally make them destroy their work at the end of most sessions.

Some of the by-products of this experiment in getting students to experience the meaning of relationships have been interesting. It has been fairly common for new students to come to the instructor after the first few months and ask why they weren't enjoying television and the downtown movies as much as they used to, and many have come to realize that films with expensive technique and cheap content can be less satisfying. Apparently the mechanized lecture can raise critical standards in more than one area. Last spring the freshmen and juniors (who had been trained in a more conventional manner) were sent out for an hour of painting on the campus. The freshmen work made one wonder what the juniors were doing in an art school. The high speed production methods of the new course, strange as it may seem, had resulted in a visible deepening of the esthetic content of the student's work.

The result of all this, as far as I am concerned, has been a strengthening of the initial conviction that what we have learned in industry could take on many rich and varied meanings in education. The conviction, naturally, carries with it a desire to see many kinds of experiments in education as a way to test it. However, despite the quite remarkable performance at Georgia, I suspect that the main initiative will not come from the field of education.

Educators as a group seem to lack the necessary vision, courage, energy—and funds. This may sound like a blanket condemnation, which it is not, but contacts with men in industry and in education have tended to dampen my optimism about the latter. It is far more likely that the initiative will come from industry (as in the case of Bell Telephone) because it will be the first to grasp the scope and importance of the problem. Industry is familiar with the experimental approach and it has learned not to shy away from the calculated risk.

For my own part, there was the wonderful discovery at some point in time that the best way to make something happen is to do it. Within the next couple of years some "sample lessons" will be made and tried out. The nice thing about these personal experiments with ideas and techniques is that they can't "fail." You see, just doing them contributes so much to one's own education. . . .

ART

SOME NOTES ON RELATIONS BETWEEN THE VISUAL ARTS

*Written quite a long time ago, in an effort to cope with
some rather large questions. I am not sure that the same degree of
certainty would be present now.*

I think it was in the year just after the war ended that the papers came out with an announcement that Pablo Picasso had become a member of the French Communist Party. I remember being interested by the news: it seemed utterly incredible that a man approaching seventy, who turned out as much work as Picasso, could find the time or energy for political activity. Also, the Communist Party was getting pretty unfashionable again, and if people were joining, not many were sending announcements to the press. Then I forgot all about the whole thing.

Six months, or perhaps a year, went by and there was another item about Picasso and his politics; he had done a portrait of Thorez, then the big wheel in the French party, and this portrait was being widely used for propaganda and electioneering purposes by the Communists. This seemed reasonable—after all, one would hardly expect Picasso to watch the polls or pass the plate at meetings.

The third item was a full report of a speech by a leading French Communist politician on the work of artists within the party's ranks. Inevitably Picasso was mentioned at length, and the gist of what the politician had to say about the artist went something like this—"Picasso had spent the better part of his life working for a group of degenerate snobs, but now he had put his shoulder to the wheel with the masses, and by this act of solidarity he had thereby become a great artist."

I forget how the rest of the speech went, and it doesn't matter. What was interesting was not that the statement was a lie—Picasso, one may safely guess, never worked for anybody but Picasso—but the clear indication of the relation between contemporary politicians and contemporary artist, which may be summed up for the former by "if you are on my side you're terrific." As I read and re-read this part of the speech, stunned by the egregious stupidity of the assumption, I began to realize that this was not a special case—it could have been a Democrat or Republican who said it. And that a lot of us, regardless of whether we thought of ourselves as artists or not, were in much the same boat as Picasso. People thought we were working "for" them—actually, whether we ourselves knew it or not, we were working for ourselves. Because if you want to create anything—it doesn't matter what, or how inadequate your talents—there isn't anyone else to work "for." This was the first time in my life that I identified myself with another artist, and the fact that it happened to be a very eminent one was not important—the same kind of motor was driving all of us and if mine or someone else's was measured only as fractional horsepower, that was a detail outside our control.

When I went to school to study architecture, nobody ever said a word about "artists"—not, at least, in connection with building. It was the job of an architect, so they said, to become a competent craftsman and to serve his clients well. In school and in the offices where I worked nothing had ever been said about basic motivations or the relationship of a man to his work. Also, I had spent two years at the American Academy in Rome, an institution dedicated to the proposition that painters, sculptors, landscape architects and architects formed by their very nature a collaborative group whose combined efforts could produce architecture comparable to the great achievements of the past. Yet during these two years nothing ever happened to suggest that possibly the motives prodding painters and architects had anything in common, that their aims had anything in common or that their day to day activities had anything in common. After all, a building was a building and a sheet of canvas was a sheet of canvas and never the twain should meet—except, perhaps, in the lobby of a post office. It might have been conversations with Wright, which started the feeling, that the underlying basis of the arts was essentially the same. If so, this was pretty curious because Wright, as far as I had ever been able to make out, appeared to have little use for sculpture—at least contemporary scultpure—and even less for painting. Whatever the background of ideas the trigger mechanism was a stupid statement by a stupid French politician, and I have never ceased being grateful to him, for the sense of identification with artists and the arts, no matter how remote from my own trade, has persisted and become stronger in the intervening years.

Attached to the group of architects and designers lumped together under the general heading of "modern" certain ideas and attitudes have tended to become established. There is an emphasis on the so-called "functional" approach. There is an emphasis on the "machine look" and there is a great deal of interest in the elimination of decorative detail. All of these characteristics can be observed in our buildings, in our furniture, in the industrial objects we have succeeded in producing. Because of this general orientation which I am describing deliberately in the most superficial terms, one finds a tendency to ignore values emphasized in the other arts. And one hears bald assertions that tend to bear out this assumption. For example, "it looks well because it works." Or, "a well designed doorknob is preferable to a badly painted Crucifixion."

Thus, there appears to have arisen a seeming division between the work-a-day arts such as architecture and industrial design and those arts like painting and sculpture. It seems to me that these divisions are more apparent than real. Examine the work of the leading architects of our time and you find, to be sure, a pre-occupation with functional design. As I have come to see it, however, in any half-way decent period of building there has always been a preoccupation with function, whether in a Roman bath or early Gothic cathedral. In the work of the greatest modern architects as in the work of the greatest architects of the past, one finds, however, that above and beyond this preoccupation with functional considerations, there is an enormous concern for aesthetic values and for that matter moral values too. The influence of the painter Mondrian, for example, is now so well known as to be a commonplace. The work of Mies van der Rohe is only one of many examples that might be cited to show cross-fertilization between the arts. The work of Wright with its tremendous concentration on organic unity demonstrates this same point although the sources happen to be different. In the work of Wright, also, there is a moral element which may or may not be aesthetically justified. Wright's work has always said, in effect, not only "this is the way your building ought to look," but also "this is the way you should live in a building." Similarly in projects of Le Corbusier, despite the overemphasis given his "machine for living" propaganda there is an enormous concern for what he considers aesthetic values and even greater disposition to preach on how people should live—whether in individual houses, apartments or entire cities.

In present-day architecture and industrial design one finds not only innumerable examples of preoccupation with aesthetic problems as well as functional ones, but also many instances where functional considerations are deliberately put aside in favor of aesthetic ones. Without going farther afield than my own office, I can provide a number of pertinent and horrible examples. A couple of years ago, for instance, we were working on the design of a coffee table and were particularly intrigued by the idea and the look of light weight. Now, this delight in the look of no apparent weight is a fairly new one—thirty to fifty years ago the more "substantial" a building or a table appeared, the better it seemed to all concerned. The origin of this idea obviously lies in the fields of engineering and aviation. In both of these general fields reduction of weight has an importance that ranges all the way from a saving in money to a saving of lives. Making things lighter has become one of the most widespread and important concepts underlying our entire industrial civilization. It is not surprising therefore that when a practice based on economy, speed, workability and safety becomes so widely accepted, emotional overtones begin to appear: by which I mean that finally a *look* of lightness becomes associated with the very idea of beauty. Thus it is not particularly surprising that in the design of a piece of furniture we were sufficiently intrigued by this powerful concept to make every possible effort to create in this instance a coffee table that not only *looked* light but actually *was* light. A sample of the table was then built, and it was a total failure: the table was so light that whenever touched by a hand or knee it skidded half way across the floor and became a household menace.

What happened is this: *an aesthetic notion derived from an original functional approach produced an unfunctional result.* Lightweight, we discovered, is not a universally desirable characteristic and in some instances even works against what the designer is trying to achieve. Light weight is not necessarily functional although in more and more areas it happens to be. Our mistake lay in confusing the functional aspects of this property with its aesthetic ones. To put it in other words, we were behaving in precisely the same manner as other designers from the beginning of time, all of whom were similarly affected by the ruling concepts of their time. It was because of our misconception of the properties with which we were dealing that the attempt resulted in failure.

I think there are two lessons to be derived from this kind of error. One, that in spite of the "functional" talk made by many architects, the procedures are not as different from those of workers in the other arts as they would like to make them out to be. All of us are trying to recreate the world in our image. If the painter in his work tried, among other things, to reveal something of the quality of the time in which he lived and to achieve thereby a kind of timeless

universality—and there is no other way to do it —so does the architect and so does the industrial designer. The other observation that suggests itself is that despite the important underlying similarity there are equally important differences. For instance, to refer back to the statement made above about the good doorknob versus the bad Crucifixion, it is possible that on some abstract scale of values (which, incidentally, I do not happen to comprehend) a good doorknob *is* better than a bad Crucifixion. It happens also to be true, however, that between the doorknob and the painting there are very real differences. Despite the wisdom and profundity of the greatest designer, a doorknob is, after all, still only a device with which to open a door. No matter how beautifully designed, how functionally appropriate it may be, it is most unlikely that this object will arouse more than a very limited number of ideas or emotions. Your painting, on the other hand, no matter how bad it may be, necessarily operates at a different level and in different spheres. This becomes more clear if one abandons the almost meaningless opposition of "good" and "bad" and compares two first-rate examples —let us say a piece of jewelry by Alexander Calder and a piece of sculpture by Michelangelo. Even if one were to make the assumption that this piece of jewelry was the greatest object of its kind to be produced in the 20th Century, there still remains an enormous gulf between the decorative object to be worn occasionally and the expression implicit in the monumental work of a great sculptor. The point can be sharpened further by eliminating differences in time and ability: Holbein was not only a great painter but also a designer of jewelry. It has not yet occurred to posterity to assign identical values to these two activities, although presumably the same genius could have been focused on both. It cannot necessarily be said that Holbein's painting was "better" or his jewelry "worse"—what we have here is a distinction of kind rather than quality. Going back for a moment to the earlier example, it might possibly be said that our time is somehow more propitious for hardware design rather than for religious painting. This, on the basis of the available evidence, seems to be entirely likely but it leaves the essential argument untouched.

"Our time" is, as a matter of fact, so powerful and all-pervading a factor in all contemporary art that it is hard to recognize its manifold influences except in small ways. The average citizen has heard that work in physics and mathematics during the past quarter of a century has revolutionized mankind's concepts of time and space. Most of us have no idea what these changes actually mean yet. In small ways we have begun to interchange time and space—it has become common speech now to say, "I live 37 minutes from my office," rather than "10 miles," but when we move back to modern painting and sculpture and again find time and space being handled in an unfamiliar manner our confusion is as great as when we are confronted with a physicist's mathematical formula. The difference is that we are accustomed to accept without question the incomprehensible findings of the physicist because they do seem to work whereas in the case of the arts, which virtually none of us have been trained to see, the unfamiliarity is more likely to produce uncertainty or confusion and consequently hostility and even rage.

It is known that in our time the mechanical concepts of the 19th Century are breaking down in philosophy, government and in industry itself. Throughout every important area of activity there appears to be a shift from purely mechanical operation and forms to far more complex types of control and organization. The shift from mechanical to electronic computers is one example; another is the shift in certain industries (such as refining) from simple geometric forms like spheres and cylinders to far more complex biomorphic shapes, this change having been dictated, as a rule, by change from a batch process of manufacture to a continuous process. These things, too, are familiar to most of us. Yet when we see their expression in the work of men like Leger, who has faithfully mirrored this shift in his paintings, or in the paintings of Tanguy, where organic and mechanical forms are mixed in the strangest and most weirdly evocative fashion, we again come to the limits of our comprehension. The result is not only a reinforcement of the outworn distinction between "fine" and "applied" art, but creation of a new distinction between intelligible and unintelligible art.

Your average citizen would probably not, if questioned, consider the movies to be a "modern" form of art expression because he sees in a film a meaningful continuity of images that add up to produce a "story," yet the effect of the films as an important ingredient in "our time" is almost incalculable, and I am not referring here to customs and manners as influenced by the behavior of the stars. What a movie actually does is superimpose, in rapid succession, a series of images that are not necessarily related. The resulting montage adds up to an idea or a kind of image almost too complex to be described because it is so frequently made up of contradictory elements. Yet when the same thing is attempted on a static piece of canvas by a painter such as Matisse or Picasso, where several sides of a water pitcher, say, or a human body are shown from different points of view, to arrive at the same simultaneous total image suggested by the movies, the result, again, is, for a great many people, total lack of understanding of what the painter is doing. All of which leads one to suspect that perhaps it is not so much the modern artist who is incomprehensible as the modern world itself.

It is in the area of the arts that the confusions and the prevailing diseases of our time are made manifest with unmistakable clarity. This, perhaps, is one reason why modern art is felt to be so horrifying and "inartistic." If the critics say as they so often do that such and such a painter seems unduly concerned with putrefaction and decay, so was this morning's paper. The difference is that in the paper these phenomena are disguised as "news" while in the hands of the artist they are given coherence and sometimes a force that may be unbearable. It is even more important for architects and designers than for laymen to realize that unpalatable content is not of necessity synonymous with "bad" or "degenerate" art—it may, on the contrary, represent a vigorous and healthy activity, as the phychiatrists could tell us, even if the critics do not. Picasso's "Guernica" is a truly horrible picture, and while its horror might have been matched by a written account (which I am inclined to doubt) by its very presentation and the form of that presentation it goes far beyond the unhappy fate of a group of innocent peasants in Northern Spain to become a universal symbol of activities and events that will be remembered and understood long after the specific event itself has been forgotten.

The tendency to be observed in virtually all of the contemporary arts—to go back along the road by which human culture has developed—and to find identification with the most primitive expressions known to man is a phenomenon that has been observed by more than one critic. I have found no more fruitful field for speculation on the nature of the modern world than this one extraordinary development. Why is it that our painters, sculptors and even architects have leaped backwards over the Renaissance, the Middle Ages, Classical antiquity to go back to the caves and the earliest diggings in Europe and Asia for their inspiration? There is something in this development of the most profound significance although you won't find anything about it in the newspapers. In a fairly obvious way it seems to me to mirror quite faithfully the continuing crack-up of what we call Western civilization and an attempt on the part of the artists to get back to some kind of stable foundation. But there are many questions that go far beyond this. Is this fascination with the primitive a return to the primitive or does it mark the beginning of new developments on all levels of something far advanced beyond anything mankind has seen? I remember one interesting illustration of this point made by the sculptor Lipschitz. Mr. Lipschitz showed a slide on which were pictured one of the last of the carriages and one of the very first of the automobiles. The carriage, although it represented a dying form of transportation, was anything but primitive. It was the most refined, elegant, beautifully designed object imaginable. The automobile with it was, by the same token, an incredibly clumsy and "primitive" looking apparatus. Yet we know now which really was the "primitive" vehicle and which represented a tremendous technological advance. What is going on in painting and sculpture today may, quite possibly, be a hard-to-decipher description of a similar development on a much vaster scale.

The idea of "simultaneity" already mentioned is evident in the paintings of any number of artists in addition to Matisse, Picasso and Braque. Does this reflect an unconscious habit of seeing and thinking produced by the existence of the movies or does it have a larger relation to the character of our time? The great number of radically different schools existing simultaneously —the abstractionist, the representational artists, the surrealists, etc.,—does this merely reflect the conditions of a confused time of change? Are these expressions as different as they seem from our close view of them? To what extent are these differing expressions validated or disproved by findings in physics, biology and psychology? These explorations, because of the underlying unity of the arts, do not confine themselves to the arts of painting and sculpture. In architecture, for instance, one observes a constantly shifting series of entirely contradictory trends precisely as in the other fields. In the city of New York alone, for instance, one can simultaneously view the old process of building closer and closer and higher and higher until it seems inevitable that the city will choke itself to death, while alongside one finds the beginnings of developments in urban planning which promise the most fruitful results from human and aesthetic points of view. Also existing at the same time one can find the builder who laboriously chops up the fake beams in his fake little house to create some inaccurate though nostalgic picture of an escapist antiquity, and rapid technological developments throughout the entire building industry which promise not only magnificent social benefits but possibilities of the most precise and refined expressions.

Once the tightly interlocked relationships of all the arts are accepted, the relationships of the arts to life itself can be grasped. Not only do these arts stem from the modern world as it is rather than as we think we see it, but because of the unfamiliar manner in which this world is presented, we are led to understand it somewhat more clearly. Finally, one learns to accept even the front page of "The New York Times," not for what it purports to be—a collection of the day's news—but as a surrealist document no less remarkable, horrifying, unexpected and contradictory than the most highly publicized efforts of Dali or Max Ernst.

The fact is there is a kind of truth in any art production whatever the level on which the object was conceived. The present-day automobile, from a design point of view, is about as unattractive an object as could possibly be conceived, yet its very ugliness reveals something which could easily be concealed in a written statement. That the arts are unified on a basis of truth or reality, whatever you choose to call it, is an interesting, revealing and remarkably important fact, yet it does not (or should not) obscure another fact, which is that the degree of truth implicit in the work depends as it always has upon the profundity of the artist. The small artist tells a small truth, the big artist tells a big truth. The big truths in our time are almost beyond the limits of our toleration—not to say comprehension. Both tend to pass by unnoticed. For always in this relationship there exists not only the artist, but the eye of the beholder.

VENUS, PERSEPHONE, AND SEPTEMBER MORN

In 1490, at the age of 46, Sandro Botticelli finished his large allegorical painting, *The Birth of Venus.* Commissioned by Lorenzo di Pierfrancesco, one of the di Medicis, it ultimately found its way to the Uffizi Galleries in Florence. For the better part of four centuries it has been considered a masterpiece.

When Paul Chabas sent his *September Morn* to the Paris Salon of 1912, it was received with unrestrained enthusiasm and awarded a medal. Millions — literally — of reproductions of the picture have been made since that date, in books, postcards, magazines, and calendars. Even without the convenient ban imposed by Anthony Comstock and his Society for the Suppression of Vice, the painting would have been popular. The critics, on the other hand, have missed no chance to damn it as an atrocious expression of Victorian sentimentality.

In 1939, Thomas Hart Benton's *Persephone* was shown for the first time, was subsequently published in Life Magazine, and is now in the artist's collection. While there has been some discussion about it, no one to date (except Thomas Craven) has suggested that it is a masterpiece.

What makes one picture a masterpiece and another rubbish?

Why are some paintings still interesting centuries after they were made?

How can one tell if a new painting—say Benton's Persephone—will last?

Why is Botticelli considered better than Chabas?

Who decides these things?

The three pictures shown here were put together with a view to answering these questions, which come up in one form or another every time one looks at a painting. One great advantage we have in this inquiry is that time has already passed judgment on two of the three. When a picture has been in circulation for more than four centuries and is still taken seriously, it obviously has qualities that make for permanent appeal. And when a picture has been around for a generation, but its use has been restricted largely to souvenir postcards and calendars, it is equally obvious that it is not prized very highly. In the case of a relatively new picture, such as the Persephone, the only way to arrive at a judgment is to make up our own minds about it.

Passing judgment on works of art is an activity which in modern times has been left largely to the critics. Unfortunately this procedure has a great many things wrong with it. For one thing, it is impossible to enjoy a picture through the eyes of someone else: any fool, given sufficient time, can learn names, dates and "correct" opinions, but enjoyment is a personal matter. For another, the critics have frequently been completely wrong, so we can't always count on them to know what they are talking about. Moreover, a great part of their technical jargon is unintelligible to the layman. If the average citizen is going to get any pleasure at all out of looking at pictures, he will have to start by discarding second-hand opinions, and he will have to use his own eyes. Not being a specialist in these matters, he will probably start with something pretty obvious. The most obvious thing about these three paintings is that each has a central female figure without a stitch of clothes on.

It is generally agreed in our society that if a male sees a naked woman, or a photograph of a naked woman, he may be expected to have

93

a predictable series of reactions, which are simple and quite direct. But let this same woman be exposed in paint on canvas, and the same male, by one of those interesting conventions of modern behavior, is supposed to react in an entirely different way. What was a more or less desirable female has now become Art (with a capital A) and anyone who ignored this subtle distinction would be considered a very vulgar fellow indeed. Against the background of this pious nonsense is the inescapable fact that when a painter chooses to do a nude instead of a bowl of bananas his choice cannot stem entirely from considerations of form and color.

This approach to representational painting may seem a little earthy by comparison with the textbooks, but it can take us a long way towards understanding. Looking at *September Morn,* for instance, it is not hard to see why this picture has appealed to so large a segment of the population. Here is a shy maiden, with her weight very agreeably distributed, caught at the edge of a lake without her bathing suit. Few females, young or old, have viewed the picture without a pleasant glow at the idea of making such a discovery themselves. Moreover, the subject is so obviously a lady — even though unaware of observation, her attitude is modesty itself. Women have never objected to *September Morn,* interestingly enough. Apparently the situation, from the feminine point of view, is not too unpleasant to contemplate.

Despite a strikingly similar arrangement of the arms, the attitude of Venus is not modest at all — she is far too unselfconscious. True, as soon as her shell lands on the shore, she will be covered by the magnificent flowered cloak which is being held ready for her, but not for concealment from prying eyes. We know this from the three watching figures, none of whom are in the least perturbed by her nudity. There is something else about Venus: she has an extraordinarily alluring face, with so haunting a quality of dreamy detachment that the observer, like the watching figures, tends to take her nakedness for granted. This by no means removes the element of sexual desirability, as the venerable Roger Fry once pointed out, but the appeal is on an entirely different emotional level from that of *September Morn.* And returning to the latter, we now see a very striking difference between the two figures: the girl in *September Morn* hasn't any face. There is only a vaguely indicated

Botticelli's "Birth of Venus"

profile and an equally indefinite mop of blond hair.

This is important. The contents of the picture include a clump of weeds and some blue patches suggesting sky, water and distant land. Obviously, the painter was not interested in the girl's surroundings. There is no face, so it seems equally clear that he was not concerned with the kind of person she was. All that is left is a body — any young body — in a provocative pose. His purpose, then, was evidently titillation. Once the observer gets to this point there is nothing left for him to look at, react to, or think about. That is why *September Morn* has been relegated to the calendars.

The haunting quality of the face of Venus has often been remarked upon, yet the face is "beautiful" only if you happen to like the smooth Italian oval and reddish blond hair. In the original one notices a pinkish tint on the top of her nose, less suggestive of glamour than the tag end of a cold. The spirits of the Wind might have been modeled after San Diego welders or Brooklyn taxi drivers. The profile of the attendant maiden shows a very plain face with an overly large jaw. What we are getting at is the observation that Botticelli's people are rather common and ordinary people and their appeal is based not so much on the standards of a Powers model as on some kind of inner vitality which is far more intriguing and infinitely more enduring. How Botticelli did this is a fascinating question. To have seen and painted beauty into these everyday faces, he must have seen them with the understanding that comes from a genuine love of people, and it is this love and emotional perception that run through the whole painting. Spring flowers floating over the sea are repeated exuberantly in the cloak and dress of the figure on the shore — the very folds of her dress have been drawn with a wonderful kind of delight in their richness. The waves, painted with an almost childlike formality, have a gaiety that is shared by the plump, stiff leaves on the trees at the right. To look at this painting and to sense something of the boundless joy and vitality in it is to see the world again with the eye of a child or poet. It is a vital enlargement of one's own experience. This is one of the reasons people still go to look at *The Birth of Venus* after more than four centuries. It is also one of the reasons it is considered a masterpiece.

Now what of *Persephone?* Comparison of the

Left: detail from Botticelli's "Birth of Venus." Left below: Detail from the portrait of Maria Luisa of Parma, Queen of Spain, wife of Carlos IV (1751-1819) by Francisco José Goya y Lucientes. Below, right: Chabas' "September Morn."

Copyright 1939, Thomas Hart Benton, courtesy of the Associated American Artists Galleries and "A Treasury of Art Masterpieces," edited by Thomas Craven. Simon and Schuster, New York.

Thomas Hart Benton's "Persephone." "... it is unsurpassed by anything thus far produced in America." Text by Thomas Craven from "A Treasury of Art Masterpieces," Simon and Schuster, New York, 1939.

Below: Henri Matisse: "Portrait".

first two pictures has already answered some of the questions with which we began. No painting comes to be considered great art if it is trivial, or if its meaning is confined to as elementary a level as that of, say, *September Morn*. And since art is produced by people for people, it is a collective judgment made by many observers over a long period of time that finally establishes a given picture as a masterpiece or something else. The process is a democratic one in a very important sense — not only that a kind of majority decision is involved — but that each participating individual arrives at his decision in a completely free and independent way. This is the way we have to look at Benton's *Persephone*. Whether the opinion arrived at is correct or not does not matter too much: time has a healthy way of rectifying errors in judgment.

Persephone, like the Venus story, is one of the great classical myths. It is the tale of Pluto, God of the Underworld, who sees the beautiful daughter of the Earth Goddess Ceres, is smitten by love and carries her off to his dark kingdom. In addition to being a wonderful story, it is a richly symbolic statement of the common desire of humanity for light and beauty. Benton, like many painters before him, has seen fit to recast the characters in terms of his own time, and for the locale he has chosen his native Middlewest. But more has happened to the story and its protagonists than a change of scenery. Pluto has become an ugly, moronic farmhand and Persephone, a model with plucked eyebrows, a nice hairdo and a vapid face. The question of her sexual desirability does not come up in this picture — it is thrust at us. The peeping face is like a pointed finger saying, "See — naughty picture!" The figure to which our attention is called with such emphasis is rather a curious one, for it was apparently intended to be voluptuous and succeeds only in being excruciatingly awkward in position. The thighs, clumsily hooked on to bony hips, look flattened out, as if they had been run through a wringer, while the identical placing of the two legs is boring. The painting does have an impact, but only because its treatment calls attention — not to Persephone, but to her nakedness. In so doing the artist has drawn attention to himself. Why does he try too hard to call attention to Persephone? We would see her anyway. Why does he fail so awkwardly in his attempt to make a woman's body alluring? Why is the legend so distorted and degraded? If every stroke of Botticelli's brush testifies to an overflowing joy in living, this painting reveals only a fear of it. Just as Persephone's face suggests nothing behind a well-made-up facade, so everything else has the same kind of superficiality. The leaves on the vines are lifeless, ugly, half-rotten; the tree has neither grace nor structural solidity; the wheat field and blue water have all the obvious pictorial quality of a postcard. In attempting to portray a great and tragic legend, Benton has succeeded merely in producing an ambitious painting.

A moment ago some leaves were described as "lifeless, ugly, half-rotten." This is valid criticism only in relation to a specific picture. There is, for example, a famous series of portraits of the Spanish royal family by Goya, whose subjects might be described fairly accurately in the same terms. The difference is that *Goya was not lifeless:* he saw qualities normally obscured beneath the regal trappings and revealed them with an intensity that even today carries with it the impact of a physical shock. It isn't that we care much today about Charles IV and his diseased little brood, but that it is almost impossible not to be interested in what Goya had to say about them.

Exactly the same thing is true about the *Venus.* Botticelli and his contemporaries had a feeling about classical antiquity which we simply cannot share. The early Renaissance in Italy was a kind of springtime in the history of mankind; the glory of Greece and Rome had suddenly been discovered; the voyagers were enlarging the world; and infant science was giving nature new meanings. To the excited, alive group in Florence of which Botticelli was a member, the story of Venus might well have been taken as a concrete symbol of the rebirth of art and culture. To us the story of Venus is just a story. But it is still possible for us to become infected with some of Botticelli's overwhelming creative passion through the way he painted faces, bodies, and draperies, through the way in which paint was applied, or colors, lines and shapes have been arranged. Another point: today we take the representation of movement in a painting for granted — for the men of Botticelli's time it was a great discovery. There had been nothing like it in painting before. The art of the Middle Ages, Greece and Egypt, whatever its positive qualities, had been essentially static. When the *Venus* was done, movement was a new and wonderful possibility, an enormously intriguing problem in technique and esthetics. The fast-moving curves which occur throughout the painting still communicate the painter's excitement of discovery after the passing of four and a half centuries. The sense of movement is not fully realized: there is a lingering hint of the characteristic stiffness of medieval art, but a good part of the fascination of the picture comes from this mixture of attitudes. It is almost as if the new technique gradually coming into being were an echo of the awakening of Venus herself.

Two significant facts should be evident at this point. One is that the enjoyment of art takes place on a series of graduated levels, and this fact indicates a clear-cut basis for arriving at a personal evaluation of a given work. *September Morn* washed out at the lowest level — the *Venus* doesn't seem to wash out at all, for the speculation is provokes, whether on the desirability of Venus herself, or the outlook of the Italian Renaissance, is literally endless. The other point is that the qualities which arouse interest in a work of art are completely human ones, based on the communication of feelings from artist to observer. These qualities are not restricted by period, place, technique or subject matter. We can sense them as sharply in primitive African sculpture or a cubist still life by Picasso as in a picture which, like the *Venus,* tells a story. But we do not find them in *Persephone,* and there is a sharply pointed statement by John Dewey that explains why. "If one examines into the reason why certain works of art offend us," says Dewey, "one is likely to find that the cause is that there is no personally felt emotion guiding the selecting and assembling of the materials presented. We derive the impression that the artist . . . is trying to regulate by conscious intent the nature of the emotions aroused. We are irritated by a feeling that he is manipulating materials to secure an effect decided upon in advance." In other words, people don't like to be pushed around — even by an artist.

As long as we talk about art in general we can talk about attitudes, qualities and reactions in general. But the moment painting is considered *as painting,* new and special factors enter which have distinct meaning in themselves and thereby open up new levels of experience for the observer. Matisse once showed a painting to a visitor who remarked that she had never seen a woman who looked like that. The painter's retort, "Madam, that isn't a woman; it's a picture!" was entirely to the point. A picture is a flat surface on which shapes and colors are arranged in an infinite variety of ways, and the arrangements are always subject to laws which apply only to pictures. It doesn't make the slightest difference whether the thing depicted is recognizable — say a barn in landscape — or merely an abstract composition. If there is any vital weakness in our attitude toward art in general it is this inability to understand that a painting is an independent creation with a particular meaning of its own. We have all been trained by social example to expect a picture to "tell a story" or to recall a person, place or mood, and it is hard to understand that the basic function of subject matter is none of these, but a means of stimulating the artist to create an object which will then pass on some of his feelings to the observer. The "subject" of the birth of Venus, as we have seen, has little meaning for modern man, certainly nothing comparable to what it had for Botticelli. Nevertheless, we can enjoy the picture.

It is possible to go a step further and look at these pictures as if they had no recognizable subject matter at all. In *Persephone,* for example, it is interesting to watch what happens to the movement of one's eye over the surface. The eye is instantly riveted to the shape of the reclining figure, and it moves back and forth within the outlines of the shape. It then has the option of breaking out of this confined area to the basket, the farmhand's face, the cornfield or the waiting wagon. But because the central shape is so emphatically presented, it is hard to look very long at any of these areas and the eye is continually wrenched back to the figure. Doing this for even a short period of time is fatiguing — it is a little like looking at a movie whose scenes are out of proper sequence. The reverse is true of the *Venus.* In the first place, the flesh tones of Venus are similar to those of the Winds and the gown of the attendant. Should the eye happen to fall on the tree trunks, it is led up to the leaves, back to the central figure and across to the wings of the Winds, or down to the dress and cloak and again back into the center. The cattails in the left-hand corner perform the same function in a less conspicuous way. In composing his shapes, Botticelli has done more than keep the eye moving over the whole surface of the canvas in an easy, pleasant way — he has regulated the time it takes for the eye to get from one place to another.

If one follows the tree trunks down to the foot of the attendant, it doesn't jump from there to the figure of Venus: there are the flowers in the dress and also the folds in the cloth which tend to slow down its movement. Even the edge of the red cloak is elaborately curved to delay the eye in its inevitable passage back to the central figure. To find a modern counterpart of this masterly timing — it is more commonly described as "composition" — one would have to turn to a film by Eisenstein. Color has been used in the same way. The most important color accent, the hair of Venus, is repeated with variations in the underside of the shell, the cattails and the hair of two of the flanking figures. These observations could be extended indefinitely, and if the original were at hand we could even concern ourselves with the manner in which the paint was stroked on the canvas, for this too is part of the picture as a work of art. It is very significant that whatever our approach to these pictures, each levels out at about the same point. Thus *September Morn* seems equally trivial whether the yardstick is color, sexual desirability, composition, or paint quality. The reason for this is that there is no such thing as technique or formal value divorced from overall concept — the artist always forces his skills to come up to the level of his emotional grasp of reality. In the enjoyment of painting, this fact is important because it leaves the observer free to find his own way into the picture. What he must do, however, is make sure that it is his *own* way. Inevitably it will follow that to each succeeding picture he will bring more sensitive perception and a steadily increasing appreciation of the many levels on which a work of art has meaning. The fun comes from making these discoveries under one's own power, and not from holding what are currently considered to be the correct opinions. It would be far better to be wrong most of the time and still get pleasure out of the process. Otherwise one is in the unenviable spot of Benton's farmhand, eternally condemned to vicarious enjoyment of what could be a genuine experience.

ARCHITECTURE

The Villa Savoye, just outside Paris, remains, after twenty years and much controversy, an inspiration to vacation-house designers

In this and the following piece, expressions of great admiration for two great architects.

CLASSIC HOLIDAY HOUSE

Twenty years ago a French family named Savoye commissioned an architect to design a suburban house. The Savoyes owned a meadow pleasantly situated at Poissy, about eighteen miles outside Paris, and had no preconceived ideas about the house except that it should incorporate features of a vacation house as well as the comforts of a year-round residence. Their architect was Charles Edouard Jeanneret-Gris, a forty-year-old Swiss who had adopted the name of Le Corbusier and was reputed, among architects, to be something of a crackpot.

Two important elements of the Savoye project distinguished it from the ordinary building venture: the architect was unconventional, and the family was willing and financially able to let him experiment. The result was a building that bore little resemblance to anything identifiable as a house—at that time. The Villa Savoye became the center of professional controversies that raged from Tokyo to Rio and, even today, two decades later, it has little in common with the average U. S. house in appearance, construction or conception.

As an example of residential architecture the Villa Savoye is undeniably "different." But this is the least interesting thing about it. Whenever one departs from the normal, there are usually two reasons: accident, in which case it can be ignored—or novel response to existing circumstances, in which case it may be significant. Le Corbusier's design belongs to the latter category. His "existing circumstances" were the known techniques for building, and the living requirements of a family in the 20th Century. His re-

sponse was a novelty of approach that is still being explored. This one dwelling is a storehouse of ideas still as provocative as ever, still to be considered as the core of today's best architectural thinking.

SLAVES TO TRADITION

Most people, ready to convert their dream houses into realities, turn to books and magazines for solutions to problems of room planning, storage, lighting, decorating and so on. This is practical in one sense, yet it has the disadvantage of obscuring larger considerations. A good house is far more than the sum of its working parts, and this is particularly true of vacation houses where equipment, appliances and elaborate planning devices are of less concern than they would be in the all-year residence. One of the remarkable things about the Villa Savoye is the consistency with which a bold concept of living has been expressed throughout. If there are any of the usual architect's compromises in this house, they're indeed hard to find.

To understand what Le Corbusier achieved in this house, try to recall the architectural scene in the late 20's. In America as well as France the architect of that time was primarily a learned gentleman who possessed an expensive library illustrating historical styles. For schools, city halls, banks and office buildings he was expected to produce designs recognizably Greek, Roman, Italian or French Renaissance. For country houses and golf clubs he copied buildings of the English Georgian period, although some successful designers looked even further back to the

Above: *Villa Savoye exterior, below:*
living room with terrace visible through
the sliding windows.

abbeys and castles of the Middle Ages. It was almost universally agreed that one had to copy *something*. What was described as progress in architecture usually amounted to modifications of existing styles. The modern-versus-traditional-design controversy of today scarcely existed then because "modern" meant at most a slight simplification of period details. Where new equipment, such as the elevator, came into use it was harmonized with the old by applying a decorative veneer in the appropriate style.

There were some exceptions to this general preoccupation with archaeology. From the 1880's on, Louis Sullivan, Frank Lloyd Wright and a number of lesser men had designed buildings that could only be described as modern, and they had invented, while Le Corbusier was still a schoolboy, many of the elements so spectacularly displayed in the Villa Savoye. In almost every country of Europe, too, small groups of architects had begun to rebel against the traditional. Le Corbusier organized these scattered efforts into intelligible theory, defended it in brilliant writings, and made it visible in a number of actual buildings. So completely did he succeed in the Villa Savoye that in spite of the many developments of the past twenty years, certain aspects of his design have yet to be surpassed.

The Villa Savoye is a square block of building set in the middle of a flat meadow surrounded by woods, like many an English country house. Beyond the setting, however, the resemblance ends, for the traditional English house tends to merge with its surroundings, while the Villa Savoye seems unrelated to its site. The light-colored walls of the second floor do not even extend to the ground—instead, there are round columns which look as if they had been designed to keep the house from having any more contact with the earth than absolutely necessary. To complete the illusion, such first-floor walls as exist are of glass or dark-painted plaster. Thus, at the very outset, we find a sharp break with the accepted practice of merging house and landscape. House and land have about as much to do with each other as an airplane and its runway.

DESIGN FOR LIVING

The arrangement of the house, compared with more familiar patterns, seems at first glance to make no sense whatever. None of the usual first-floor rooms are on the first floor. There is a garage, to be sure, but the rest of the first floor is taken up with maids' rooms, a chauffeur's apartment and a laundry. There is also a large entrance hall and, leading from it, a circular stairway. But this stairway is inconspicuous and secondary: the main "stair" is a *ramp*.

On the second floor some of the traditional first-floor rooms appear. The ramp, having doubled back on itself, reaches a long hall which leads directly to a living-dining room extending almost the width of the house. Long, horizontal windows, virtually continuous, open on two sides of this room, and part of another wall is glass-paneled, room height, and can be slid open. The kitchen and other services, except for being on the second floor, are where one would normally find them. At the opposite end of the hall from the living-dining room are located two bedrooms and a boudoir. A third bedroom opens off the hall, but there is no master bedroom evident. What arouses one's curiosity, however, is the large central open space adjoining the ramp. This space would be a room if it had a roof on it, or a garden if it were downstairs, or a conventional roof terrace were it not for its juncture with the living room's glass-paneled wall. Those familar with many of today's vacation houses will recognize this extra area as the "outdoor room." The outdoor room of the Villa Savoye was one of the first modern uses of this device for more spacious living, and remains a wonderfully satisfying expression of the idea.

An outside ramp leads from the second-floor terrace to the top level. As one ascends the ramp, the house looks even less like a house, for its walls begin to take on the broad curves seen in the superstructure of ocean liners. Le Corbusier, incidentally, was a tremendous admirer of seagoing architecture and in his most famous book, *Towards a New Architecture,* he included photographs of ships to help prove his point that buildings could be functional without being smothered with traditional details. Some of the curved walls on the third floor set off areas for sun bathing, and behind the largest of these walls we finally locate the master bedroom, placed in its own penthouse, with a fireplace in the boudoir, a pair of huge dressing rooms and a bath.

It is difficult to imagine anything much more luxurious than the Savoye bedroom penthouse.

The shapes of walls and rooms on the third floor may seem more arbitrarily fanciful than anything in the house, but any engineer would tell you that curving a light wall is an effective way of giving it strength. Still, I feel sure that Le Corbusier used them principally because he liked the way they contrasted with an otherwise rectangular pattern. Reproductions of his paintings reveal almost identical combinations of forms.

ARCHITECTURAL ANSWERS

The unusual design of the Villa Savoye raises numerous questions. Why would an architect build what might easily have been a one-story house, on three floors? And, especially, why would he do this on a site large enough for ten such houses? Why put an out-door room on the second floor, where it costs a lot of money, instead of on the ground, where it is relatively cheap? Why use a ramp instead of stairs? Why, in so agreeable a setting, build a house that appears to abhor nature? Why put a building on dry land on stilts, anyway? And finally, what makes the house so important an example of modern architecture?

Consider the last two questions first. To Le Corbusier, a house—or any building for that matter—must first of all be totally functional. He once remarked that one might be proud of a house "as serviceable as a typewriter." As part of the transition toward a functional kind of structure, he abandoned the age-old method of wall-bearing construction in favor of structural skeletons in which walls are treated as skins of glass or insulating material. This idea of a steel or concrete cage is familiar in the United States, but the method is used in large buildings and almost never in houses. By stripping off the first-floor walls and leaving his columns (the stilts) exposed, Le Corbusier made it dramatically, almost shockingly clear that the walls of this house were not holding it up. The house, in fact, supports the walls.

Skeletal construction is a modern idea, and for its full realization it requires modern materials and techniques. The characteristic quality of industrial production is precision, and throughout the Villa Savoye one finds every effort made to convey this impression. In the spacing of the columns, in the windows, even in the concrete blocks used to pave the outdoor room, there is repeated use of standardized units characteristic of modern production. In a basic sense, therefore, the house is contemporary. All its major elements—the glass walls, horizontal windows, the

Above: Ramp leads to roof gardens. Below: Space below the main level at entrance.

open plan, use of outdoor space, and so on—have been accepted by the architects who came later.

Why did Le Corbusier design the Villa Savoye so that it seems to ignore its surroundings, even to abhor nature? To answer the question one must take into account several factors, and the conclusion one personally reaches will have much to do with the kind of house he himself would want. Le Corbusier saw the house as an industrial product—or, more precisely, as a product that *should* be industrially made, and would be, if people were more intelligent. Considering the fantastic prices demanded for the handicraft product today, I doubt if many people are disposed to argue this point. If one sees a house as a factory-made object, then it will not look "natural" compared to, say, a log cabin or an adobe hut. Nor is there any reason why it should. We have all seen photographs of shiny aluminum transports flying over mountain peaks, yet we never question the difference in character between "nature" and the airplane. The same holds for the Villa Savoye in its meadow, except that in the case of houses we are not accustomed to this kind of contrast.

There is another interesting point in connection with the relation between house and landscape. This has to do with the American attitude toward the land. We have built some of the world's biggest cities and most complete urban concentrations, but our nostalgic feelings about the rural scene have only increased in the process. Let the average city-bred couple acquire an acre in the country and they are automatically "farmers." Probably there is no harm in this self-deception, but it has a distinct effect on the design of vacation houses and other nonfarm dwellings, because if a man pretends he is a peasant instead of an insurance broker he is going to want a house to match the role.

HOUSE ON STILTS
The same holds if his budget allows him to masquerade as a country gentleman. The French on the other hand, have spent far too many years working their limited land in a business-like manner to enjoy such illusions. Consequently, an upper-middle-class resident of Paris is unlikely to indulge in bucolic fantasies when he is transposed periodically to pastoral surroundings. Thus it would be correct to conclude that the Villa Savoye is a more appropriately French expression of luxury country living than

American. Nevertheless, its value as a demonstration of principle is not diminished because of cultural differences.

The remaining questions concerning the house almost answer themselves. It seems clear, for example, that the architect arranged the house on three levels instead of one because the underlying idea of a skeleton structure could not have been expressed so forcefully in a one-story design, and there was no desire to make the house appear to merge with the ground. In the house on stilts, Le Corbusier always saw other advantages, and he never tired of explaining how this scheme created a covered garden at ground level, living space at a slight elevation, and a roof garden away from dampness and insects. In the Villa Savoye, he didn't quite practice what he preached, because the entire ground level is either service rooms or driveway. And once, in describing the house as he planned to build it, he said, "The view is pretty, grass is a nice thing and so are the woods—we'll disturb them as little as possible. The house will sit in the middle of the meadow, like an object, without spoiling anything." So we may conclude that even the machine-for-living attitude is not necessarily devoid of a feeling for nature.

Regarding the disposition of the living spaces within the house, their size and number make it quite clear that the owners wanted their country retreat to be a luxury house. There is no published record of the cost of the Villa Savoye, to my knowledge, and if there were I doubt if it would prove anything, since French and American construction techniques are different, and because prices have risen so much in the last two decades. But the quality of luxury achieved in this house is worth observing, because it is not necessarily related to costly materials or equipment. The frame is concrete, walls are stucco over hollow tile, there are no expensive interiors, and mechanical appliances are probably fewer than one would find in the average U. S. household. The quality of luxury comes from the manner in which space has been enclosed and related. The entrance hall is no vestibule, but a large area with an interesting shape. Access to the floor above is a leisurely stroll up a ramp, with changing views of the outdoor room near the top. On a pleasant day one may sit either indoors or out by merely sliding back part of the glass living-room wall. The view from the outdoor room is framed by wide, horizontal openings in the wall; it is different from what one sees at ground level, and it can be varied further by going up the outdoor ramp to the sun traps on the roof. The penthouse suite creates an entirely separate living area, away from servants, children and guests. That all of this takes place in a building whose lack of frills reminds many observers of factories or hospital operating rooms is beside the point, for it reflects only a difference in tastes. The American decorator's dream of an overstuffed heaven represents one widely accepted method of treating an interior—but only one. The Villa Savoye happens to reflect another philosophy, sharply expressed by Le Corbusier when he said, "To take care of any lack of taste on the part of the owners, I built the house in such a way that no one could put too much furniture in it." Arrogant, if you like, and not the usual way an architect treats a client, but it leaves no doubt that the Villa Savoye came out as Le Corbusier wanted it.

THE LESSON OF VILLA SAVOYE

Disregarding the question of taste, the absence of trimmings is a real advantage, for there is nothing in the house to distract one from an examination of its remarkable plan and exciting space relationships. In the twenty years since it was designed, it has become a classic and there is hardly a modern architect alive who has not studied it and succumbed, in one way or another, to its influence. For the layman who is more concerned with an immediate solution to his living problems than with architectural theory, it is an enormously valuable house to study. It lends itself easily to the modern vacation-house idea, and it helps the layman to understand the recent developments in vacation-house architecture.

The main lesson of the Villa Savoye, so far as I am concerned, lies not in the details of the structure but in its suggestion that architecture can give freedom to living, that "function" can be described in psychological as well as physical terms and that the expression of fantasy is as legitimate as the provision of closets. In terms of the vacation house, where social inhibitions can lose so much force, this is quite a lesson.

If you are planning to build, as the slogan goes, the Villa Savoye would be a good job to paste on Page 1 of your scrapbook, And, incidentally, that scrapbook isn't a bad idea.

Living room at Taliesin, Spring Green, Wisconsin.

Residences, built by a great architect for himself, make the landscape look as if it had been designed to fit them.

"I have always been willing to go without necessities," Frank Lloyd Wright once remarked, "as long as I might enjoy the luxuries." **One** difference between Wright and other people who may have expressed the same idea is that he has lived it. There was a winter toward the end of the depression, for instance, when funds were so low that his house was close to the freezing point. Providentially, a client turned up with an important commission, and a check covering a sizable retainer. Wright used the money to buy a harpsichord instead of coal. He has always considered living—in the fullest possible sense of that misused word—more important that the deferments and substitutes so urgently recommended by contemporary society. That is why Wright lives in two of the most luxurious houses in America. He built them when he had money, and he kept on building them when he was up to his ears in debt. He is still working on them.

It is some forty-five years since Wright, acting on his conviction that living in cities was a contradiction in terms, moved out to southern Wisconsin and began the house he named Taliesin. It is almost twenty since he and his family and some thirty young apprentices moved out to the Arizona desert and began Taliesin West, a fabulous winter home and workshop. The existence of these two great houses may be responsible in part for the prevalent notion that Wright is a wealthy man. He is unquestionably one of the richest individuals who has ever lived, but not in terms of bank accounts. What money he has had was always earned with his own two hands, and the only use he ever found for it was to spend it. In an age that has practically canonized savings banks and life insurance, this attitude is disturbing. It is even faintly suggestive of immorality. But even his thriftiest critics have had to admit that the money was always spent with exquisite discrimination and in a manner equaled only by the princes of the Italian Renaissance. When he completed the Imperial Hotel in Tokyo, Wright received a fee of $380,000. He returned home broke—but the owner of one of the great collections of Oriental art. If further illustration is needed, these houses supply it.

The conventional picture of luxury in houses has been made familiar by the habitations of the milk-of-magnesia magnates and their brethren. Marble baths, gold-plated faucets, telephones in every tree stump, interiors stuffed with brocades, carloads of automatic gadgetry—and probably, if one is completely honest, a shabby little den on the second floor where the surfeited owner can sit with his shoes off. Wright's houses present a different picture, for their luxury is internal. Their quality comes from the manner in which space is enclosed. Lao Tze, some six hundred years before Christ, remarked "Doors and windows are cut out in order to make a house; the utility of the house depends on the empty spaces." Wright is one of the few architects in history who have comprehended fully the implications in that statement.

In these houses there is little emphasis on the so-called "necessities." The plumbing is adequate, but only adequate. Equipment is kept to a bare minimum. Furniture is more likely to be hard than soft. Materials are rough and inexpensive, put together almost entirely by amateurs. Seen in this context, the luxuries are unexpected: a window high in a stone wall that lets through a shaft of sunlight for a few hours; a Chinese screen set up on a wall of rough stone; and above all, space. The "garden room" at the desert camp is around seventy feet long, and it opens out to include a walled garden several times that size. Broad terraces of smooth concrete link rooms and outdoors so closely that at times the camp seems as big as the desert itself. The original house in Wisconsin wraps itself around a series of courts and its windows embrace the entire countryside. Both houses if laid together would extend nearly a quarter of a mile. There is no problem here of room to swing a cat—one could swing a dinosaur.

When Wright began building Taliesin he wrote that he wanted to build a "natural" house.

The word is important, for it makes intelligible the startling dissimilarity between the house in Wisconsin and the house in Arizona. Taliesin is built into a hill. In summer it is all but hidden in the trees. At all seasons its size is elusive. Its colors are subdued. Taliesin West, on the other hand, is barbaric in its contrasts. Like a crustacean, the house has its structure on the outside, and this structure creates a jagged outline as sharp and savage as the cactus that surrounds it. Since Wright's work has often shown contrasts as unexpected as those between his own two houses, he has been accused of trying to be sensational. Such criticism overlooks the fact that the difference between the landscapes of Wisconsin and Arizona is sensational, and the houses reflect that difference with such extreme sensitivity that the impact on the beholder is a very powerful one. We have lived so long in the prefabricated monotony of U.S. cities, and have accepted so passively the dry bones of building "styles" that lost all meaning centuries ago, that "natural" architecture is bound to prove strong medicine.

Wright's work (these two houses stand with the best of it) is a perfect example of what happens when a great and creative personality rejects the values of his time and sets his own standards. The results look strange at first because they do not stem from the old rules. The idea of change embodied in them frightens people, arousing hostility toward the artist, who usually is left to die of neglect or is hounded to death. Later on his work is copied, bought by museums, and put into the history books. Wright, now eighty-seven, was too tough to succumb, and has lived to see the times begin to catch up with him. Taliesin, a "sensation" in 1913, has been copied all over the world, so that today it looks almost familiar. The same, in another decade or two, will be true of the desert camp. But the importance of Wright's houses is not that they were in advance of their time. Nor that they would cost nearly a million dollars if put together by a contractor today. The important thing is very simple: they enclose space as if it were precious, not for the sake of the space itself, but for the life that goes on within it. Architecture—as opposed to building for mere shelter—has no greater justification.

*Written as a contribution
to "New Architecture and City Planning," by Paul Zucker. An attempt to cope with
the exasperating question of monumentality and modern architecture.*

STYLISTIC TRENDS IN CONTEMPORARY ARCHITECTURE

From the vantage point of the third year of war in America, it is easy—suspiciously easy—to review the turbulent and ultimately successful progress of the contemporary movement in architecture and to evaluate its sometimes divergent trends.

That the battle for acceptance is practically over can no longer be doubted, and one of the strangest phenomena of our period is the crusader, still unaware that the battle is won, who goes on attempting to trade blows with adversaries who in some bewildering fashion are becoming his allies. The crusader, too, like his adversaries, has changed in many instances, for his unwillingness to realize that the conflict between modernism and eclecticism is approaching an end is directing his opposition towards the processes of life itself, with reproaches to his one-time heroes for having progressed beyond the limited formulas of the 1920's.

That this confusion should exist—and exist in the minds of many more than the noisy group constituting the ultra-left in architecture—should not be the occasion for any surprise, for the success of modern architecture has come about with incredible rapidity. It reached its first peak with the Chicago school and Sullivan and Wright, only to succumb to reaction; it hit another with the completion of the theoretical work of Le Corbusier and others; a third was attained less than ten years later with the completion of buildings and projects such as the Barcelona Pavilion, which are now the classics of our time; the fourth was the period just before World War II, when there was not a country in the world which had not in one way or another acknowledged the force of the new ideal and the attractive logic of its best completed expressions.

Architects and critics in Europe had better than three decades in which to watch efforts develop into broad trends: there was some chance for meditation and evaluation. In America, however, the movement, once it had really started, developed with literally breathtaking swiftness. It seems hard to remember now that it was only about twenty years ago that a magazine considered putting out an issue devoted to modern U. S. houses and gave up the venture because adequate material could not be found. Frank Lloyd Wright after all, was not rediscovered by his countrymen until the late 30's.

To match this extraordinary transformation, there seems to be at least one comparable example: this was the Italian Renaissance, whose earliest manifestations had a similarly explosive quality. Brunelleschi's exquisitely fresh Pazzi Chapel was built in 1520, only sixteen years after the completion of Or San Michele, forty years after Siena Cathedral. The Palazzo Rucellai, another landmark, was finished in 1451. The shift from the medieval to the renaissance outlook was, historically speaking, sudden and complete.

The parallels between our time and the middle 15th Century are valid, but they cannot be carried too far. The revolutions in structure, for example, that have taken place during our lifetime, played no significant part in the renaissance world. And more pertinent to our theme, we have seen nothing comparable, in our time, to the assurance, gaiety and rich inventiveness with which the renaissance masters glorified the leaders and the ideals of their society.

One great source of strength in modern architecture has been the firmness with which all temptations to slip back into an old and easy eclecticism have been rejected. In all countries, during the past several decades, the leaders of the movement have said "no" as often as women on a diet. For a time, any kind of enrichment was looked upon as something a little sinful, rather like a plate of bonbons. After the Civil War and Victorian periods there was need, unquestionably, for a certain restraint. But in the search for a satisfying continuation of the great tradition in architecture, there was visible a tendency to grasp the guideposts left by the pioneers, and to convert them into crutches.

The contemporary architect, cut off from symbols, ornament and meaningful elaborations of structural forms, all of which earlier periods possessed in abundance, has desparately chased every functional requirement, every change in site or orientation, every technical improvement,

to provide some basis for starting his work. Where the limitations were most rigorous, as for example in a factory, or in a skyscraper where every inch had to yield its profit, there the designers were happiest and the results were most satisfying. But let a religious belief or a social ideal replace cubic foot costs or radiation losses, and nothing happened. The absurd memorial to Thomas Jefferson was castigated by every articulate designer in the country, and quite rightly, but far more significant was the fact that nowhere in the contemporary group did someone arise with a new design. Faced with the problem of the monumental building—the building in which function and structure become secondary problems—the modern architect seems to lose his creative faculties and he becomes a critic.

That there has been a pretty uniform tendency for people to try to leave, in some form or other, an enduring proof of their impact on the world, is clear enough from the history books. In the more conventional of these volumes it seems that the history of architecture consists of nothing but monuments to something or somebody and that nothing else is sufficiently important to be included. The notion of sacred and profane in architecture is by no means dead at the present time.

Whether the monumental building—whose primary purpose is to commemorate an event or express a belief rather than to satisfy some utilitarian requirement—is more or less noble than the places of production and commerce, does not seem important. The fact is that it has been demanded steadily in the past and will in the future. The first evidence should appear in the years immediately following the war. In the face of these demands the contemporary artist, whether architect, painter or sculptor, will be helpless unless, like his great predecessors, he can somehow integrate the imponderables of sociology, economics and philosophy with his art. The training of the architect, at any rate, has made no provision for such integration.

The contemporary architect, "free" from the stultifying rules of a century of limitation, is today in danger of being bound more tightly than ever by a new set of limitations. To take the place of static symbols and copybook forms, the architect turned to planning problems, engineering realities and functional solutions. Everything was submitted to the gloriously revealing light of logic. If the program was complete enough, it was said, all the closets and stairs and rooms and walls would fall into place almost automatically and you would have a perfect architectural solution to a perfect architectural problem. The factory is the living symbol of this attitude: logic and the accounting department give all the answers. Intuition and emotion are safely out of bonds. Or perhaps not so safely, for structure and function have become crutches. And he who goes on crutches is not free to run.

In discussions that have taken place on the subject of the problem of monumentality, reactions of those participating have taken several clearly defined forms. One is that we *have* created our monuments, that we have actually, though unconsciously, expressed our faith in some kind of cooperative industrial society by our works: by the dams, bridges and factories. To this group there is no problem, because the problem solved itself before we became conscious of its existence. The Romans, they pointed out, probably expected to be remembered for their temples and law-courts; but what we think of today are the roads, the baths and the aqueducts. And perhaps, they add, tourists will some day pay a quarter to see the ruins of the Radio City Music Hall in much the same spirit that tourists hire guides to see what is left of the Coliseum.

A second reaction is that the problem does not exist because monumental building is not in the spirit of our time. (This is based on the concept of monumentality as inseparable from great weight and permanence of materials.) It is pointed out that every visible trend in building today is towards the ephemeral, the quickly obsoleted and easily removed. In structures where skin stresses take the place of brute weight, where standardized frames make the bones of a service station and a school practically interchangeable and therefore indistinguishable, there is no place for the monumental building. This last is a little like arguing that Lincoln and his assassin were qualitatively and historically equal because they had skeletons of similar design and construction. Nevertheless, the point is that the monumental building is an anachronism in our time.

There is still a third reaction, which might be labeled utilitarian. Here the answer is simplest of all. Why argue about memorials to Thomas Jefferson or Will Rogers, we are asked. Any monument would be inappropriate, for when so many people need housing, park space and the other elementary decencies of modern existence, the conspicuous waste of any structure purely monumental in its conception is an affront to society. Within this body of opinion one does not find elaborate analogies to earlier periods, for the argument is essentially political and somewhat tenuous. It would be difficult to condemn Chartres because the people who built it lived in miserable hovels—which they did. It happens to be true of both human society and nature that neither has been so niggardly in the use of its resources as to refuse extravagance in the midst of poverty and decay. The argument is weak because it confuses two needs. If a community needs housing or playgrounds, let it make a clear issue of these needs and try to satisfy them. Those who say to build housing and call it a war memorial are merely trying to satisfy their own limited objectives without fighting for the program as a whole, and on its own merits.

Actually, what we have in this contention is not so much a proposed solution of the problem of monumentality as an attempt—essentially political—to capitalize on a temporary situation to obtain a few insignificant social amenities.

This much is clear from a consideration of the problem as a whole: it is full of contradictions.

There is a contradiction between the still-powerful urge on the part of a social unit to commemorate itself, thereby achieving a kind of immortality—and the tendency in architecture, which is towards the ephemeral.

There is a contradiction between the demand for monumentality and a general lack of faith in the institutions normally glorified in monumental architecture and sculpture.

There is a contradiction between the admittedly high social ideals of the contemporary architect and planner, and the fear with which they shrink from everything but the most utilitarian problems.

Yet these contradictions must be resolved; are in the process of being resolved. In the trend from the single, individualistic building to the more complex organism of the sub-community there is a hint of one answer. For here it would be possible to maintain that continuity of expression so important to the concept of monumentality, at the same time that the parts were becoming obsolete and being replaced. Within the new concept of the community that is growing up—as a place where the citizens can have dignified and fruitful intercourse with one another, there is a germ of an ideal quite as worthy of monumental expression as the earlier ones: a renewed vision of society as an organism regulated by its members in their own interest.

It is this, in fact, which disposes of the contention that we have unconsciously solved our problems in the design of our factories, for the structures devoted to production cannot have the quality which we are discussing and seeking. The Roman roads are not an expression of a traffic system, but of what was then a new world outlook, which stemmed from a system of social unification without previous parallels in history. It is only in their broadest implications that our industrial plants, highways and dams will have any meaning for posterity.

The monumental expression in architecture, which will become increasingly pressing as a task for the contemporary designer, will be solved, and not by a move back to the past. Like what we have already achieved in the new architecture, it will continue a tradition deeply rooted in the people, their ways of living and more significantly, their aspirations. To continue the tradition, architecture will have to throw away its crutches, move up to another plane, and express itself in another scale. But express itself it will. We have been preoccupied with closets and minimum shelter and undersized bedrooms and all the minimal paraphernalia of a penny architecture long enough.

HOUSES

DOWN WITH HOUSEKEEPING

The home is better than ever now that architects are coming up with wonderfully fresh and useful designs, employing fantastic gadgets that can make life not only less arduous but fuller.

Ten years is a long time these days, and even the house, slow as it is in accepting change, is no longer quite the same thing people were putting up with in the year HOLIDAY's first issue hit the newsstands of the world.

By way of introduction, try a few random facts. In Boston, the custodian of so many shreds of our traditions, there are more TV sets than bathtubs—and this is no implication that Boston has fewer bathtubs than it requires. Among the families subscribing to a single large home magazine, 1,220,000 own power lawn mowers. Spectator sports, according to a business publication, are being pushed to the wall by—of all things—competition from the home, with TV, the workshop and garden as the big weapons in the domestic arsenal. Also, it appears that there are six times as many private swimming pools as there were a half dozen years ago. In 1955, around 100,000 prefabricated dwellings were erected, and in the same year 95 per cent of all heating systems installed in homes of all prices were to some extent automatic. There is also something (a very large something) known as high fidelity. A sizable group of economists now rate 73 per cent of the United States' population as middle class or better.

And so on, including the tangential fact that air conditioning will be installed in 80 per cent of this year's Cadillacs.

When a society becomes rich it generally spends a large part of its money on building. For the Romans it was aqueducts and military roads, for Louis XIV it was Versailles, for the lucky Joe Palooka of our own time, it's a ranch house complete with electric sink and dishwasher, carport and no down payment. A middle-class society builds middle-class houses. But at no time in history has anyone seen a middle-class house quite like the one we are building now.

For one thing, its style is not clearly defined. There are virtually no period (in the sense of reasonably faithful reproduction) houses built today, and while the recognizably modern house has gained ground everywhere and is still the "style leader," the great bulk of our new houses incorporate a blend of features borrowed from a variety of times and places. Several factors are responsible for this, notably our desire to merge indoor and outdoor living activities, which changes the exterior appearance of our homes. Another factor is the emergence of the merchant builder, the man who puts up houses in large batches for general sale. When one builds for a market rather than for a known individual, the tendency is to try to please everybody, with the result that most current dwellings are uniformly tasteless and thus inoffensive—architectural equivalents, so to speak, of the contents of a can of pressed ham. A further influence on house appearance has to do with building costs, which are high. This has resulted in efforts to simplify construction and trim, and in a preference for factory-built components such as windows and kitchen cabinets which can be installed with a minimum of labor.

Even closer to the essential character of the new housing is the prevalence of power assists applied to household chores. Today it is a rare citizen who owns fewer than twenty electric motors harnessed to some domestic task or other, either reducing labor or increasing comfort. The steady trend in household machines is exactly the same as in factory machines, that is, toward automatic operation. Thus our heating is automatically controlled, and so are cooking, air cooling, dishwashing, refrigeration, laundry, and so on. This trend is so pronounced that you do not have to be a science-fiction fan to envisage a house that takes pretty complete care of its occupants with no effort on their part beyond servicing the machinery involved.

Consider house cleaning, This has shifted pretty much from the broom and dustpan to the vacuum cleaner, a tool any American housewife at any economic level looks upon as a necessity. But if we borrow an idea familiar in technical circles—that the only thing better than a tool is something that removes the need for it—we can design a house that needs virtually no cleaning. All that is necessary is a filter system that will remove dust particles from the air, even the very small ones making up cigarette smoke. The devices capable of doing this are in wide industrial use and their cost is not too high for domestic use. What I am describing here is no theoretical possibility. Our office designed such a house before World War II, and it was built in the middle of Manhattan which, all local propaganda to the contrary, is one of the dirtiest spots in the nation. It worked. We used to check the house at two-week intervals, and even in places impossible to dust, such as under the strings of an open grand piano, there was never enough of an accumulation to soil a white cotton glove. Of course, there is more to house cleaning than dust elimination, but this is one more step in the evolution of the automatically self-maintained house.

As another example, examine the job of bedmaking. Here is a chore—and a tiresome one—that hasn't changed in centuries. Yet it is no technical problem at all to eliminate bedmaking. What you do is get rid of the bedclothes. With a proposal of this sort one encounters a highly emotional factor: people have strong feelings about bedclothes, in spite of the fact that everyone has at some time in spring or summer tossed them off and slept happily. Whenever I suggest, especially in mixed company, that it is possible to sleep uncovered every night, the reaction is as if I had proposed the revival of polygamy. The fact remains that it is no problem to eliminate bedmaking. The answer could consist of a bed

or pallet with a mattress pad made like an electric blanket and a ceiling also equipped with a radiant-heating panel. Anyone who has ever been skiing knows how warm one can be in cold air on a sunny, windless day. The radiant heating I speak of functions in the same way as the sun. My office is currently designing an experimental house for a Midwestern exhibition, and I think we may incorporate this arrangement just to see how many denunciations are thundered out of local pulpits.

Cooking? It is already on the way toward being pretty automatic, and the distance that remains is being covered rapidly. The meals you get on the airlines, the TV dinners they are selling at the supermarket, these are merely two small-scale sniffs of things in store for us. These prefabricated meals, by the way, also tend to eliminate the scrubbing of pots and the washing of dishes, thus modifying in another way the functions of the kitchen. I agree that you can get a better meal at the Colony, but this isn't quite the point. The direction in which we are moving is clear for all to see.

What happens to people when something as time-consuming as cooking has all the work taken out of it? When beds don't have to be made? When houses clean themselves? Does the race go to pot, get soft, forget the primitive knowledge that tells a man to come in out of the rain? There is no cause for alarm. When automatic oil burners made their appearance, Father cleared out the old coal bins, swept the floor and started building a boat. It is no coincidence that, as soon as cooking became easier, people started buying charcoal grilles like mad. Now that we know we are capable (technically) of making this planet a very comfortable place to live, men are planning space ships and dreaming about worlds never meant for human habitation. The same thing always happens. Nothing is so ingenious as the human animal when it comes to making work. The picture of today's house confirm's this with great force: take the labor out of one area and people put it right back somewhere else. There is a difference, of course, and it is pretty wonderful. The work one *chooses* doesn't seem like work.

We are still too close to a 19th Century background to be fully aware that change and insecurity are not the same thing. Increasing mechanization, the trend toward automatic operation, the elimination of traditional household tasks and the increasingly casual attitude toward possessions are all facts. It would be reasonable to conclude, as many have done, that "gracious living" is on the way out. If gracious living means crisply ruffled bedspreads, snowy table linen, gleaming silver and crystal, lighted candles under chandeliers, starched waitresses and the rest, it may indeed be on the way out. If, however, gracious living has to do with the way people behave with one another, and with their aesthetic judgments regarding houses and their contents, I fail to see why it should be seriously disturbed by a technological revolution or two. Also, to go back to the endlessly enchanting perversity of the human animal, it is a safe bet that when the totally automatic dinner-maker hits the market, the number of people, male and female, who will begin baking their own bread, and sweating over recipes that would have stumped Escoffier, will be slightly in excess of the present combined number of Democrats and Republicans.

What happens when the New Prosperity and the New Leisure hit the old (*circa* 1940) homestead? The answer is extraordinary, and nowhere is it revealed more clearly than in the storage space required in new houses. When a family's income increases, it buys something. In fact, if current figures on installment credit mean anything, the family buys something before its income increases. Anyway, the "something" is always an item considered a necessity. In an era of rapid technical advance, the nature of a necessity changes very quickly. Today's "necessity" was a convenience yesterday and a luxury the day before. Let us select a necessity about which no one can argue: the garbage can. Our family buys a grabage can because it needs one. Presently, however, it hears about a disposal unit you can attach to the drain in the sink. This device has an electric motor operating a grinder, and leftovers can be dumped into it and flushed down the waste pipe. So another investment is made.

At this point we encounter an extraordinary fact: the electric disposal unit *does not eliminate the need for a refuse container of some sort*. It can grind up bones, but not tin cans. In the same way the dust-eating filter machine described earlier does not eliminate the vacuum cleaner,

but merely reduces the frequency of its use. The vacuum cleaner has never eliminated the broom, the dustpan, the whisk broom, the mop, the dustcloth, the pail. Do you begin to see why the modern house contains so much storage space?

But this isn't all. Let us go back to our not-so-imaginary family with an increasing income and asusme that all "necessities" are now under control. At this point the master of the house (well, he used to be the master) goes out and buys a bag of golf clubs. More storage. But not much—after all, a full set of clubs can be stored in a space about one foot square. However, caddies are expensive, so it makes sense to get one of those carriers. More storage. Possibly by moving the power lawn mower (another necessity) farther back into the garage——

Golf is more than a game, it is a way of life. It involves joining a club of some sort. Clubs multiply social contacts. Social contacts, when expanded, can translate themselves into an interesting variety of things. New dresses for parties (new hanging rods for the new dresses, new closets for the new hanging rods). New clothes and shoes for the golfer. More cocktail and highball glasses. An ice bucket. (A better refrigerator?) New porch furniture for father's new friends. If the dinner is at home, how does mother make like a gracious hostess without the help of a dishwasher?

Maybe you think that this extension of the consequences of purchasing a bag of golf clubs is carrying things pretty far, but there is nothing silly about it. Ask any architect who has faced the job of providing space for his client's possessions. Almost any purchase nowadays can start a chain reaction that may end in blowing up the house, if not like a bomb then at least like a balloon. Are you acquainted with the man who was given a power drill for Christmas and is now equipping a complete workshop? If you aren't, practically everyone else is. In the dictionary the camera is defined as a device for capturing an image on a light-sensitive emulsion. This is hopelessly inadequate. A camera means a 35-mm camera, a movie camera, a view camera, extra lenses, tripods, lights, projection screen, enlarging and developing equipment, and ultimately a darkroom. Someone has to find space for it.

Once I was on a railway platform in Germany, waiting for a train that was late. A few dozen GIs were also waiting, patiently seated on their suitcases, all reading comic books. Being rather stuffy about these matters, I was somewhat depressed by the sight of so many adults immersed in reading matter that should bore a teen-ager, until I realized one inescapable fact about this peaceful scene: all these people knew how to read. People who can read buy books (including comics), magazines and newspapers. Reading material requires storage space, of course, and reading itself needs a place. A place where disturbances are at a minimum. It is hard to read next to a television set going full blast. If you have a society of people who can read, who listen to the radio, look at television and play records on their new high-fidelity sets, the house plan has to make room for these conflicting activities in one way or another. Thus the living room becomes a multipurpose room, bedrooms double as sitting rooms, playrooms and so on, a new type of room (the family or activities room) emerges, and, as the physical shelter becomes inadequate for the demands made on it, living tends to spill into the outdoors.

So the expansion of wealth and free time has done two things to today's house: it has increased the number and kinds of possessions to the point where traditional storage devices are overwhelmed, and it has given all sorts of activities new scope, creating the need for a variety of spaces in which these activities can be pursued. High-fidelity equipment is more than a gadget to be stored. Its existence disrupts the traditional house plan, just as television brought a host of new problems for architects and homeowners. In the living room of the house where I grew up, the only activities provided for were reading and conversation. A piano occupied an adjoining alcove, and when I practiced everyone fled to the kitchen. Today, thanks to the new leisure, such an arrangement no longer functions adequately.

On top of the shift in adult activities in the home, there is also the changed attitude toward children. We now consider it bad practice to tell the little dears to shut up, so in the new house we set apart an area where they can make all the noise and mess they want. We may even build on the so-called "bi-nuclear" plan—actually two separate houses connected by an entrance hall—but simple "zoning" of the house plan is less drastic and far more common. The idea is the same: to provide physical separation for activities which conflict. Since most of these conflicts stem from the fact that two generations are living under one roof, the house tends to divide itself into adults' and children's areas, with further subdivisions of each as the price bracket goes up.

As the activities multiply, especially among adults, certain household areas are put to uses which are mutually exclusive and thus a source of inconvenience. A bathroom, let us say, can be drafted into service as a darkroom, but since each use cancels out the other the tendency is to set up separate spaces for each. A television set turned on makes other activities in the same room difficult. Committee meetings demand a room that can be closed off. Gardening, even on a limited scale, seems to require an entire outbuilding for its equipment. All these call for a more elaborate house plan, and hence they affect the over-all design of today's house.

What of tomorrow's house? A good example, built last year, included the following features:

Television in five locations.
Six separate outdoor spaces, including a walled garden, dining garden, dining terrace with rotisserie, and so on.
A "formal" motor entrance (garage converted into the front hall of the house).
A family playroom.
A complete home entertainment system, including tape recorder, several radios, four speaker enclosures.
Workshop.
Tool house.
Private plunge off master dressing room.

Even from this list, which is not by any means complete, it is clear that this house is no more "real" than Detroit's dream cars are "real," but the very exaggeration of conveniences helps clarify the picture. The dream house does two things at once: it reveals what people consider desirable, or even essential, and by displaying a host of new features it creates corresponding new "needs" in people's minds.

The $64,000 question now is how can people get all this for $64,000 or less? One answer, I suppose, is that if present economic trends continue until the year 2000, and more and more "luxuries" move into mass production, the problem will take care of itself. There is no doubt that the present trend in house building is taking us ever closer to full industrial production of houses and their contents. Last year prefabrication business accounted for roughly 10 per cent of all house production, and this percentage has no place to go except up. The current prefab is not much more than a rationalized version of a hand-built house, but, as the business grows and competition increases, it is reasonable to expect that the consumer will get more and better housing for his money. In the meantime, manufacturers of major appliances are driving strongly toward the development of "packages" of all descriptions, from prefab storage walls and kitchens to double-duty units that heat or cool the house according to the season. Both trends indicate that we are moving toward the time when we will be buying Ford- or Cadillac-type dwellings—and loving it.

I say this because people today are no longer interested in a house as an heirloom-type possession, but rather in its ability to service a growing variety of interests and activities, and in its capacity to store equipment, whether machinery or sporting goods. With so radical a shift in attitudes, it becomes not only possible but absolutely certain that industry-built shelter will find more and more acceptance. No doubt at this point "gracious living" really goes down the drain, but as a population we are very clear about what we want from a house, and the best examples currently available leave no doubt on this score. We have come a long way in the relatively short time since the two-story portico was the symbol of affluence and social status, but the mint juleps are still available—in the "entertainment center," the "family room" or out on the back terrace. If the period house is following gracious living down the drain, that is because what it had to offer is no longer worth the price. You can't merge indoor and outdoor living using windows of the 17th Century Salem variety, and if hand-carved cornices cost as much as air conditioning we buy the latter. It doesn't really matter that, in the search for contemporary answers to contemporary problems, we sometimes come up with absurdities or monstrosities. A period of change requires experiment—and claims the right to fail. What matters is that we seem to have decided what we want, and that is the freedom to choose work instead of drudgery. Work of one's choice can become creative play, and in this situation the human animal begins to discover his full capacities. His house today can help bring this about.

The most interesting of all houses, by one who had never seen one . . .   **THE JAPANESE HOUSE**

I believe it was in the fifth or sixth grade that I first became aware of the Japanese house. We had been given a book entitled *Little Friends From Far and Near,* or something to that effect, and there were about a dozen pages that were given over to the Land of the Rising Sun. All was quaintness, picturesqueness and unfamiliarity. Not only were lanterns made of paper but so were the walls of houses. There were no chairs or sofas in the houses, and this seemed less strange then than it was to seem later, for at the age of ten we suffered no discomfort sitting on the floor.

I still remember some badly reproduced prints showing the Japanese hunched on their knees on mats, and looking, in their flowered kimonos, exactly like the dolls sold in the dime store. Even then, however, the Japanese house had attributes of respectability as well as strangeness: its occupants were always drinking tea, just like the Ladies' Club on Wednesdays, and arranging flowers, like the Garden Club on Saturdays. What the book failed to tell us about the house was that, exotic as it seemed, it met the requirements of Japanese daily life, economy, social tradition and climate with such exquisite appropriateness that as a design for living it had never been surpassed.

It may be that this would have been a little over the heads of grade-school children, though I doubt it. The truth of the matter, however, was that the generation which wrote our textbooks was incapable of understanding the Japanese house. These people were too deeply enmeshed in the portiers. lace curtains, antimacassars and overstuffed furniture of their own houses to comprehend simplicity, and too habituated to the process of wholesale imitation that governed American architecture to recognize anything genuine when they saw it. So they did the best they could and wrote about the remote, charming little people who lived in toy houses next to miniature gardens; who waved their fans with quick, birdlike gestures, and bowed to each other all the time. What gaps the books left for us were filled in by Gilbert and Sullivan. If the picture thus created has changed greatly in the years that followed, it was not because something new had been added to the traditional Japanese dwelling, but simply that the most advanced architects of the Western world had so changed their ideas about how people might live that house design literally underwent a revolution. And, as in the case of other revolutions, it was presently discovered that many of the "new" concepts and principles had been in operation many centuries before.

This is why the Japanese house no longer looks like a toy, but seems more a remarkably provocative solution to many problems architects are trying to work out today, particularly, perhaps, to fitting a house to the holiday or vacation mode of life.

A HOUSE THAT IS ITSELF

The Japanese house, like our own, is a wood-frame structure, but it resembles the barn of Colonial days more closely than it does present-day American dwellings. Our houses are constructed of a great number of relatively light pieces of wood, covered by sheathing to make them tight and rigid. The Japanese house is made of a small number of heavy members which are set far apart. As in the U. S. barn, the framework can still be seen after the house is completed. This characteristic articulation—of expression and structure—is quite important, for it is the underlying element that gives the house its particular look. By contrast with the Japanese house, our own has a structure as carefully concealed as Victorian legs.

It is curious that wood should be so universally employed as a building material in Japan, for the country is not particularly rich in forests, while there is plenty of stone, clay and brick. The reason for the persistent use of wood lies not so much in habit or tradition, though both are strong, as in the whole concept of the house as a special kind of shelter from the elements, which in Japan include not only heat and cold but extraordinary humidity, typhoons and earthquakes.

Viewed superficially, the house does not seem particularly effective against any of these. Its wood framework is not braced like ours, and as a result is far from rigid. Moreover, instead of a heavy foundation wall and cellar, the entire support for the building consists of individual rocks, one for each post, pounded into the ground. Between this sketchy foundation and the wood posts above there is no attachment whatever. Faced with the problem of making this house stable, the Japanese long ago decided to concentrate its weight not in the ground, as we do, but in the roof, whose load of tile, or thatch, and massive beams keeps the structure in place on its underpinning. In a gale the house can sway and creak perilously, much like a loaded fruit tree; without being blown down. A good part of the weight of the roof is due to the fact that it is much larger than the house, for instead of hugging the walls like the Colonial gable, the eaves project from three to six feet. The reason for the eaves, however, is not to gain weight—this could be achieved more simply in other ways—but partly to protect the walls from deterioration.

When we think of the walls of a house we are accustomed to visualizing a weatherproof skin tightly enclosing the interior, and where openings such as doors and windows occur, we go to some pains to seal them as closely as possible. It is only in modern houses that the solid wall has been giving way to sliding membranes, usually of glass, and this corresponds closely to a practice the Japanese have followed for centuries. Rarely does one find more than two solid walls on a Japanese house—the others generally are sliding screens of wood and translucent paper or glass. The solid walls, moreover, do not serve to brace the structure, as do ours; they merely fill the voids between the posts. Here again we have a direct parallel with much United States factory construction, except that the filler materials used in the Japanese house are naturally lighter and less costly. A mesh of woven fiber or bamboo is inserted between the vertical posts and then both sides are plastered with mixtures of mud, clay, lime and sand. Like the posts themselves, the plastered walls are exposed both inside and out.

Mud is not impressively durable when exposed to rain, and rain in these islands is a torrential downpour during June and July. The projecting roofs not only protect the solid and paper walls from disintegration but allow the rooms to be kept wide open in bad weather, thus lessening some of the discomforts of the oppressive humidity. The roofs have another function, currently being exploited in our much-publicized "solar houses"—they keep out the sun during the hottest months and allow it to come in during winter, when the sun is much lower in the sky. Solar heating has been a commonplace in these houses for a long time, and this is fortunate, for the Japanese house traditionally has nothing resembling a heating plant.

The house also lacks a cellar, since there is no continuous foundation wall to enclose one. The Japanese first floor (there is rarely a second) is not only uninsulated but is raised a foot or two off the ground and all the winds of winter can blow freely under it. As a result the interior is far from comfortable by American standards, but this construction has two advantages: ground water that accumulates during rains can drain off under the house, and the ventilation keeps the floor beams from rotting. It would be difficult to imagine a more economical and practical solution in the design of a summer house.

The Japanese have one kind of insulation that helps to decrease the discomfort of cold floors. This is the standard mat which covers all floors except those in the kitchen and bath. About two or three inches thick, it is composed of straw, covered by woven matting. This mat provides one explanation for the custom of leaving street shoes in the entry: under the pressure of leather soles or wooden clogs the mats would go to pieces rather rapidly. The Japanese mat is probably the most versatile piece of architectural equipment ever devised. It serves as floor insulation, as carpet, bed, chair, sofa and, in some instances, dining table. Furthermore, it is standardized in length and breadth (roughly three feet by six) and therefore is used as a unit of measure in all plans for houses.

Our own methods of house building are so thoroughly chaotic that the significance of this "mat-module" may be missed. What this kind of standard means is that virtually all elements of the entire building can also be standardized, and that any skilled carpenter, given a simple mat layout, can build an acceptable house. Our own attempts at prefabrication rely on standard units of measurement, but our problem is that an acceptable module for a wall panel may not correspond with the stock sizes of windows, bathtubs, stoves, and so on.

The interior of the typical house is a rectangle and is divided into two smaller rectangles. One of these contains the kitchen and other services. The other is a large open living area, broken up as desired by light sliding screens covered with paper. The actual number of rooms in the house, therefore, varies with the hour of the day, the time of year and the activities going on. To clean and air the house one removes the mats, stacks them outside in the sun, sweeps the floor and slides open the screen partitions to ventilate the interior. There is no problem of maintaining furniture or of moving it around, for there isn't any, outside of a few rudimentary pieces, such as low tables or armrests. All storage space is built in. Even decoration is concentrated. There is an alcove, about three feet deep and six or nine feet wide at one end of the main room. In this alcove, known as the tokonoma, the owner sets a picture, a flower arrangement, or both. Adjoining this alcove is another, equipped with a few shelves for decorative objects. These little displays are changed periodically, but our custom of placing pictures and bric-a-brac indiscriminately around the walls of all rooms is unknown. A Japanese would probably feel that this random placing of a large number of decorative objects not only destroys their intrinsic meaning but also ruins the unity of interior design.

The structure and plan of the Japanese house are by no means the whole story, but taken by themselves they are most revealing. What we have here is a house with no attic or cellar, no foundation, no fireplace, no furnace, no chimney, and practically no doors, windows or exposed furniture. Measured by our standards of comfort it is a poor man's house, and it is true enough that even before the war the average Japanese was a poor man. But if the house were dismissed at this point, and on this basis, we should miss a good deal of its meaning. For one thing, it is also the rich man's house. In other words, the bare, stripped-down character of the house is due not merely to a lack of money and materials—it also reflects accurately the tradition of the Japanese society as a whole. For instance, every child is taught to use the familiar kneeling posture instead of sitting. Under such circumstances, no matter how much money one has, any kind of chair is superfluous. Children are also taught to keep warm by wrapping themselves in their kimonos and huddling over charcoal braziers. One might pass this off as primitive, which it is, but one Japanese pastime, the winter party, involves opening wide the sliding walls of the main room so that all the occupants can enjoy the beauty of snow in the garden while they talk. The fact that we have not been conditioned to withstand the rigors of this kind of existence is not to the point; the Japanese have, which is why even the rich man's house shows almost as little concern for the so-called "necessities" as does that of his less wealthy neighbor. It should be fixed clearly in mind that poverty has a different meaning in Japan. It is neither shameful nor a situation to be remedied as soon as possible.

WHERE MASS AND CLASS MEET

Our custom of segregating residential neighborhoods by income is not followed in Japan—houses of the rich, the middle-income groups and the poor can be found in the same areas, and, due to the inconspicuousness of all house exteriors, it is sometimes difficult to tell which is which. I am not trying to present these contrasts as social virtues opposed to vices; it would be equally easy to describe Japanese ways as exquisite in their refinement or meaningless in their backwardness. My only concern here is to show how a series of facts is reflected with extraordinary precision in the design of a type of house.

One of these facts is the attitude of the Japanese toward Nature, which has influenced his feelings about house design as much as has his economic condition. For example, while the woodwork in a house is precisely cut and finished, one post in the main room usually is left in its original tree form. The contrast between accurate workmanship and the natural shape of the single tree-like post is considered very beautiful. We express the same feeling when we place, say, a piece of driftwood against a finished plaster wall. The difference is that we don't build the contrast into the house, although, as we shall see presently, some of the modern designers are trying to do exactly that.

Anyone who has ever bought a piece of old furniture and removed its finish knows what is meant by "the beauty of natural wood." Nevertheless, to protect this beauty we cover the wood with shellac or lacquer. The Japanese, as a rule, do not do this; they prefer the appearance of clear grain to a protective coat that changes the natural color of the material. As a result, their house interiors often have a somewhat unfinished look, and the fragrance of slowly evaporating wood oils. They contain almost nothing that isn't "natural." Not only is the wood frame left untreated but also the paper screens, the woven mats, the sand-finished walls, the lightly planed wood ceilings, the screens of reed and bamboo. Seen in juxtaposition with the garden, the house always looks like part of it, and in a very real sense it is, for it is built of the same materials.

A great deal has been written, much of it nonsense, about the Japanese garden, and we have done ourselves little good by our many imitations of it. It is possible that the Japanese garden, with its little bridge, little pool, little stream and dwarf trees, is a miniature landscape loaded with cosmic symbols, as some writers have insisted. For our purposes, however, other considerations are more important. The Japanese garden, like the house, is a poor man's creation with a history of great antiquity. The garden has to be small, for few urban houses have much land around them, and the average citizen, who has to work long hours at low pay, isn't going to set up gardens that require elaborate maintenance.

SPIRITUAL GARDENS

Another clue to the garden design can be found in the house itself, which shows clearly that Japanese taste rules out profusion and ostentation, that great delight is taken in small objects, and that contrasts are enjoyed more when they are subtle. The garden in Japan, therefore, is a direct expression of the conditions that made the house what it is. Just as the "natural" way to build a house is to cut wood into straight pieces and put them together, the "natural" design for a garden respects the materials used and attempts to accentuate their intrinsic qualities. Since a man walks in a straight line only if he has been trained in the army, garden paths do not follow straight lines. Vistas and changes of direction are more important than getting to the house in the shortest possible time. Even ground textures are selected with great care, so that as a person passes over sand, rounded boulders, flagstones, gravel, and cobblestones, he can enjoy a series of subtle physical experiences as well as the changing view around him.

The lessons that can be learned from the house in Japan have nothing to do with copying its superficial aspects. It has already been demonstrated that imitating an alien style always ends up wtih the dead bones of a period. To understand this one has only to walk through any city and observe how meaningless are the Roman fronts tacked onto banks and railroad stations, and how tiresome are the attempts at "individuality" in the residential areas. Any effort to reproduce the Japanese house, or its parts, would merely result in a freak, because the Japanese way of life is not ours. Nevertheless, there is something valuable to be learned.

Perhaps the first thing that strikes one who examines the plans and photographs of these dwellings is their delightful design for summer living. Big roofs keep the sun out. Removable walls let the breeze in. Separate rooms can be merged into one large open-air pavilion by sliding back the paper screens. Housekeeping could not possibly be simpler. All the materials used suggest not only economy, but ease and informality. Most refreshing, of course, is the total absence of clutter; against such a background anyone should be able to relax. The appeal of the Japanese house, in other words, is not based on style or pitcuresque detail but on its charming expression of a special approach to shelter. That this charm is felt, despite the differences that exist, is evidence essential human requirements cut across all ideological and cultural lines. In studying the Japanese house we encounter a remarkable series of coincidences, for without much direct influence we have been developing a modern house in this country that bears a strong resemblance to it.

FREEDOM FOR OUR HOMES

Trace the trends in U. S. house design, and it becomes apparent that all the familiar architectural forms of our childhood seem to be disintegrating. The tight little rooms that helped keep the early New England houses snug broke apart into the barnlike interiors of Victorian mansions, made big and open by the fluid warmth of central heating. Despite the temporary reversion to Colonial styling after World War I, the house in its more advanced forms continued to open up. Partitions tended to vanish, or to become movable. Storage furniture, such as chests and bureaus, began to give way to built-in chests and cupboards. The outer walls, once solid with wood and masonry, and pocked with small windows, became translucent, transparent, movable. The eaves moved out again, now sheltering glass walls with summer sunshades. Inside, the shapes of walls became simpler, and architects began to experiment with the textures of natural materials—redwood, cedar, cypress, brick and field stone—and to use these textures to contrast with the slick perfection of painted plaster. Excess decoration disappeared. And finally the garden moved indoors—literally—as the house walls opened to include it.

Told without pictures, the story of our modern house could be a passable description of its Japanese counterpart, and this is all the more remarkable because the two came into existence under entirely different conditions. The same thing can be said of the modern garden. The two best landscape architects in the western hemisphere, Thomas Church, of San Francisco, and Roberto Burle Marx, of Rio de Janeiro, are both designing gardens which strongly resemble those of Japan—not in detail, but in principle.

AN ORIENTAL LESSON

To understand the Japanese house (or, by extension, the modern house) we must put aside the particular set of ideas with which we were raised, particularly the idea that a house must be a solid box, tightly enclosing a series of fixed cubicles. Once this fact is grasped, it becomes possible to visualize a house as a kind of open stage, standing free in space. The floor of the stage is slightly above the ground, and its roof is held up by as few supports as possible. Applied to this light framework are a few solid walls (toward the street, for privacy) but most of the outer covering is light and movable. Inside there is even more freedom, for rooms can be created—or erased—as one desires. Fixed areas include the bathroom, kitchen and built-in storage units. Furniture and accessories are light, and treated like theater "props"—they are brought out when needed and then put away again. In this type of dwelling, no matter what "performance" is in progress, the stage can always be arranged appropriately and with ease. Nothing could be further from the kind of house most of us live in. And nothing could be closer to the kind of house we are gradually developing.

The lesson of the Japanese house, therefore, is of very special contemporary interest. It is an almost perfect prototype for vacation living. It is a masterpiece of standardization, but it shows that standardization does not have to mean monotonous uniformity. By separating house structure from house enclosure, it makes possible great freedom of movement for the occupants and creates an ever-changing relationship to the outdoors. Product of age-old culture, it demonstrates that modern man is not quite so different as he sometimes like to think. It has proven conclusively that a house can be a work of art—without stuffing its insides with "art." It teaches that the beautiful way to handle materials, whether paper or wood, rock or shrub, is the natural way. It suggests that you can get attention by whispering as well as shouting, that simplicity is not the same as bare emptiness, that poverty is not necessarily ugly, and that for full living people require a flexible enclosure, not a strait jacket.

It is curious that we are learning this lesson from our late enemies.

An expression of a deep-seated
conviction: houses, like education, like everything else
we use in quantity, have to be tooled.

PREFABRICATION

Americans are funny people: we discover mass production, trumpet its limitless virtues in all directions and propagandize the rest of the world in attempts to make it follow suit. But when people right among us took the propaganda seriously and applied it to our largest and most important product—the dwelling—then "prefabrication" became a nasty word.

The early prefabricators took quite a beating before they discovered that there was a nation-wide taboo on houses made in factories.

The idea was so tempting, the thinking was so logical:

1. All Americans buy detached houses as soon as they can afford them.
2. The houses, within very narrow limits, are pretty much alike (wood construction, three bedrooms as a rule, identical baths and so on).
3. Therefore houses, or at least the great bulk of houses, can be described as standard products; and, since standard products can be mass-produced giving high quality at lower cost . . .

Conclusion—So can houses.

The idea was great, but for a quarter of a century it failed to work.

Many important factors were neglected in the original thinking. Disparities in building codes, trade union opposition, financing problems, the difficulties in making and transporting so bulky a product were among them. A major (and largely hidden) factor was emotional: The house was a sacred cow, a symbol of social status, an outward expression of personality. People already uneasily aware of the gray uniformity gradually enveloping their work, tastes, habits and thoughts resisted the attack on the house as if industrialization in this area were the final assault on their own disappearing individuality.

Today, this battle is being lost, as all such battles in our time must be lost. Last year 93,000 prefabricated houses were built, as against 50,000 in 1950.

Again, the reasons are fairly clear. Large merchant builders are taking over the house field from the small contractor, demonstrating that standardization and volume production can give greater value per dollar. For this group prefabrication means saving in time and money and hence a competitive advantage. So today we have a house-manufacturing industry. It is pretty primitive technologically, to be sure, and still much too anxious to hide the fact that its product is no longer handmade. But it is an industry nonetheless, and one due to develop with great rapidity in both size and techniques.

If the battle is being lost, this does not mean that the loss is ours. Why should we get full value when we buy factory-made products such as razors, nylons or cars, and be denied it, as we are today, when we build houses?

There is a persistent myth that factory-made houses are in some way cheap and inferior; yet our entire industrial history shows over and over again that this simply has to be nonsense.

How would you like to buy (and pay the price for) a handmade home laundry?

To see the real meaning of the industry-made house, we must somehow shed ourselves of the fear that we as people have to become standardized when we accept standardized tools, toys or shelters. The creaking platitude "clothes make the man" no longer holds when everyone can be well-dressed. Einstein lived in a nondescript little house on a side street in a small town; Buddha lived in a cave. So what? I suspect that if the day comes when possession of everyday things becomes largely meaningless because everyone can have pretty much the same basic necessities, the uniqueness of human personality will begin to be really appreciated.

The problem today is not whether to prefabricate or not to prefabricate. This question has already been settled. The simple, observable fact is that the building of homes is becoming an industrial affair. The problem is how, through these industrial methods, to bring the house up to the technical level of the refrigerator, the automatic machine tool, the automobile, and to use this technique to enhance human values.

We are entitled to this kind of performance in our dwellings simply because we have demonstrated so abundantly elsewhere that we know how to achieve it. But not with carpenters or masons. For us, 20th Century people who have made an irrevocable commitment to the machine, there is only one choice. The swift growth of prefabrication in building means that again—as in transportation, food and clothing—we have already chosen.

AFTER THE MODERN HOUSE . . .

Thoughts following an attempt at collaboration with Buckminster Fuller. The text is based on a talk presented to the Fashion Group of Chicago on June 17, 1952.

The modern house is close to fifty years old, but despite its respectable age it is still far from a conspicuous or accepted part of the American landscape. Banks and builders in many localities are still afraid of it. Some communities have regulations to prevent its construction. Nevertheless, it has increased in numbers and its influence on home furnishings and interior design has been extraordinary.

From this preamble one might conclude that the modern house has come to stay, and that it is only a matter of time before it becomes our dominant house type. In one sense this is probably true, but I have a different view to present for your consideration: it is that the modern house is already obsolete. I believe that powerful pressures to hasten a change are in existence. There is visible evidence to suggest the probable nature of this change.

All of us are familiar with the modern-versus-traditional controversy: The modern house looks cold; it is an operating room or a goldfish bowl; it would be fine for a desert or a beach, but not where you and I live. For the modernist the ties; it is cluttered and too hard to maintain. What both groups have overlooked in the partisanship is that the *similarities* between modern houses and period houses are much greater than the apparent differences.

Since this point is basic to my argument, I shall develop it briefly. The traditional house is so planned that a number of rooms are allocated to services, sleeping and general living activities. These rooms are separated by partitions of wood studs nailed together and covered with plaster or wallboard. The shell is also made of a nailed wood frame, sheathed and finished in shingles, brick, wood siding, etc. Holes are left for doors and windows. Through the shell, partitions and floors, electricians, plumbers and heating men make more holes for piping, wiring and ducts.

If I were to describe the typical modern house, I could do so in the same terms. The plan is slightly more open in the living areas, the windows are larger, but that is about all. Both types are handicraft products, equipped with a number of mass-produced items. If you counted the number of such items, I suspect that the period type would come out ahead.

In a society approaching total industrialization, handicraft products with a utilitarian purpose suffer because they give diminishing value at increasing cost. Everyone knows that this is true for houses, and the fact holds whether the design is period or modern.

Among those who favor the modern house, one sometimes hears reference made to the automobile as a comparable object, and there is an implication that the period type resembles the buggy. Except in an ideological sense the comparison is not valid, for the motor car and the buggy are entirely different in concept, materials, engineering design and production. If one wants to find in building a parallel to automotive evolution, it is to the factory or office building one has to turn, not the house.

In industrial building there is no traditional-modern controversy. Can you imagine anyone suggesting that a new plant be designed to resemble a New England factory of the water wheel era? And yet from a design point of view a modern factory is a truly radical building, far more so than the modern house. Oddly enough, the more extreme it is, the better people like it. What is the modern factory? Speaking generally,

the factory: flexibility in a conditioned interior

*Conditioned shell enclosures in industrial building: Mies van der
Rohe's Metals Research laboratory above; Saarinen's G.M. Technical Center (next page)*

Opposite page, left: The Crystal Palace—a prefabricated cage enclosing people, gardens and interior structures (but hardly "conditioned")—preceded the conditioned shell of modern factories (Albert Kahn's Toledo Scale Factory and Dodge Factory, center). Multiplication of a few structural parts and absence of finishes speeds up assembly. The flexibility of unobstructed interior space makes factory methods widely applicable to commercial building. The Atlanta building, designed by I. M. Pei (right) was a large shell built on speculation, later occupied by Gulf Oil Co.

Wright's Johnson Wax Building which
refines interior space with sculptural columns, dramatic skylight.

Mies van der Rohe's Concert Hall Project (above) shows the dramatic architectural possibilities afforded by free-floating elements within a large space enclosure. Inside a trussed steel and glass cage he has arranged several lightweight vertical and horizontal planes — walls and ceilings—which, entirely free from any structural role, develop visual and auditory harmony and shape an exciting interior space.

it is a hollow shell, built almost entirely of synthetic materials. Inside there is a floor unobstructed by offices, washrooms or columns. Electric power, water and compressed air are accessible everywhere. The design objective is a totally flexible arrangement in a perfectly conditioned interior. The interiors of the best new factories make one think not so much of a building as a clean, orderly community under one roof. These plants are ornaments to their communities—factories like Albert Kahn's Toledo Scales and Dodge Half-Ton Truck plants, and others, like Mies van der Rohe's Minerals and Metals Research Laboratory, which are not factories in function but which are in principle. They represent *the master type of space enclosure of our time.* Inevitably they must affect all other structures, including the house, because they enclose space more beautifully, more economically, and lend themselves to industrial production. Almost all of a factory shell today is produced in factories—the building job is largely an assembly operation.

What comes after the modern house, I suggest, is not a house at all in the familiar sense, but a space container, a precisely engineered and manufactured shell providing a space conditioned to serve the requirements of the occupants. By "conditioned" I mean warmed, cooled, ventilated, humidified, dehumidified, daylighted, artificially lighted, acoustically treated and a number of other things. It may sound complicated but the know-how and techniques exist.

The interior of this shell could be arranged with complete freedom, since all partitions would be lightweight and movable. One might visualize it as a year-round garden, for instance, with brightly colored little sleeping pavilions scattered around in it. If this living space, perhaps fifty feet in each direction by two stories in height, is compared to the average living room, the picture isn't so bad.

To get a visual idea of what I mean, observe what is already happening in the houses of Charles Eames, Mies van der Rohe and Philip Johnson, Bruce Goff and others—houses which begin to span the gap between the modern house and this newer concept of controlled shelter.

I mentioned pressures which would tend to bring this development about. One is the efficiency of factory construction. Another is the fact that houses are getting so cramped, due to their cost as handicraft products, that people have to find a way out. Prefabrication has been offered as such a way, but the results to date are not impressive. The weakness of prefabrication, as I see it, divides the shell into transportable units and then transfers a certain amount of work done in the open to the inside of a mill. This is fine as far as it goes, but it doesn't go very far. To effect a shift from handicraft to an industrial product—particularly with a product as complex as a dwelling—the whole concept of the product has to be recast.

If my hypothesis about the conditioned shell is correct, the conventional notion of "architecture" as applied to the planning and design of dwellings will become relatively unimportant and will tend to be replaced by a combination of interior and industrial design. Such a fundamental

Charles Eames: industrial vocabulary, personal style

Philip Johnson: a single spatial unit clearly organized into areas of use.

Soriano: a house made from standard modular parts, as spatially flexible and quickly assembled as a factory.

Paul Nelson's model of a Suspended House, designed in 1938, is an hypothetical demonstration of how—once the concept of a shell enclosure is accepted—interior volumes and curves might be organized for flexibility and contrast.

Mies: glass enclosing a fluid space makes nature always visible, but never tangible.

Polevitzky: a trussed cage surrounding both man and nature.

The conditioned dome would combine the structural simplicity of basic shelter, the spatial flexibility and rapid assembly of the modern factory in an economical enclosure which would be adaptable to any combination of complex living patterns. This scale model of the Fuller dome (actually 78 feet in diameter by 26 feet high) is covered with transparent plastic for study purposes; in reality, the covering should be translucent, to transmit light but check direct rays. If technical problems could be solved, the covering might ultimately be a material which could be made to vary from transparent to opaque in accordance with moods and seasons. The five arches between the points on which it rests would be transparent.

In the controlled atmosphere of the dome, the interior area may easily be arranged to suit the particular needs and patterns of the inhabitants. Traditional habits, however, could soon disappear in the light of the potentialities suggested by the bubble house. It could be like living in a garden, with the "house" organized into isolated, colorful pavilions, where the necessary privacy and enclosure could be found. The pavilions are thought of as extruded aluminum or steel frames covered with plastic-and-fabric sandwich material.

change in anything as important socially and economically as housing would, I believe, give all the design and furnishing industries new opportunities of staggering dimensions.

Whether these conclusions are correct or not, I can assure you they were not arrived at in the comfort of an armchair. For some years I have been active professionally both as an architect and industrial designer, and there is a profoundly frustrating difference between the two. The industrial designer works to develop a prototype, spending much time and energy to make it suitable for economical production. An architect has a relatively limited time to solve a very complex set of problems, and when he has done so his design is picked up by a motley crew of masons, plumbers, carpenters and others who then proceed to execute it in a thoroughly unpredictable fashion. Furthermore, his design is a one-of-a-kind thing, and on the next house he has to start again from scratch. And no matter how conscientiously the architect may work, he cannot possibly deliver value in the final product: both design and production costs are too high.

With this thinking as a background, I began work on a theoretical house project some months ago, using my own family requirements as a guide. The first step was to plan a conventional modern house, and when all space requirements were taken care of I had pretty close to 5,000

Life in the conditioned bubble could mean perpetually camping out in the perfect climate under ideal, even luxury, conditions. The kitchen above is a low, uncovered unit standing in a year-round garden. Some pavilions have colored triangular flippers which raise or lower to control top light.

square feet of house. At present-day prices, this meant a cost of $75,000 to $100,000 exclusive of design or land or landscaping. When I isolated the space problem from all the others, it led rapidly to a study of factory structures which, as I said, are essentially space containers. A factory can be built in most places for $7 or $8 a square foot (compared with $15-$20 for houses) for structure and services in excess of what a dwelling would require. I guessed that a house shell might reasonably come to less.

The interesting thing about the space container is that all heavy interior construction can be dispensed with. A large, properly conditioned interior could be fitted out with the necessary kitchen and bathroom equipment and most of the privacy requirements could be taken care of by glorified pup tents. In other words, it looked as if a luxurious interior could be developed using industrially produced components, without excessive cost. It also became apparent that the most serious single family problem—the need to expand space as the family grows and the need to contract later when the children grow up— could now be solved, if the space were large enough to begin with, by the addition and removal of sleeping compartments.

Interested primarily in pushing a line of research as far as I could, I then decided to try one of Buckminster Fuller's beautiful dome structures as the shell. The dome appears to offer more space enclosure at even less cost than the conventional factory shell, and also suggests the possibility of a beautiful interior.

This project has now been developed to the stage of the large model shown here. If Mr. Fuller is to be given the entire credit for the beautifully articulated dome structure, I must ask you not to blame him for the inadequacies of the interior design. This summer my office, in collaboration with Mr. Fuller and a selected group of students, will pursue a study of the many problems and possibilities of this new kind of dwelling. With luck, by fall we may have a second model suitable for use as a scale prototype. However, if we do arrive at a workable full-size dwelling I have no idea whatever of presenting it as anything other than what it will be: a laboratory experiment at working scale. I do not believe that we shall have an immediate panacea for today's housing problems. If you still want an automotive parallel to a house, I can give it to you here: General Motors' Le Sabre car, like this shell structure, attempts to project present knowledge as far as it can go. But the Sabre, despite the immense body of experience and limitless funds behind it, is still not offered as a consumer product. If General Motors is going to need more time for research, I think that we, with a somewhat smaller budget and working staff, may legitimately claim the same privilege.

THE SECOND HOUSE

This is the age of the second everything. It opened officially and most inauspiciously with the second chicken in every pot. While this hopeful forecast may have cost Mr. Hoover more votes than the combined total of his other errors, the vision, though unhappily timed, was prophetic.

In 1956, 5,000,000 U. S. car-owning families had two automobiles. "At least" two automobiles is the way the report is phrased. In 1957, the builder who tries to sell a house without a second bath has to try very hard indeed (there is a marginal group of customers who will still settle for a bath and a half). And who is still without a second telephone?

The second television set was hailed as the miracle to rescue a new industry from the doldrums, and the family from constant warfare over channels. Hi-fi fans, who at present seem to embrace the entire male population, are moving from high fidelity old-style to something called "binaural" or "stereophonic." Whichever term wins, they both mean you need two of everything to hear what is being played. And now, if the tales of travel agents are to be believed, there is a developing social phenomenon known as the second vacation.

The second house fits into this expanding category of "seconds" but it is a thing (perhaps "event" would be more accurate) which belongs in a totally different order of magnitude. For the second house is not merely a shelter in addition to the one the family thinks of as home: it is also a generator of duplicates. A couple with three children *and* a second house probably owns 12 beds, 48 sheets, 24 blankets and pillowcases, two automatic laundries. The beds are only the beginning, and anyone can take it from there.

A survey of five widely circulated magazines indicates that between six and sixteen percent (depending on which publication) of their subscribers own a second house. At a convention of highway officials, the duputy commissioner of the Massachusetts Department of Commerce had this to say: "We have talked about two- and three-car families as a very likely possibility in the near future. It is also conceivable that the highway system will bring about a two-house family because of the reduced time of travel between places of residence and places of recreation and leisure. The four-day work week and the three-day weekend may soon accelerate this social effect. . . ."

What is this social effect? It is, as far as one can make out, a further expansion of the mobility so characteristic of our time. Like other phenomena representing social change, this one could also be viewed with alarm. The change, however, is one of quantity and not of kind, for there is nothing intrinsically new about the second house. The rich have always taken what advantage they could of the refreshment that comes with a change of background. The perennially fascinating events in "Mayerling" took place in a second (perhaps it was a third or fourth) house. Marie Antoinette's favorite retreat was a kind of make-believe farm. The events in Newport, Bar Harbor and Palm Beach which so fascinated the masses around the turn of the century all took place in second (at the very least) houses. All that is new today is that great numbers of middle class people are staking out claims in what, not so long ago, was an area of absolutely inaccessible luxury.

"Luxury" means many different things to different people, and it is this multiplicity of possibilities which make the problem of the second house so fascinating and so tricky. Speaking as an architect who has had to cope with the problem more than once, I am strongly of the opinion that, in the event you are contemplating such a venture, it is far less important to **decide** what the second house *is* than to determine what it is supposed to *do*. It would be dealing in platitudes to observe that the second house is a response to a felt need, but it is surprising how difficult it is to so define the need that a successful house is the result.

Traditionally, the second house is a vacation house; it is also predominantly a warm-weather vacation house. Traditionally—and logically—the vacation house goes in a vacation place, that is, a place related to water, mountains or woods. Also built into the image is the expectation that a vacation place be cooler, and quieter. Now where did this idea come from? It came from the fact that the only people, for all practical purposes, who could afford to think about a second house lived in cities, which, in the era before air conditioning and paved streets, were even more uncomfortable and noisy than they are now.

Today there is probably more money residing in suburbia and exurbia than in the cities, and in many of these areas the classic requirements of a vacation place are already being met: good air, lower temperatures, reasonable quiet, swimming pools, plenty of grass and trees, and so on. For this large and prosperous group, well equipped to pay for the pleasures of a second house, what is the second house supposed to do?

Provide more lawn, more trees, more quiet? It is an interesting question, and the second house would be more interesting too, if the question were answered intelligently more often. To listen to the wives in this group, one frequently gets the impression that for them the absolute limit in holiday luxury would be a compact urban apartment, complete with air conditioning, room service and no children underfoot. This may not correspond with the average male citizen's dream of a second house, but it is an intelligent and even illuminating response to a particular set of circumstances. Things have indeed changed since the days of the Mizners.

Other things have changed too. Most curious, perhaps, is that now that the second house is available to a great many people, it is no longer enough. The world has gotten too small. There are too many fascinating places which can be easily reached.

When I was a small child, my parents had a summer cottage on Long Island Sound. It was an event when they got the house, and there were months of planning, packing and unpacking. When we finally took off, our Hudson Super Six touring car was loaded to the gunwales. My father came down for weekends, driving thirty-six miles each way. All this represented an achieved limit, of a kind, and within it we were not only content, but rather impressed.

Now my own family has a second house. It is almost three times as far from home, reflecting not only the improvement in roads and cars, but the growing shortage of suitable land near cities. It is not only a summer house, but is used intermittently throughout the year—a far more complex affair, with its automatic heat and other equipment, than the summer cottage of childhood. Today's second house tends to be as fully equipped (in some respects better equipped) than the "first" house.

One might think that with this embarrassment of riches the many families who now follow this pattern of living would be more than happy to shuttle endlessly between home base and the second house. But this does not appear to be so. Our summer neighbors across the street are spending half the summer in Wyoming. In the past twelve months my wife and I toured the canals of Holland in a motor cruiser and the Bahamas in a schooner. There were quite a few other tourists around in both places. The second house, achieved within a framework of rising liv-

ing standards, ceases to be an end in itself and becomes one of a larger series of options. One interesting consequence of treating a house in this casual off-and-on manner is that it tends to evolve, not as a house but as a machine. It has to, unless one has the caretaker and staff to open and close it.

Another possible consequence of treating a house as only one of a series of options is that it be planned with periodic rental in mind. Many yacht owners enjoy a luxury afloat that would be slightly beyond their means if they were not able to charter the boat when they had no use for it. The second house frequently tends to fall into a similar category. Designing a house with rental in mind presents no special difficulties, any more than in the case of a boat. It means giving a little extra attention to questions of maintenance and providing ample lock-up storage for personal possessions.

There are two times in life when people start thinking seriously about supplementing their year-round living facilities. One is when the children start coming; the other is when the children start going away. The first group generally requires a larger house than it can afford; the second can usually afford a bigger house than it needs. Both situations add up to a house on the smallish side. Needless to say, exceptions to these statements are legion. Nevertheless, it is reasonable to consider the second house as a relatively compact affair.

There is a second general characteristic: it has to do with the fact that the second house reflects a desire for a change of pace. All too frequently this is left to the surrounding landscape for solution, while the house itself reflects the monotonous mediocrity of the suburb from which the owners have just escaped. It is very much too bad that the most interesting opportunity afforded by the second house, the chance to achieve a total change of atmosphere through intelligent planning and some lighthearted architectural experimentation, is so often passed up. This does not necessarily stem from undue conservatism on the part of the owner: a lack of awareness that the opportunity exists is far more likely to be the reason.

Consider, as an illustration, a family planning to build a summer house in the Wisconsin north woods. Wisconsin, for a good part of the year, can be a fearsome place: winter temperatures take zero as a starting point and move down from there, and four-foot snowfalls fail to make newspaper headlines. A house built to endure in Wisconsin must, naturally, take these conditions into account. However, for summer living in Wisconsin a house lifted bodily from Florida or the Southwest would do very nicely indeed, and its typical features such as sliding glass walls, through ventilation, screened patios and the rest would contribute mightily to the joys of vacation living. If the house were also to be used as a ski lodge on occasion, the features could still be retained while supplementary provisions for heating could be made as desired.

What this example says is that the second house need not conform to a given regional type. In fact there are excellent reasons why it should not. The best expression for the second house, in by far the larger part of the country, would show a rather surprising and unexpected kind of hybrid. This proposition is not as alarming as it may sound, for the process is already under way in all types of houses. The conditions which fostered the rise of the regional type of house are rapidly disappearing. People don't feel as regional as they used to—they move around too much. So do building materials and equipment. It is cheaper in Pennsylvania, for instance, to build a wall of Pacific Coast redwood than to use the abundant local stone. Improved communications have a good bit to do with the process of hybridization now going on: if a builder in Maine sees a three-months-old California house in his magazine, what is to prevent him from being influenced by it? The difference between the year-round and the second house, in this respect, is that the latter has fewer limitations.

Somewhere above I ventured the opinion that the second house is due to evolve more as a machine than as a house. Such an expression is unpalatable to many, but it is still hard to see how the trend can be otherwise. It stems not only from intermittent use, which demands a good deal in the way of automatic heating equipment and other apparatus, but also from the fact that women need vacations too. Whether a house is an all-year affair near the city, or a holiday place somewhere else, it is still a house, which means that rooms have still to be cleaned, beds have to be made, people have to be fed. If the second house is to provide a vacation as much for the housewife as it does for her husband and children, then it follows that the need for

mechanical servants is virtually unlimited. The 19th Century image of a vacation as a return to nature and the simple life is still with us, but for the housewife of today there is no simple life without quantities of equipment. All of which gives one pause, for a full complement of automatic household machinery is anything but inexpensive. The question here is exactly the same as it was at the beginning: what is the second house supposed to do?

Equipment is not the only burden on the second-house budget. There is also the matter of space. Unfortunately, it is always at the moment when space is most needed that the least money is available. What answers there are to this problem lie in an understanding of where space goes in a house, and where it can be most easily manipulated.

The service block in a house (kitchen, baths, heating) occupies a minimum of space, and while ingenuity can sometimes compress it, the savings never amount to anything. Where the bulk of the floor area goes is into living areas and bedrooms. Especially bedrooms. In a year-round house it makes excellent sense to provide children with bedrooms which are also study and play areas, and citadels of personal privacy to boot. There is no such need in the second house. Dormitory set-ups complete with double bunks are not only adequate but frequently welcomed. If your children do require complete bedrooms in both houses, all you have to do is pay for them. In areas where swimming forms part of the daily routine, the whole bathroom plan can be greatly simplified. For purposes of general living in the second house, a large, complete living room is often superfluous. Outdoor living is an agreeable reality when the second house is in full operation, and outdoor space can be exceedingly inexpensive. If bugs are a problem, a ceiling of screen cloth is a standard, simple device for creating a usable outdoor room of any size. The luxury of space, in other words, is attainable in the economy-size second house if the space is created outside. Any time a porch or a patio can take the place of a constructed room, you are ahead of the game.

How much is an economy-size second house? There is no answer, of course, without more information, but these figures may serve as very general yardsticks. Service areas such as baths and kitchens tend to average out at $25 to $35 per square foot. You can spend much more but not much less. General living space can be constructed for around $10 per square foot, but with heating and insulation $15 is closer to a safe minimum. Outdoor living areas can be built for $2 to $8 per square foot, depending on what you do in the way of paving, fences, trellises and so on. Again, it is easy to spend more. If the budget dictates a minimum of house now, with the hope of more later, do not expand the house by adding a room or a wing. Add a separate building. I know it sounds extravagant, but any other way leads straight to insolvency. There is nothing in building quite as expensive as tampering with an existing structure.

A few years back I watched a friend go through the procedure of getting himself a new beach house. Some carpenters arrived and in the course of a few days erected a large platform on heavy posts. We then waited for them to get going on the framing of the house to go on the platform, but they packed up their tools and went away. More days passed and a truck arrived, bearing the name of a large New York department store. Panels of assorted sizes were disgorged and on the following afternoon the platform supported not one house, but two. Each was tiny, and contained only a single room, but they looked cheerful and there was plenty of room left on the platform for sitting out. The house was actually two prefabricated units, made for use as garden tool sheds, but as a beach house the whole thing worked admirably. The following season, feeling the need of an expanded social life, he went back to his department store and presently had a fine guest house about fifty feet away from his own. His few neighbors considered him impossibly eccentric, but when I discovered how very little his luxurious little three-unit house had cost him, I was not so sure.

The beach house was an admirable example of a user analyzing his requirements and then meeting them without concern for proper traditional procedures. He too discovered that the economical way to expand was with separate building units, but there is more to this method than a cost advantage. Decentralized building permits zoning, for instance. This means that if you use the house as a whole during the summer, but need only cooking and sleeping facilities on an occasional winter weekend, you can conve-

niently heat one building while leaving the rest alone. The same holds for air conditioning. If married children want to move in for their vacation, the decentralized plan offers much more in the way of privacy for everyone. And if the house ultimately gets too big for your needs, it is far simpler to sell a small unit and have it moved away than to attempt to saw the old family mansion in half.

Size presents all kinds of ticklish problems in the second house as well as the permanent home. It is never exactly right. When the family is growing up there is never enough room. When the children start bringing home friends from school there is even less. When they go off on their own it becomes an echoing barn. Buildings are too static and rigid to cope completely with anything as dynamic as a family, but the second house, if it makes full use of the possibilities of interplay between indoor and outdoor areas, and treats necessary structural enclosures with as much flexibility as possible, can at least come close.

The final problem to be met by the second house has to do with its transformation from "house" to "home." As a rule it is not anticipated when the house is built, and yet the transition can be supremely logical. The permanent home is generally built—or bought—to meet a difficult set of requirements. It has to be accessible to the place of work. It has to be in a certain kind of neighborhood. It has to be within reach of school, church, stores. In the great majority of U.S. cities the advantages of location stop right there. The second house, however, is located on the basis of an entirely different set of values, which are human rather than economic or social. Beauty of surroundings, lack of congestion, freedom from traffic and other disturbances are among the criteria.

At retirement age, those factors which made home what it was, where it was, have largely evaporated. The original requirements of accessibility, proximity, social compatibility are no longer operative. Is it surprising that the second house begins to look more like home? Why should it be? The second house is the place where from the beginning, free from the limitations of the workaday house, you can build in all the qualities that have to do with good living.

PLANNING

PLANNING WITH YOU

WHY PLAN?

Most American communities, large and small, have grown without any plan. That was not so bad until they got too crowded. To make matters worse, along came the automobile. Now it is so difficult to get around that you have to park your car half a mile from the store where you want to shop.

Another thing which this crowding has done is so to inflate the cost of desirable land, both commercial and residential, that it too must be overcrowded. Look at the tangle Main Street is always in. No matter where you live, the chances are you have not enough ground to really enjoy your house, have a nice garden and a place to sit out with a little decent privacy. If you live in a large city, probably you have no place to sit out at all except in a distant, public park. And it's much worse, of course, for your children. Where do they play—in the street? And how many streets must they cross to get to and from school? Bad business, isn't it?

It is really bad business in another way. More and more families are finding living under such conditions too much to put up with. So they move out of town into the country. Here they find life more as they like it and sometimes less costly, but they give up many conveniences and social opportunities. Every family that moves out of town takes its taxes with it, so the town not only loses the people but their needed financial support. And that is definitely bad business.

Most, and probably all of these troubles could have been avoided had we been smart enough years ago to plan properly for our needs when the big shift to city and town came. Because we were not, we are paying heavily now for our lack of foresight. Must we go on this way forever, or is there still time to do something about it?

The time has come for us to get smart about our cities and towns.

REPLANNING TO SERVE CHANGED NEEDS

City planning is nothing new. Centuries ago, cities were planned and built. Their remains can be found in Egypt, France, Iran, China. Specialists still study these ancient communities, not to copy them, but because their patterns so faithfully reflected the life of the time.

Take one example—the picturesque fortress towns of the Middle Ages. Everyone who has read about King Arthur's Court remembers the

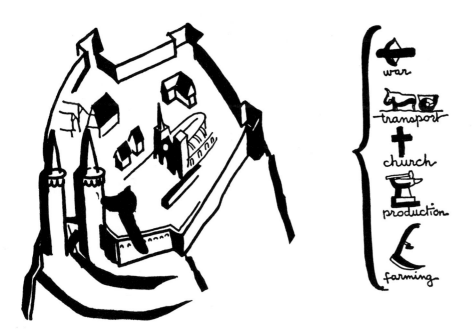

pictures of towers and battlements perched on rocky crags. But those who built them were not interested in being picturesque. The medieval town was one of the finest schemes for living and defense ever developed. Its hilltop location was inconvenient, but safer. Its walls were armor against catapults and battering rams. The houses inside were put close together because this meant that less wall had to be built. When artillery was invented the walls lost their usefulness and the cities grew beyond them.

Now let's skip a few centuries and look at our own country. Our colonial villages were not arranged like medieval towns, yet they too suited the needs of the people who lived and worked in them. Because many of the early settlers were refugees from religious persecution, the church was their first thought. Life was hard and building was a slow process, and so the church quickly became more than a religious edifice—it also housed the town meetings, the nucleus of our democratic form of government. Near the church the houses were clustered, partly for protection, but chiefly because people in a new and empty land wanted to live close to each other. It made trading, handicraft manufacture and social intercourse easier. The Common around which the shops, houses, church and school were grouped was a social center, a parade ground, a grazing field, and it gave light and air—breathing space—to the community.

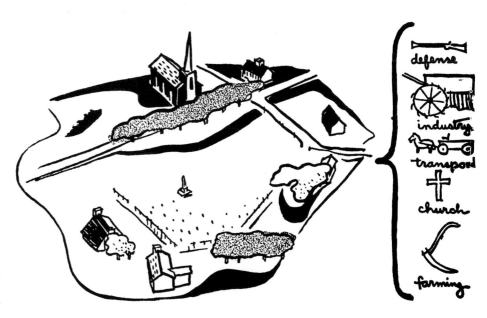

You can still see another early form of the American city in small midwestern communities where the highway runs right through the center of town and is flanked for a few blocks by stores, a public building or two, and houses. This practice of building on the highway was all right when travel was by coach. As cities grew and automobiles began to appear, it became a source

houses and
business mixed

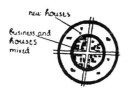

new houses

business and
houses
mixed

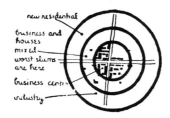

new residential

business and
houses
mixed
worst slums
are here

business center

industry

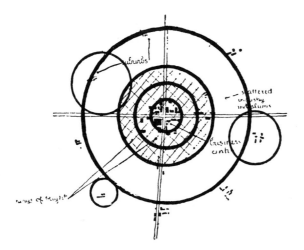

suburbs

scattered
industry
and slums

business
unit

ring of blight

of great congestion. The up-to-date city builds by-pass roads so that through-traffic goes around the town and does not add further tangles to already crowded local streets. This is just one way in which the 19th century pattern of the American town is gradually changing to conform to new ways of living.

WE NEED A "BACK TO TOWN" MOVEMENT

The diagrams you see here show what happened to the American City as it grew from a tiny settlement on two sides of a dirt road to a community of 10,000 100,000 and 1,000,000. It grew by adding rings, just as a tree does. At first, shops and houses were so few they formed one solid little core. Then, as the business district grew, houses were forced farther out. As the business and then industrial centers expanded, the old residential neighborhoods began to decay, often becoming slums, and those who could afford to, again moved—still farther from the center. When rapid transit came in, this movement became a stampede and the ring of worn out buildings around the solid core of valuable business property grew larger and more and more decrepit.

It would be hard to find any town whose plan looks exactly like these diagrams. Sometimes there would be a body of water to close one side. Sometimes it would be a hill. But whatever shape the town took as it grew, it showed the same characteristics.

Today, except for war centers, most cities have practically stopped growing. Existing streets and sewers often are more than adequate to serve present and future needs. Most of our towns must turn in toward the center again. There is room, if the blighted sections can be torn down

158

and rebuilt, for all the things a modern city needs—decent housing, parks, schools with land around them, and other amenities. Rebuilding *inside* our towns can give them new life. Dropping property values can be stabilized. Slums can be eliminated. City costs can be reduced.

WHY CITIES DECAY

One reason our cities and towns decay is because people build the wrong thing in the wrong place. Most of these people are just as good citizens as the rest of us. They are simply trying to make money by building something on a piece of ground which they own. Unfortunately, one mistake can start a neighborhood downhill. For example, as new residential districts developed in towns, shops and filling stations grew up with them. People nearest the shops moved away.

Other things cause decay too. Someone puts up a new, large office building where it is not needed. Tenants move out of older but still good buildings, leaving them vacant. A few people profit temporarily through these expansions, but in the end everybody loses. Our cities and towns have decayed so badly that many of them are bankrupt or soon may be.

This process is terribly wasteful. It destroys property values. It breeds slums. Blight had gotten in its deadly work on sections of London long before the blitz came.

These conditions have long been recognized and some effort has been made to control them. Many communities have long had Planning Boards and almost all have zoning regulations and other legal restrictions. All of these efforts have been right in principle and have prevented a bad situation from getting worse. They have fallen short because they have told people what they cannot build, but have done little to encourage the right kind of development.

HOW CAN WE FIX DECAY?

The way a dentist does—by cleaning out the infected area and guarding it against further trouble. Our cities show many examples: Chicago has filled in its lakefront and created a handsome, accessible residential neighborhood and splendid waterfront parks. New York has taken many tax-delinquent properties and turned them into playgrounds. San Francisco has turned an old exposition grounds into a fine park. Hartford, Connecticut, has rejuvenated decayed residential districts with insurance company office buildings set in their own beautifully landscaped parks.

Many attempts have been made by our cities to eliminate blight, but they are small and scattered.

159

A planless program is no solution; it merely creates a new set of problems. Where do we tear down and where do we build? Where do we put the parks and schools and new residential areas? Tearing down and building up, in other words, must be part of an overall plan. And that plan must not only correct past mistakes, but prevent future ones.

WHAT IS WRONG WITH PLANNING?
1. *Does it mean regimentation?*

No. It means coordination, which is quite different—for this means cooperation in a completely democratic manner to serve the best interests of all the citizens. Planning provides a framework, not a set of immutable decrees. Democratic planning gives plenty of room to the individual.

2. *Is it expensive?*

Compare its cost with the cost of not planning. Billions of dollars worth of real values have been destroyed by the process of decay which, as we have seen, occurs in all of our cities, large and small. The choice is clear. Without planning, any community is bound to lose out. With sound planning, any community can better itself.

3. *Is it visionary and impractical?*

No. Every successful business man plans. When businesses expand to become great corporations, they have entire departments devoted to nothing but planning. The larger the business, the greater the necessity for planning. And planning even a small community is big and important business. All planning means, after all, is figuring out the best way to get the best results with the smallest expenditure of effort and money.

WHAT THE MODERN CITY NEEDS
A great many things our parents never dreamed of. It needs roads—not the tangle of traffic jams and stop lights it has now, but a network designed for free, fast-moving traffic. It will need proper provision for air transport—private and commercial planes and helicopters.

It needs protected neighborhoods where people can buy and build with an assurance that their investments will not go sour. It needs neighborhoods which are more nearly self-contained, where the shops and other sub-centers of the community can be grouped in a convenient and attractive manner.

The city needs a stable and convenient business center with plenty of parking space. It needs good schools full of light and air with adequate playgrounds around them.

The modern city must have breathing spaces, just as the colonial village did. These are parks, playgrounds, open squares, plazas—again free from the hazards and noise of automobile traffic.

It needs light and air for every dwelling, every office building. This does not mean more space—it means using the space we have more intelligently.

Above all, it needs order and beauty—for this is something all people react to, and their lives and thinking are better for it.

These are some of the things the planners say the city needs. Most citizens would agree. Many say that these are fine objectives for any community but impossible of realization.

As it happens, they are being realized. Many cities already have the beginnings of a network of express highways. Separation of pedestrian and automobile traffic is something that has been used in parts of many American cities. Some have at least a start on airports. There are restricted neighborhoods where the types of houses and sizes of lots protect the inhabitants. There are good schools, beautifully designed, amply provided with the necessary ground space around them. There are splendid parks and recreation areas in the towns from one end of the country to the other.

Certain sections of certain towns are handsome to look at and agreeable to live in. There are cities with fine community centers, superb municipal swimming pools, golf courses, tennis courts and other facilities for the health, instruction or relaxation of adults as well as children. But they are never all in one city. If one American city had all of these elements, it would look to any of us like a dream of the world in the future. But it would not be a dream, for it is already here piecemeal.

CLOSE-UPS
Let's look at some of these details more closely.
1. *Slums*

The slum is the breeding place of crime, disease and death. It has no more place in an American community than a ghetto or a vice district.

Blight is malignant and unless stopped moves on to make slums of once good neighborhoods. Slums are not limited to our large cities. Slums are everywhere. Their removal and replacement with proper housing must be the No. 1 move in any plan to rehabilitate our cities and towns.

2. *Traffic*

We must set up brand new traffic standards in completely up-to-date terms. For example, the standard might be that in a town of 50,000, no part of the town should be more than five minutes from any other part by automobile. Think what this would mean to factory workers and business people. Of course, this means non-stop roads through the town.

But we know how to build non-stop roads. The initial cost on such a network might be fairly high, but it does no have to be built all at once. If a plan exists, the work can proceed gradually, but according to an orderly plan.

3. *Shopping*

Downtown merchants are complaining because their patrons are leaving them for the new neighborhood centers. Some shrewd storekeepers have capitalized on the virtual impossibility of downtown parking by building modern stores on the outskirts with ample parking space for all patrons. Unless the downtown stores cooperate on a plan for convenient shopping, they are certain to see their business decline.

4. *Parking*

Sooner or later, it should be required that any individual putting up a building to which people come in cars must provide the space for parking these cars—off the street. Loading by truck must be off the street. In large buildings such as department stores, theaters, hotels, etc., patrons should arrive and get out of their cars—off the streets. The new Statler Hotel in Washington, for example, does exactly this. So does the Waldorf-Astoria in New York, which was built on some of the most expensive land in the world. And also in New York, in the Starret-Lehigh Warehouse, trucks and even trains are brought inside for loading and unloading.

5. *Recreation*

Facilities for recreation must include not only one big park—generally hard to reach from many neighborhoods—but facilities easily available to all the dwellings of the city. These include playgrounds for children and recreation areas for adults.

6. *Appearance*

America, the richest country in the world, has some of the ugliest cities. Our best looking communities are those in which each building considers its neighbors. Planning will give our skilled architects the chance to create fine looking buildings, fine looking streets and fine looking towns.

7. *Health*

The health of a city is intimately tied to its plan.

Slums are the most serious menace to community health. But any kind of overcrowding is bad, whether people live or work under congested conditions. Few communities, especially the larger ones, have enough light and air. This involves not only the space between buildings, but the design of the buildings themselves. Noise is another threat against health. Experts know how to reduce it. Smoke is unhealthy, and can be eliminated.

An unbelievable number of places lack decent water and decent sewage disposal. Does it surprise and shock you to know that 49.2 per cent of all the houses in the U. S. are badly in need of repair and that an even higher percentage have no inside toilet?

Scarcely any community has enough hospitals and clinics for properly caring for its sick and injured.

But the real answer to community health lies not in curing sickness but in preventing it. Make it easy for people to live healthier lives—open up the city to sun and good air, provide recreational facilities for adults as well as children, make streets and roads safe against accidents and outlaw overcrowding.

When any city has done particularly fine civic planning, all of the inhabitants are quite aware of it and proud of the results. People know good things when they see them. But no one has seen a city really designed for living properly in the 20th century.

What would such a town be like?

This town, let us say, is a community of 75,000 people, located anywhere. Approaching our imaginary city on an express parkway, we notice that the highway no longer goes through the town but skirts by it. It is banked by trees instead of billboards, dilapidated hot dog stands

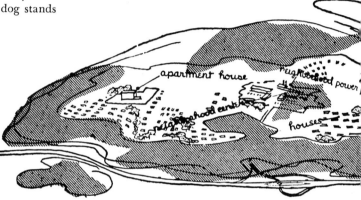

and the usual junk that clutters up most of our roads.

From the parkway there is a turnoff which leads directly, without the interruption of cross traffic, into landscaped parking spaces which surround the business center.

Leaving our car, we proceed to a covered sidewalk which leads directly into Main Street. Unlike other Main Streets, there are no cars on it. In place of the old pavement and trolley tracks there are long stretches of lawn, paved walks, benches, fountains, flowerbeds and trees. Our new Main Street is for pedestrians only.

This kind of a Main Street could be created right in your own town. To get it, it would not be necessary to tear down all of the existing buildings, or even many of them. By eliminating dilapidated structures that have outlived their usefulness, clearing out the ring of commercial blight which surrounds the business district of most towns and taking advantage of existing open spaces, plenty of land can be found for the

parks and parking spaces needed. And all this could be done gradually, as conditions permit.

None of the buildings is particularly large or high, nor are they all alike. But the riot of signs is gone, and the individually designed shops are planned so that each harmonizes with the other. All Main Street shops are double-faced, one side facing the street itself, the other facing the parking areas. Along each row of shops are arcades which keep the sun off the show windows and provide shelter for shoppers and office workers. Here and there is an outdoor cafe and restaurant. What were once side streets have become small squares where people can move about quietly and with complete comfort.

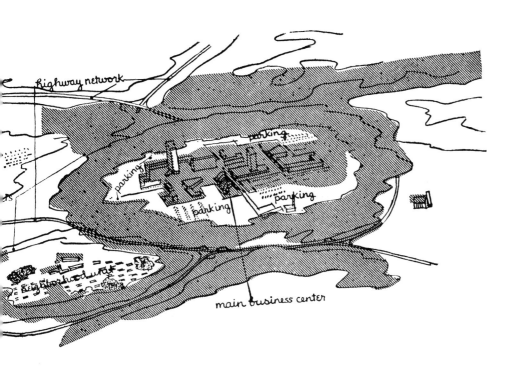

CITIES FOR CIVILIZED AMERICANS

You do not have to be an expert to know the difference between a beautiful city and an ugly one. Americans have gone abroad by the millions and have marveled at the boulevards of Paris and the splendid parks inside the city, at the wonderful squares of Rome with their fountains and surrounding fine buildings. Here, tourists make pilgrimages every year to rebuilt Williamsburg and the villages of New England. Of course, these towns are not planned for today, but their beauty and quiet order pleases everyone.

The best place to see the business section of our imaginary town would be from the top of its tallest office building, which has perhaps 10

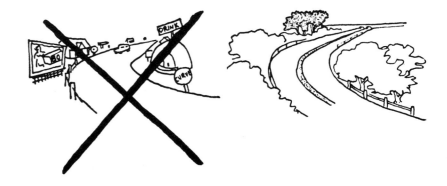

or 12 stories. From the roof terrace we can see down to Main Street and side streets, where pedestrians stroll unworried by automobiles. We can see that no building shuts out the light or air of its neighbors, and we can see the large parking areas, from which it is easy to get to the shops, theaters and offices. Around the parking areas is a belt of lawn and trees and beyond this is the road which circles the entire center. This small greenbelt is a recreation area. Here businessmen and workers can meet their families and friends, relax, chat and dine.

Outside the ring of commercial and recreational activity are the homes, which again are surrounded by their own little greenbelts with the playgrounds, schools and other community facilities. Streets within these residential areas are for local traffic only, and they are supplemented by pedestrian walkways.

Where these walks meet one of the streets they either go over or under. There are no crossings at grade level. A child could safely be left to play as he pleases within one of these neighborhoods.

The neighborhood shopping center is a miniature of Main Street. It too has its surrounding parking space. The shops cluster around a small plaza. Here we might also find the church, the fire station, high school, community building and other services.

In these neighborhoods we find both apartment houses and single family houses, but they do not clash with each other for the town building regulations require that there must be a minimum amount of ground space for each family. Consequently, if someone wishes to put up an apartment house for 50 families, he must provide equivalent space for these 50 families, which means that all apartments are set in miniature parks which enhance rather than detract from the fine character of the neighborhood.

Such a park apartment has ground space for outdoor activities, and all tenants are assured permanent protection against encroachment on their view and sunlight. The owner of such a building is not penalized by the tax board for providing these amenities, for the community understands their desirability. Obviously both apartments and individual houses are excellent investments, for as the years go by, values remain stable. And occupancy of such neighborhoods remain relatively stable; there is no decay to

drive people out. The variety of dwelling accommodations provide for the requirements of families young and old, large or small.

Each neighborhood has a certain number of people in it. There might be 2,000 or perhaps as many as 5,000. But once a neighborhood is filled to the edges of its own small park belt, no more building can be done until houses or shops within it are torn down to be replaced. If the population expands, the neighborhoods do not expand, but their number increases.

Our imaginary city is no fancy residential suburb, but a complete community in which the people work as well as live. The factories are located away from the houses, but not very far away. Many of them can be reached on foot and others by bus. Because the factories have installed smoke-eliminating devices (which have been on the market for years) their surroundings are clean. They too have trees and lawns around them.

This is a pretty picture, isn't it? But it is not a visionary one. All of these elements already exist in fragmentary form. They need only be assembled to form complete, modern gracious and beautiful communities if there is a plan. Because only the plan can tell the wisest way to spend the money which has to be spent anyway.

MAIN STREET: NOW AND POSTWAR

Most of us are so accustomed to the cities we live in that it rarely occurs to us to look at them in a critical or constructive way. We know that they are far from ideal in many respects. Slums are a part of practically every city and town; there is almost never room to park near shops or theaters; streets are too narrow in the business districts; and what little space there is has to be shared by trucks, cars and pedestrians. Even in residential sections, children are exposed to the dangers of automobile traffic. In the congested areas of larger towns, the buildings do not conform to any plan, but fight with each other for light, air, prominence and tenants.

Competition for attention has turned Main Street into the ugliest thoroughfare in the world, with garish fronts next to over-age derelicts, with signs of all sizes and shapes creating a picture more discordant than the most raucous and cheap of amusement parks.

If by chance there were a town near your city or mine, newly built, and properly designed for the people who must live and work in it, we would soon become acutely conscious of the ugliness and inefficiency of the average city. But there isn't. All U. S. Main Streets suffer from the same disease, and we naturally tend to think of the bad planning of our business districts as something quite normal.

It is a curious fact that most business districts in small or large cities, congested as they are, really have plenty of room. Even on Main Street itself there are generally vacant shops and offices, buildings which have been only partly occupied

Yesterday . . . a show place

for years. Around the corner, we find more old firetraps, which should have been torn down years ago. In some cases, they have been torn down and the land used for automobile parking, in order to pay the taxes. Perhaps the most interesting single fact is that these obsolete buildings and parking lots are always found in the same place. They are almost invariably spotted in a ring which forms the fringe of the business district. There is a good reason for this.

All U. S. cities began as small towns in which the business and municipal center consisted merely of a handful of buildings along a street. Within easy walking distance of this center, the houses were built. As the city expanded its production and trade, the center grew, and soon the best of the residential districts were engulfed by shops, filling stations and light industries. Naturally, the people who had built their homes in pleasant open fields were not too happy about the turn of events, and those who could, moved farther out.

The retreat from the center took on tremendous proportions with the coming of the automobile; and real estate speculators, who had had visions of an indefinitely expanding business area with steadily rising values, awoke one day to find that stores and theaters in outlying districts were competing vigorously with merchants in the center. The "expanding" center began to contract. And the first spots of blight began to appear on the fringes. The three sketches tell the old, story. What to do about it is the biggest problem our cities will have to face after the war.

Today . . . a "white elephant"

Tomorrow . . . a rooming house

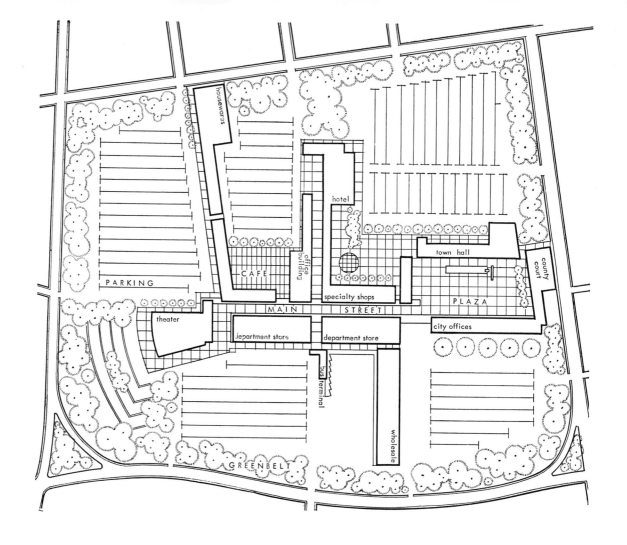

housewares

hotel

office
building

CAFE

PARKING

theater

town hall

county
court

specialty shops

PLAZA

MAIN STREET

city offices

department store

department store

bus terminal

wholesale

GREENBELT

Decay, in nature is not a disaster. It is part of an organic process of change. Many of our most valuable mineral resources are the result of decay. Any gardener making a compost pile knows that the decayed vegetable matter will enrich his soil. So with our cities. Blight occurs in cities at almost the exact places where building should be cleared out anyway to make room for sun, air, and automobiles. The drawing at the top of this page is not a planner's dream as much as the projection of a trend. It was made from the plan of an Eastern city with a population around 50,000.

In the new plan, the most congested blocks right in the heart of the city were changed to a park-like promenade for shoppers, by simply closing them to traffic and planting grass in the streets! And by placing new buildings so that they block Main Street at each end of this section, traffic would be diverted around the outside of this area over existing streets that skirt the new parking lots.

Many large parking areas were placed where such lots already exist. A number of the old buildings were left, others were remodeled, some are new. The most remarkable feature is Main Street itself, where instead of honking cars and clanking trolleys there are now lawns, fountains, trees, benches and playgrounds for children. Fantastic? Not to the hard-boiled planner who sees many straws in the wind which point to this as a logical solution to many of the troubles cities are having. Let us look at the plan more carefully. In the first place, note that a car can be parked within a very short distance of any building. This is something that both shoppers and downtown merchants want badly. In the second place, note that there is no crossing of pedestrian and automobile traffic. Aside from its convenience, such an arrangement saves money. It eliminates stop lights and traffic police; it saves gas—a lot of it—for stop and go driving is wasteful, and it prevents accidents. The costs of shipping by truck are lowered, since time is saved. And there is a great saving of general wear and tear on the dispositions of drivers and pedestrians alike. So this one becomes a happier city to live in.

The great economic advantage of this postwar Main Street, however, lies in the fact that it stabilizes values which are reflected in tax returns. Shops and offices so easily reached by car and bus are profitable, and they may be protected from future depreciation by municipal controls over building. A small greenbelt surrounds the business center, not slums, and this too helps stabilize existing values, as it sets a limit to both over-expansion and encroachment.

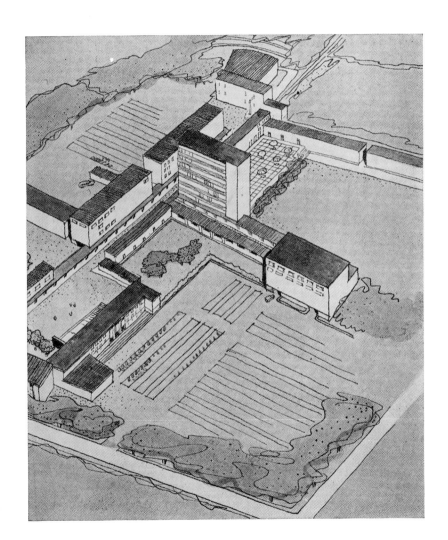

At this point, we look at our town a little more closely, not from the air any more, but from the streets themselves, as the inhabitants might see it. Our first close-up shows a view of Main Street, looking toward the high wall of the new theater. Gone are the street car tracks and the clattering trolleys—the noisy buses and honking cars have disappeared. In their place is a tree-lined promenade, and pedestrians can walk in comfort and safety along the full width of the street. Occasionally there are spots of shrubbery and flowers in the paved areas, while lawns and flowered borders are freely disposed along the length of the street. Sidewalk cafes could easily become a part of this quieter, more pleasant Main Street; there would be plenty of room for tables out of doors if the community wanted this gay arrangement.

Making over Main Street does not mean tearing down the center of town and starting from scratch. In the sketch, for example, we see the department store's 50-year old building facing a low shop and office building of more recent vintage. The only new building here is the theater, which blocks the street and provides an end to the vista. The theater is a little unusual in its placing, for the stage end rather than the front faces the street. There would be good

reason for this, as most of the people who use it will come not from Main Street, but from the parking lot which adjoins the building.

At the other end of Main Street is the Municipal Plaza, once an open square criss-crossed by tracks and overhead trolley wires. Now it is a quiet square surrounded by public buildings, the most impressive of which is the new Town Hall with a long pool in front of it. Pools, like smooth grass areas, are among the finest ornaments of a city, and there is no reason why the new Main Street should be without one. At the end of the pool is a fountain, adding movement and pleasant sound to the quiet picture. Behind

the fountain is a massive monument, a sheer wall of smooth dark granite. Carved on it is the plan of the business section, a very reasonable thing to do, for the pride of the citizens in their achievement is very real and completely justified. Other buildings around the Municipal Plaza, which do not appear in the sketch are the old County Courthouse, city offices and the regional headquarters of the REA—the rural electrical cooperative—which has become so large a part of the community life of America's outlying cities and towns.

One of the most striking features of the new Main Street is the use of arcades. These shelters have much to commend them. They permit comfortable movement in bad weather. They encourage "window shopping" even in the rain. They keep the sun off show windows filled with perishable merchandise. And if anyone wants to walk in the sun, he can always go out into the middle of the former street. Such arcades would be relatively inexpensive, for they could be prefabricated in standard sections, making excellent use of the beautiful, lightweight, rust-proof metals which will be available in abundance after the war. The view on the opposite page was not taken on Main Street, but on the narrower side street devoted to the smaller specialty shops. The metal shelters, however, are identical with those on Main Street.

Here, as in the other views of the business section, we see old and new buildings. The tall structure whose narrow end is on Main Street, is a new building, ten or eleven stories in height, with a roofed-over terrace occupying part of the top floor. Many of the shops are new only in the sense that they now have arcades; others have had their fronts remodeled. Perhaps the most interesting feature of this street is the enclosed playground for small children, one of several built and maintained by the local merchants. These very desirable play areas are also definitely worth while from a business viewpoint, for a harassed mother with several children in tow is not a good shopper.

This is the end of our tour. Perhaps some of us, in the years after the war, will be able to make a real tour of the same kind, in a real town. Planting grass on Main Street, of course, does not solve all a city's problems. Some may ask, "If you freeze Main Street in this fashion, what can be done to handle increased business as the town grows? To this there are several answers. One is that our period of frantic city growth is over, as far as the country as a whole is concerned. Where growth seems certain, provision can be made for enlarging the center, if the total area is kept large enough to start with. And a business center can expand vertically as well as horizontally.

Perhaps the best answer is that much business expansion in the future will be in the residential neighborhoods, for no matter how good **Main** Street is, the best place for the grocer, druggist,

cleaner, movie theater, and so on, is as close as possible to the homes which have to be served.

A stabilization of Main Street, consequently, if accompanied by wisely controlled neighborhood shopping centers, might well be the soundest solution for all concerned. Sooner or later, the basic soundness of such a scheme will make itself widely felt, for the automobile—despite gas rationing and rubber shortages—is here to stay. Our cities have not been designed for the car. And since one must change in favor of the other, it seems fairly safe to predict that it will be the city.

To transform the entire center of a city as described here may seem at first like no more

173

than a rosy dream, wonderful to think about but too costly to be attempted. Nothing could be farther from the truth, for this plan was worked out to produce the greatest benefits for the least money in virtually any city or town.

Few buildings would need to be torn down in addition to the most dilapidated firetraps that are already a burden on the community. In some cases only two new buildings would be needed— and one of these could be a theater that would serve as a business investment. Most of the new construction would consist of the arcades and modernized store fronts, so obvious an advantage to the merchants that there would be a strong business incentive for them to undertake it themselves once the plan as a whole is adopted.

The promenades and landscaped parking areas, in addition to ornamenting the community, would probably cost no more to maintain than the present inefficient streets. With the inevitable increase in values that would follow, every one concerned would benefit financially—the municipality, the public, the merchants and business men. It is not too soon to start thinking and planning now for such a transformation of your city's shopping center once the war is won. By obtaining a plan of your own city as it is now, you and your neighbors and friends could begin discussing the possibilities of a project like this, and become perhaps the moving force behind such a civic improvement.

INTERIORS

THE DEAD-END ROOM

*A first exploration — for me — of the
connections between
psychology and house planning.*

An architect with a medium-size practice in a medium-size New England town, has so dealt with his clients that they still speak to him after they move into the houses he designs for them. This happy state of affairs, having existed for many years, not only provides a satisfying trickle of new clients, but also offers continuous opportunity for discovering what happens to his houses after families have been living in them. Recently, in the course of a dinner party at the house of a particularly well-pleased pair, this architect made a discovery which differed from previous observations in that it startled him into reconsidering his fundamental ideas about home planning. The discovery resulted from a series of observations of no apparent consequence:

The house in question is rectangular in plan, two stories high, conventional in exterior and interior appearance. Every city and town in the United States has dozens or hundreds pretty much like it. In the center of the house is the front door and stair hall, with a large living room on the left and a gun room beyond. The gun room is nothing more than a sitting room with a rack of guns in it. The living room is a pleasant, open space with plenty of daylight, equipped with a large plant-filled bay window at one end and a row of double-hung windows at the other. Seating is comfortable, with three sofas within range of a generous fireplace. A dining alcove opens off one side of the living room. So much for the setting.

On the evening of the dinner party, the architect arrived about fifteen minutes early in order to look around and, having disposed of his coat and hat, went into the living room. Tacitly allowing for the fact that a room just before a party offers a better-than-usual appearance, the architect viewed his handiwork with pride, and he contemplated with satisfaction the many signs of his client's good taste in furnishing. If he had the room to do over, he reflected, he couldn't do better. Wandering on, he entered the gun room, picked up a magazine, sat down and idly leafed through it and was presently given a drink by his host. A few minutes later, when the other dinner guests arrived, they, too, wandered into the gun room, sat down and were given their drinks. At one point in the general hum of conversation the architect picked up one thread: someone was commenting on the quiet charm of the gun room and again he felt a prideful stirring. It was a good room — simple paneled wood walls, just enough dark blue-green paint, a well-designed fireplace, unobtrusively expensive furniture. "A really successful room," he thought,

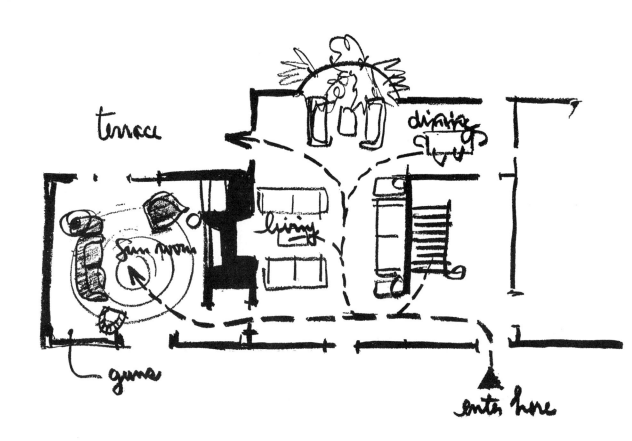

terrace

dining

living

sun room

guns

enter here

178

"considering that it is barely fourteen feet square." "Fourteen feet square" suddenly recalled conversations with clients when the house was still on paper. A small room was what they had wanted, he remembered. They were going to use it as a retreat in the dark winter evenings. There were never going to be more than four people in it at one time, and yet there were eleven here right now! Why were they all in here? Why were people perched on chair arms and the coffee table instead of sitting comfortably in the living room?

After dinner the living room *was* put to use. Each guest found a place to sit; each chair had a table of some kind within easy reach; plenty of space for ash trays and coffee cups. The question of living room versus gun room began to fade out of the architect's mind. There was nothing strange about it; it was obvious that people on arriving had gone to the room where they had seen others. As simple as that.

With the coffee cups cleared away, the guests stirred and sat back to talk when, almost imperceptibly, a movement began. The host and two friends went into the gun room and did not return for a while. A girl got up to retrieve a compact she had tucked into her husband's coat pocket. She did not return either. Soon, without any summons, everybody was again in the gun room, and they were still there at midnight, when someone announced it was time to be going home. The living room, designed expressly for gatherings like this, had been used for about thirty-five minutes out of the three hours.

Among those whose business it is to concern themselves with problems of home planning, a great deal of consideration has been given to the relation between the use of space and its cost. Only recently has this become important. Too often, in house-building today, space is what is left after one has paid for automatic furnaces, laundries, bathroom fixtures, and streamlined kitchens, and the efficient use of space is being scrutinized more and more intently. The bedroom, for instance, is occupied for about eight out of twenty-four hours. Architects have been aware of this and many have recommended, in consequence, that the sleeping area be reduced to minimum size. The same with the kitchen, and the dining room, which is used least of all, has frequently been eliminated entirely. This has been extended to relatively costly homes — the one just described is a typical example. In place of the dining room, various kinds of alcoves have been developed as extensions of living space in addition to taking care of meals. The open plan, characteristic of so many modern houses, is in part the result of merging rooms to produce larger over-all living space. Yet in the case of the gun room versus the living room it seemed a trend was reversing itself: the large, relatively open room was consistently passed up in favor of a small, totally enclosed room, not really adequate for the number of people who chose to occupy it. The whole thing made no sense, and the architect who watched it happen was bothered. Many discoveries can be traced to a minor irritation.

To see what happened and why, one must again look at the plan of the two rooms. One is large, one is small. Both are admittedly pleasant rooms, but the small room is used more often. Why? The plan show one significant difference between the two rooms, aside from their relative size. The gun room is a *dead-end room* — there is only one way in or out. There is a second difference: the living room does not have a single corner where people can sit. One corner is taken by the hall entrance, one by the dining alcove, and the other two by the doors to gun room and terrace. The gun room, on the other hand, has three solid corners. Both of these differences have a lot to do with what we are looking for, and there is a third, which can be made visible by a traffic pattern. Note that traffic into the gun room moves into a kind of pool in the center and is stopped. In the living room, on the other hand, there is actually a corridor area at one end, a path to the terrace door and another to the dining alcove. Now this matter of traffic may seem pretty unimportant where a family of four is involved, and an occasional gathering of a dozen to twenty people. Obviously there is no traffic problem in the ordinary sense, since houses do not have steady streams of people pouring from one entrance to another. Nevertheless, in the difference between closed corners and open ones, in the contrast between static and fluid circulation patterns, possibly in the essential nature of the dead-end room, must lie the answers we are looking for, because there is nowhere else we can look. We also know that the episode described at the outset is no isolated experience: most people have encountered the same thing at some time. Another clue lies in the behavior of the guests, which was not deliberate or purposeful, but instinctive. In other words, whatever the impulse that moved them from the living room into the gun room, it was not one that was very strongly felt. But it moved them.

When children play, their activities fall into a set of patterns which have a curiously close relationship with the behavior of the dinner guests. Children retreat to attics, build forts in backyard jungles, take to the hay loft or, in the winter, to snow houses. The cul-de-sac — or dead-end room — has a fascination that is unique. And the smaller the enclosure, the better they seem to like it. When grownups appear on the scene, they watch these goings on with indulgent amusement, possibly with a bit of nostalgia too, little realizing that they did the same thing, when they squeezed into the gun room at the X's dinner last night. At least one school of psychologists makes a good deal of the return to the womb theory, and there may be some such urge (hard to prove or disprove) that is operating. Or it may not. Architects who like to do one-story houses are often restrained by the wives of their clients because they "don't like ground-floor bedrooms." Fear of burglars is most frequently advanced as the reason, but burglars can climb stairs just like everybody else. The feeling, nevertheless, is strongly and widely held. At this point another explanation can be advanced: man's eyes, for all their advantages, are so set in the front of his head that he is blind to at least half of the circle which surrounds him. This arrangement leaves him peculiarly vulnerable to attack from the rear, and in millenniums gone by it must have exposed him to risk every time he ventured from shelter. A wall at the back, considered in this light, is not merely something solid to lean against, but a very real protection. It seems quite possible that a solid corner, now considered a comfortable place to relax, might once have been nothing less than an aid to survival. In other words, the force that moved the dinner guests from the spacious living room into the huddled group in the gun room might be a dim racial memory that goes back tens of thousands of years to a time when a man was as likely to be the meal at a dinner party as a guest.

In the history of house design there are many examples to support the notion that surprisingly often modern man acts like a defenseless animal in search of protective shelter. The basement play room or rumpus room has been derided time and again by the sophisticated, but its popularity continues. One might say that this kind of space is purely makeshift, that it merely represents use of cellar space no longer needed for coal storage. But one might also say that people seem to get a special pleasure out of a room surrounded on two or three sides by solid earth. The basement playroom, incidentally, is usually a dead-end room. Considering the popularity of the basement, and the objections to the ground floor, one suspects that the universally popular house would have basement rooms, no first floor, and an attic.

This is not quite as ridiculous as it sounds. An entire school of modern architects has taken at least half of this idea to create the so-called house on stilts. Le Corbusier, who first developed it, is a Swiss. The pre-historic inhabitants of his native Switzerland also lived in such houses; they were built on the edges of lakes and offered good protection against marauding animals.

Any attempt to create a theory of house design on the basis of such vague feelings could quickly end in absurdity. It seems obvious, however, that any house in which these feelings are totally ignored will not be popular. We will do well to remember that the most common name for the study, library, gun room or what have you is still *den,* which is in itself revealing.

Complaints leveled against the first modern house usually resolved themselves into one sentence: "Who wants to live in a goldfish bowl?" Now this is interesting, because goldfish don't mind living in goldfish bowls. The reason is to be found in their eyes, which are so constructed that they cover a full 360°. There is no blind spot around a fish, no need for a protecting wall in a region where the eye cannot reach. The first modern houses offered precious little protection from the unseen observer. The idea of being watched while one is unaware of observation, always makes people uneasy. In several recent houses, walls have been built *outside* the house to provide just this protection from the gaze of passers-by.

Frank Lloyd Wright's approach to house design — a field in which he is unsurpassed — offers many illustrations for the popularity of the dead-end room. In Taliesin, Wright's home in Wisconsin, there are two rooms, both large, which may be classed as living rooms. The bigger of the two is enormous by present-day living standards, and yet it is never deserted in favor of the

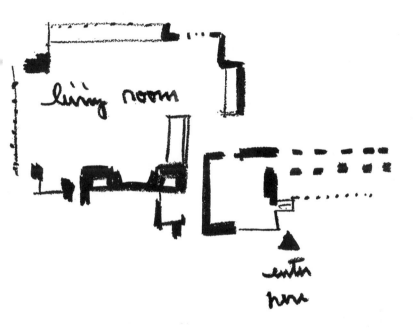

Living room of Frank Lloyd Wright's Taliesin III, Spring Green, Wisconsin, 1925

smaller. As one examines this larger interior, which is generously equipped with windows, the theory we have been developing seems to break down, but further study of the plan indicates the contrary. It also demonstrates that *the size of the room is not one of the psychological factors determining its comfort.* The gun room, you recall, had three solid corners, which had a lot to do with producing its agreeable atmosphere. Wright's big room has many more than three. Next to the fireplace, for example, there is a couch set with its back to the entrance. Normally this placing would not be well liked, but here the couch is backed up by a large bookcase wall which reaches to eye level. Anyone sitting here, has therefore, a solid corner with one wall of wood and another of stone. This is not a corner *of* the room, but a corner *in* the room; the effect is the same. The plan shows too that the room itself is not a simple rectangle, but a complex and very subtly divided interior which functions as a series of half-enclosed seating areas. In spite of the large number of windows, none of them are set where anyone can look in, which gives the same feeling of protected enclosure as a solid wall. Just as the whole room is a dead end in relation to the entire plan, the areas inside it are smaller expressions of the same planning concept.

In any number of Wright's houses the corner is handled again and again with great emphasis on the principle of the cul-de-sac. Even in relatively small houses there is usually at least one alcove somewhere which satisfies admirably the desire for a feeling of protective enclosure. Wright's clients have been conspicuous for their enthusiasm about their houses, and without discounting the many other important factors which contribute to their feeling, I am convinced that one reason is that Wright always finds a way to put walls at their backs.

Whether one prefers the racial memory theory or the back-to-the-womb idea as an explanation of the general preference for the dead-end plan, the net result is the same; either provides an instrument of immediate and practical value to the architect. Understanding the general psychological principle, we can now begin the job of evaluating an entirely new factor in home design. In the past the psychological need for enclosure was pretty much taken care of by the technical limits set on buildings. Rooms had to be small and totally enclosed to conserve heat; windows were small for the same reason. The delightful fireplace alcoves in Colonial living rooms and kitchens helped keep people warm. Low ceilings also produced a feeling of snugness. In houses today these limitations have largely disappeared, and the danger is that indiscriminate open planning and a desire for economy and easy maintenance may destroy some of those qualities in living space that people prize most highly — though least consciously. It is not possible to fill a house with dead-end rooms, nor is there reason to enclose them all in the way we used to. In planning the house we already have many valuable yardsticks: we measure the steps from stove to sink; we check bedroom walls to see if the beds will fit; children's rooms are placed out of range of living room noises. To these and many others we can add a new one. It couldn't be simpler. All we have to do is keep in mind that people still remember, however dimly, those far-off days when a cave felt like a good place to live.

MODERN DECORATION

A cliché hunt, with the aid of a battered typewriter.

The plywood-and-rubber-plant school of design, one disgruntled reader of *Interiors* called it. I doubt if he coined the phrase, for the designation has been too obvious for too long. The who-wants-to-live-in-a-goldfish-bowl style was the way it looked to Irvin S. Cobb a couple of decades ago. But people aren't so afraid of glass walls any more. I read in the papers that each of the 10,000 identical houses (or is it 10,000,000?) in Levittown, Long Island, has its identical large picture window, which means that modern decoration is now in. This observation is fully confirmed by any issue of either of the thirty-five cent home magazines.

Times have changed—and rapidly. It was only about eight or nine years ago that an architect of my acquaintance bought a station wagon because he had designed a number of modern houses he wanted published. His clients owned no modern furniture or accessories, so to get the interior shots he had to have, he loaded into the station wagon the photographer, his cameras and lights, a lrage rubber plant (the plywood walls were already in the houses) a couple of Aalto stools and armchairs, a modern coffee table, and a few pieces of prehistoric-looking pottery. I found out about this drastic procedure in looking through the photographs of the houses. The taste in furniture, accessories and plants shown by his clients was remarkable in its uniformity. Then the story came out.

It seemed to me then that the directness with which this architect solved the problem of modern decoration (at least for photographic purposes) was very impressive. All you needed to get into one of the more advanced architectural publications was a station wagon, a discreet selection of furniture and other props, a good photographer, and a rubber plant sufficiently rugged to stand all the traveling.

In fairness to my friend, it might be added that he had little choice in the matter. As late as 1941 it was not the easiest thing in the world to find good modern furniture—and as for fabrics and the rest it was virtually impossible.

The ease with which these interior transformations were made still has a kind of horrible fascination for me. The disgruntled reader mentioned at the beginning—a decorator by profession, I gather—also shares this feeling. His letter reads in part:

". . . if the interiors you advocate become the rule, the vast majority of us will simply have

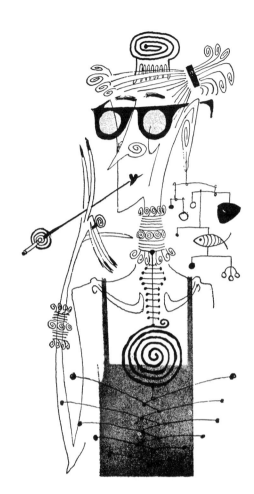

to close shop. Drapery work-rooms do not stay open making up a wisp of nylon net to hang at one end of a thirty-foot expanse of plate glass; very few people feel that they need a decorator to tell them to put a pair of Eames chairs beside a built-in sofa and a rubber plant in the corner . . ." I never thought the day would come when I would be in agreement with a decorator about anything, and the economics of decorating fall well outside the particular rut in which I move, but the fact of the matter is that I too have developed an acute dislike for modern decoration, a dislike tempered only by boredom. To make matters worse, it is unsettling to find oneself not only a critic, but one of the culprits as well. Just when this feeling began to manifest itself I do not recall, but there was a time, also before the war, when I became aware of one of the chief characteristics of modern decoration. There was in existence, in the late '30's, a small, lively architectural magazine started by a student group. I became mildly involved in its affairs for a brief spell and attended meetings of the editors in their various apartments. The curious thing about the apartments was that they were all, in essence, the same apartment. Each interior was chalk-white, each homemade couch was covered in monk's cloth, the radio was always an Ansley Dynaphone (the Ansley was the only radio-record player that came in an undecorated blond box). Invariably there was a Miro on burlap (or some reasonable approximation thereof) set with careful lack of symmetry over the fireplace, and the latest modern chair. The third encounter with the same apartment at different addresses gave one pause. Here was no style within whose limits individuals expressed themselves freely— this was a uniform. It was like the Calder jewelry worn by a certain kind of female to proclaim that she loves modern art. Or (this was what bothered me most of all) it was like the Georgian or French Provincial settings faked up by the decorators for the more prosperous suburbanites. If one of the real potentials of the modern movement was a new degree of freedom and flexibility, why were its most vocal exponents regimenting themselves with as much rigidity as the decorators, who could not so much as look at a fireplace without feeling compelled to flank it with two love seats, two matching lamps tables, two identical lamps and two undersized silver ash trays? Ten years ago thoughts of this nature were nothing less than rank heresy and they were quickly suppressed. As time went by and house jobs periodically turned up in our office we occasionally became irritated by the problems of the modern interior. We also battled with the decorators engaged by our clients to "do" the rooms. They were usually ladies who labored happily under the impression that modern was just a cute new variation on Empire or Biedermeier. And there was the intermittent struggle to find non-existent merchandise. At one point I ordered what seemed like an entire boatload of furniture from Finland, but friends grabbed it all before there was a chance to foist it on any clients like my friend with the station wagon. It was just as well, because the problem to be solved had precious little to do with this or that item of furniture, but at the time I didn't know this. As far as the interiors themselves were concerned I doubt if we produced or collaborated on a single one that ran the full gamut from A to B.

With the coming of the war and the enforced cessation of civilian building there was time to think, to meditate on past professional sins, and to look at books again. It was in the course of doing the last that it occurred to me that one might examine with profit what the masters of modern architecture had done about the interiors of their houses.

First of the projects to turn up for inspection was the famous Villa Savoye, built by Le Corbusier in a rural setting not too far outside of Paris. The house itself is a box set on stilts in the middle of a meadow—not a particularly good way to describe one of the most exciting architectural projects of our time. In terms of decoration, however, it seemed to say nothing at all. There were some metal chairs and tables, and some otherwise bare rooms. It was as if LeCorbusier had signed off with the completion of the shell of the building. LeCorbusier's own studio and apartment in Paris, in contrast, looked wonderful in a rather barnlike way, but there seemed to be no connection between what he had done and the problems that were bothering me.

Having missed the point on both these jobs, I pursued my investigations. There was the magnificent Tugendhat house of Mies van der Rohe, whose living room has four of Mies' Barcelona chairs handsomely arranged against an onyx wall. In this house the architect had clearly kept control of the job until the last dish had been installed on the last shelf, but as far as I could then see, the whole affair was more like a museum than a house. It had precious little to do with the habits or requirements of any family I had ever encountered. In the case of Wright, matters were not much better. His rooms were so designed that they seemed furnished before the furniture got in, and there was the feeling that almost anything would be an unwarranted intrusion. I gathered that Wright felt that way too, for his chairs, tables, and even beds only repeated the square, hexagonal, or circular patterns of the buildings themselves. Later on, when there came opportunities to question him about these matters, he showed no interest in furniture (in the sense of the isolated, decorative object) and cared nothing about functional problems in chair design because he considered sitting an unfunctional posture. He also disliked pictures, and had no use for them at all as wall decorations. All this was discouraging for one enmeshed in the inanities of modern decoration, and looking for guidance. It is now clear that the work of each of these men had something very definite to say about the contemporary interior, but a lot of water had to go over the dam before I could understand this. It is not possible to grasp the expression of a principle if you are concerned only with finding formulas to follow and tricks to copy.

What also seems incredible now is that not once during this period of search and questioning did it occur to me that it might be a good idea to formulate a working definition of what I meant by "modern decoration" and to try thereby to arrive at some notion of the purposes and processes involved. Instead the aimless search went back to the books—and back in time. Maybe there were clues in the quiet formality of the Federal period, in musty New England parlors, in the oval rooms of the late French Renaissance, in anything. None presented themselves. The decorators, of course, were lifting whole pieces of these rooms and their furnishings every day in the week, and inserting them into the dining rooms of Oklahoma City and the salons of Scarsdale, but the idiocy and dishonesty of this particular racket was so patent that there was no need to dwell upon it. The real answers, of course, were as firmly imbedded in the period work as in the valid modern examples—but to repeat, when you are looking for formulas you don't recognize principles. As usual it was the process of life itself that provided some of the

needed lessons. There was the beginning of a friendship with the sculptor Noguchi, and visits to his studio. A huge, square room with a skylight in the center, it sheltered both working and living space. The room was always littered with a tremendous quantity of stuff—tools, materials, work in progress, odds and ends of natural objects, a half empty box of crackers, things picked up on travels. The furniture you sat on was a plank with a rug over it or a rickety kitchen chair. The room was never the same twice, but at its very worst it had ten times as much excitement in it as the best jobs I had ever done.

Then there was the problem of remodeling a house built in the 1880's. There was no budget for exterior alterations, so it became an interior job. Two of the rooms on which work was done were a living room and a study. The former turned out to be just one more living room. The latter, to judge from the automatic reactions of people in general, was kind of terrific. The living room had a pretty consistent modern treatment; the study had no "treatment" at all. The walls with the worst plaster cracks were covered with boards, books occupied one full wall and part of another, a radio-record player and a long, low storage cabinet were made and installed by the carpenter, the desk was an extra door covered with Masonite and sheet plastic. On the walls, two pictures that had nothing to do with each other, some African masks, and a half-dozen cast iron trivets. And on all available horizontal surfaces, a clutter of miscellaneous objects—shells, cactus, skeletons, old magazines, empty picture frames.

Gradually a little light began to seep through what I had fondly imagined to be a brain. The living room had been "decorated"—it was not particularly good. The study hadn't been decorated at all—it was very good. The reactions of the people, and myself, had not been to interior design, but to something else. That "something else" was a direct and unselfconscoius revelation of personal tastes and activities. To go into the living room was to be received with a polite expression that tried for warmth but achieved only blankness. To go into the study was to be given an intimate glimpse of what a person was like—the experience was as flattering as a confidence from your best friend. Against this direct emotional communication the "decoration" carried very little weight one way or the other. Whether you sat in the study on the newest of

In this house the architect had clearly kept control of the job until the last dish had been installed on the last shelf, but the whole affair was more like a museum than a house. (Tugendhat house by Mies van der Rohe)

There were some metal chairs and tables, and some otherwise bare rooms. It was as if LeCorbusier had signed off with the completion of the shell of the building. (Villa Savoye by Le Corbusier)

His rooms . . . seemed furnished before the furniture got in . . . Wright's chairs, tables, and even beds only repeated the square, hexagonal, or circular patterns of the buildings themselves. (Lewis house by Frank Lloyd Wright)

Above: *Interior of typical Japanese house. Below*: *Kitchen of colonial house in Bucks County, Pennsylvania. Although they show many objects now considered decorative, they contain no "decoration" in the modern sense of the word.*

modern chairs or an old beer barrel was of relatively little importance. It was quite a lesson.

Pursuing the experience with these two rooms a little farther—the living room *could* have been an exciting room, too. But it would have required an equally direct and honest approach. Had it been designed for what it was, a place where the family and visitors occasionally sat around, had its necessarily more impersonal character been accented instead of covered up, this room would have said what it had to say as strongly as the study. In other words, there would have been a comparable emotional impact, though of a totally different character.

This is why the living area of the Tugendhat house registers with such force. Its four elegant chairs and the coffee table can be taken as direct symbols of the basic apparatus required for social intercourse. There is nothing else in the area because there is no need for anything else. Most people still find this kind of "decoration" a little shocking, but it isn't the decoration that shocks—it is the naked honesty of the expression. Most of us find honesty disturbing, which is probably why the entire nation expends so much energy in teaching its young to keep quiet in company. It should be added, in connection with the Tugendhat living room, that the comments above do not "explain" it. Mies is an architect of extraordinary sensibility and strongly developed personal taste. His house looks the way it does because that is the way he wanted it to look. The same attitude towards the living room problem could be expressed equally well in a hundred different design solutions.

It is this possibility of endless variation that is so distressing to the people who are looking always for tricks and formulas. It is far easier and safer to follow a formula than to develop a principle. This is why modern decoration, so-called, is largely a matter of plywood and rubber plants and why it is so devastatingly boring—although there is nothing wrong with either plywood or rubber plants.

Once the distinction between principle and formula is grasped the lessons from the books begin to make themselves clear. Your early American kitchen (page 130) changes from a charming stage setting into another powerful manifestation of a way of living. The very essence of the idea "kitchen" is built into this room. Although they show many objects now considered decorative, they contain no "decoration" in the modern sense

of the word. Note too that while the kitchen of 1649 is hopelessly old-fashioned by comparison with the kitchen of 1949, this does not lessen the enjoyment or admiration in the least, for one reacts to the essentials and not to the details.

In the photograph of the Japanese interior we have a superb instance of what takes place when the problem of interior design is attacked on the highest level: everything is simultaneously meaningful *and* decorative. The idea of decoration as something applied like pancake make-up is absent. The picture in this room is a model of the calligraphic art, but it was made to be read. The post in the corner of the tokonoma is very decorative with the bark left on it—but it also holds up a beam. The pit in the floor is beautifully placed as an accent in the matted floor, but it was built for a charcoal fire. There are four main surface textures in the space, all exquisitely related to each other, but each makes a complete and quiet kind of sense with regard to its use and to the structure of the building. It may be thought that the enthusiasm this room arouses in a modern designer stems largely from the superficial resemblance that does exist between the traditional Japanese interior and the contemporary room. It is true of course that our tastes give us more pleasure in the work of some periods and less in others. But it is equally true that to commend simplicity as contrasted with, say, complexity, is an expression in terms of formula rather than principle. The modern room can be bare or rich, full or empty, light or dark, wasteful in terms of space or economical, and still be a magnificent success or a total flop. Discussions in terms of principle can be interesting, up to a point. Then the particular problems press for attention. Which is another way of saying that we all want the quick and easy answers. Specifically, how does one design that fine modern bedroom? Specifically, how does one give a feeling of warmth to this or that room? Specifcally, how do you produce a fascinating study for someone who does not collect African masks, butterflies or seashells—or read books—or listen to music?

The specific answer can be framed only in terms of the specific solution. The general answers can be stated only in terms that most people will find disturbing and unpalatable.

Modern decoration is in its present appalling state because it *is* decoration.

By decoration I mean what most people mean

by decoration—the piling of assorted objects into a space until the occupants are no longer made uneasy by its emptiness. And, of course, the arrangement of these objects in accordance with certain current rules so that the result will be pretty to look at.

Incidentally, there is in Balzac an observation on this matter of "emptiness." In that agreeably pornographic collection known as the *Droll Stories* there is the tale of Father Amador, a mendicant friar whose religious fervor is matched only by his masculinity. Amador gains admittance to a castle whose lord and lady are having difficulty living in marital harmony. In fact their eternal bickering has made life a shambles for everyone in the castle. The lord attempts to assuage his unhappiness with the help of his prettiest maidservant, a method which does not improve things at all, as far as his wife is concerned. Into this scene of conjugal discord wanders the monk Amador, who with truly medieval directness persuades the maid to give him what free time she has, seduces the daughter of the house, and finally enjoys the more mature charms of the lady herself. Something of a religious revival then occurs and the women of the castle make it clear to the lord that the continuing presence of Father Amador is absolutely necessary for their spiritual salvation. During one of the noisy quarrels between master and mistress, Amador approaches the former with a solution: "My lord," he whispers into the august ear, "I believe you will find that when a woman's mouth is full, she is empty somewhere else."

When a room is full, the emptiness may show up in the lives of its occupants. How on earth do a study for people who do not study? How create a fascinating room for people who are dull?

Amador's patron slowly digests the sage advice, rises and conducts his lady to her bedchamber, and everyone in the castle lives happily ever after.

I think it possible that when a room is full in the sense of decoration as defined, the emptiness may show up in the lives of its occupants. How on earth does anyone do a "study" for people who do not study? How create a fascinating room for people who are dull? How would you design a room to express the thoughts and activities of your clients if their activities were Canasta and gawping at a video screen and their thoughts were non-existent? You could do it, of course. It would be a room with walls, floors and ceiling painted one color, a card table (inlaid with plutonium if they were real rich) at one end of the room, and pews at the other where everyone could kneel when the Milton Berle show went on. But I don't think they would buy it. In fact I don't think they would even like you for getting so close to the core of the problem.

Fortunately, the problem is rarely presented to the designer in such precise and horrendous terms, and the kind of emptiness I am talking about is something from which we all suffer. Fortunately, too, the designer gets absolutely nowhere by blaming his inadequacies on his clients. There is no law that makes him work for them if he thinks they aren't worth an honest try. The fault, dear Brutus, lies not in our clients . . . Come to think of it, I never did run into a client who asked for plywood and rubber plants.

It would be a room with walls, floors, and ceiling painted one color, a card table (inlaid with plutonium if they were real rich) . . . and pews where everyone could kneel when the Milton Berle show went on.

The designer can be — and frequently is — trapped
by his own enthusiasms. This trap, built largely of metal legs, was
finally discovered by a camera at floor level.

NOTES ON THE NEW SUBSCAPE

If you look up the word, as I did, you will not find it—not in Webster, Funk & Wagnalls, not in Oxford, Shorter or Longer. Had it been there, the definition might have gone something like this, perhaps.

> subscape (sub'scap) *n.* 1950. U. S. (orig. apparently obscure pub. dealing w. int. des.). From Latin sub = under, from under; and-scape, 1773, (a back-formation from *Land-scape*), a view of scenery of any kind. 1. Tech. View of the furnishings of an interior, ranging upwards from the floor to the height of a chair seat, or at most, the underside of a table. 2. *Modif.* The lowest zone within a room, averaging thirteen inches in depth and never more than twenty-eight inches.

I suspect that none of us will ever see this definition in any dictionary with a pretense to respectability, and for good reason. Nevertheless the word has some temporary value in the context provided for it.

The subscape unfolds its manifold wonders in a zone of nearly total invisibility, and it has been good traditional practice to keep it so. The best furniture builders have hidden legs wherever possible and treated them with inconspicuous decency when it was not. The best photographers have always cooperated by setting their cameras at least four and a half feet off the floor, thus distracting attention and diverting the view to table tops, lamps, bookshelves, wall decorations, ceiling fixtures and so on. The best designers have also helped by wrapping skirts of finest Circassian walnut around desks, or by so loading chairs and sofas with coil springs, eiderdown, webbing, etc. that nothing remains of the legs but fat little nubbins that can be completely hidden by the use of fringe and other devices. The occupants of rooms are also involved in the

conspiracy to ignore the subscape. Standing, they look at each other or at objects located at eye level. Lying prone they observe the ceiling. Seated they busy themselves with the paper, television or a glass. If the gaze of an adult ever penetrates the region down by the floor, it is to observe a leg (not attached to furniture) or an ankle that appears to be especially well shaped. In some instances, the obscurity which veils the subscape is momentarily lightened. The housewife trying to clean under bed or bureau periodically establishes contact, but without too much visual awareness since she is concerned with other problems at the time. Certain forms of life inhabit the subscape, notably cats, dogs and small children, but this group lacks the capacity to turn out designs based on critical observation or to put its impressions down on paper. Designers and critics are generally barred from the zone by their extreme physical laziness and by the atrophied condition of their stomach and thigh muscles. That I got through at all was due entirely to curious happenstance, and when the event occurred, it felt like the penetration of an iron curtain—or perhap's Alice's looking glass.

As I recall, this was the way it happened: a few weeks back, relaxing from the mighty labors of a designer's day, I lay down on the couch with a new magazine. Idly riffling through its rather pretentious pages, I came to a section that also appeared to be a page but was actually an artfully concealed series of folds manufactured of some spring-like material resembling paper. Like those trick greeting cards which when opened release unexpected swarms of noisily flapping paper locusts or bumblebees, the magazine

erupted and the mass of hidden folds cascaded oft the couch and across the floor. Momentarily unnerved, I lunged sideways in an unthinking effort to recapture the escaping contents and found myself on the floor with the still-unfolding folds. Fortunately the couch was of modern design and consequently not too far off the floor itself, but the jolt to my aging carcass was the last thing in my mind as I stared about me, bemused by the view as a visitor from Mars. On all sides as far as the eye could reach were the elements, structures and symbols of the contemporary subscape—a region of whose existence I had been almost totally unaware.

Here, armed with all the fresh advantages of the mouse-eye view one could see with devastating clarity some of the things that have happened to contemporary furniture. To the left, about three inches from my eye, a slender steel shaft supporting a light plywood tray. Beyond this blurred vision of polished chromium plating, eight more steel rods, this time holding up two seats of molded plywood. Still farther in the distance, two supports in the shape of braced Xs with a slab of some sort above them. On the extreme right, tangled with my elbow, a couch leg crudely shaped like an over-scaled bent hairpin. Beyond the couch a pole of brushed aluminum (far above the upper limits of the subscape this pole supports three lighting units, but these are as invisible to the inhabitant of this region as the subscape is to the normally located adult eye). Across the room, another welter of bent hairpins, arranged in a kind of counterpoint with the three black rod legs of an iron stool and the four stubby tube legs of a coffee table. To see the molded plywood chassis of a

Most characteristic of the new subscape are its wide open spaces. Vast reaches of unencumbered floor extend in all directions, interrupted only by stems of metal. The terrain is ideal for the movement of infants, toys, vacuum cleaners, cats, dogs and inquiring photographers. The silhouetted object in the foreground is one of the steel underpinnings of a couch. It seems appropriate, somehow, that the gateway to the modern subscape should be an arch turned upside down.

Matthsson chair in this jangling underworld of steel and aluminum produced the same kind of shock as would the appearance of a Stutz Bearcat on Chicago's outer drive at rush hour.

My second descent to the subscape took place shortly afterwards, this time by intention and with proper clothing and equipment. The latter included a reflex camera with a short focal length lens (use of a view camera for the subscape is impossible unless one chops a hole in the floor for the photographer) and a brace of photofloods which worked only part of the time, unfortunately. Illumination at subscape levels, whether by day or night, is very poor, lighting engineers showing no concern for the seeing requirements of dogs, infants or photographers.

Two observations suggest themselves as a result of this exploration of a close but oddly unfamiliar region. One is the platitudinous comment that there is value in the shock that comes with seeing familiar objects from a strange point of view. I make no apologies for resurrecting so ancient an idea, for it is still one of the most potent and least-used tools in the design process. The other is that in one important area of modern furniture design the unanimity with which designers have been replacing wood supports with metal is rather remarkable. Whether this tendency is "good" or "bad" I have no idea, and I suspect that it is neither. The development itself is a fact; it certainly exposed the prejudices and preferences of a whole group of designers; it may indicate some social and cultural trends that will doubtless be clearer to posterity than they are to us.

The emerging metal subscape should not be dismissed as an upstart. It has ancestors, just like the earlier and heavier subscapes. Its progenitors include the tubular furniture of Bauhaus origin, now strongly entrenched in beauty parlors and "dinettes." Also wrought iron garden furniture of the 19th Century, now accepted in the dining room and making tentative passes at the rest of the house. And let us not forget the delicate and playful wire chairs and tables of pre-World War I ice cream parlors. Not as fancy a family tree, perhaps, as something based on Louis XV, but people are becoming more tolerant in these matters.

The new subscape also has a great many relatives in the modern world, some of them quite imposing. These include the new skyscrapers,

199

heavy blocks set on a base of thin stilts; they include Calder's mobiles, in which large shapes are held up by the thinnest of supports, the doodles of Joan Miro which exhibit the same characteristics, the newest elevated highways, the Horton spheroid found in the vicinity of refineries and chemical plants, diagrams of molecular structure—the list is a long one and remarkably varied to boot.

The metal subscape, unlike its predecessors, is very open. It includes few large, solid barriers to vision. Compared to earlier interiors (many of which suggest the canyons of the Wall Street district) this one is more like a young forest without underbrush. It also exhibits a great sympathy for, and understanding of, women who have to operate vacuum cleaners. And it provides a vastly increased *lebensraum* for young children and dogs.

Whether one likes it or not, it is at any rate here. I'd say here to stay for a while were it not for Korea and Korea's possible successors. Perhaps it will become a gently nostalgic reminder of the brief breathing spell between metal shortages. In any event, it is still around and can be observed—in discomfort—without a diving helmet, though rubber knee pads would help. I found it worth the visit.

Most of the chapters that make up this book were originally published elsewhere. Appreciation is expressed to the following magazines and publishers for granting their permission to reprint the articles noted:

Interiors (Whitney Publications Inc.):
Ends and Means
The Enlargement of Vision
Some Notes on the Relations of the Visual Arts
Venus, Persephone and September Morn
After the Modern House
The Dead End Room
Modern Decoration
The New Subscape

Industrial Design (Whitney Publications Inc.):
Design as Communication
Art-X
Captive vs. Independent Designer
Obsolescence

Holiday (Curtis Publishing Company):
Classic Holiday House
Down With Housekeeping
The Japanese House
Second House

Fortune (Time Incorporated):
Wright's Houses

Architectural Forum (Time Incorporated):
Planning with You

House and Garden (Conde Nast Publications, Inc.):
Prefabrication

Revere Copper and Brass Company:
Main Street

American Fabrics:
Structure and Fabrics

Philips Academy Bulletin:
High Time to Experiment

Philosophical Library (From a symposium edited by
Paul Zucker "New Architecture and City Planning):
Stylistic Trends in Contemporary Architecture

The following photographers and sources have supplied illustrations for this book. The majority of the photographs and drawings not otherwise credited are by the author or from the author's collection.

Culver Service: p. 98
Charles Eames: p. 22, p. 25, p. 26
Ray Garner: p. 24
Hedrich-Blessing: p. 136, p. 138, p. 141, p. 189
Metropolitan Museum: p. 94, p. 97, p. 190
Museum of Modern Art: p. 22, p. 23, p. 104, p. 106, p. 108,
        p. 110, p. 141, p. 189, p. 190
Simon and Schuster: p. 98
Julius Shulman: p. 140
Ezra Stoller: p. 137, p. 140, p. 141
U. P. A.: p. 24
Williams and Meyer Co.: p. 188

Associate editor: John Pile
Layout: Carl Ramirez and John Pile   George Nelson and Company
Cover design: Roger Zimmerman